186990

Nicaragua v. United States: A Look at the Facts

Robert F. Turner

Special Report
1987

A Publication of the
INSTITUTE FOR FOREIGN POLICY ANALYSIS, INC.
Cambridge, Massachusetts, and Washington, D.C.

PERGAMON·BRASSEY'S
International Defense Publishers

Washington London New York Oxford Toronto Sydney Frankfurt

Pergamon Press Offices:

U.S.A.
(Editorial)

Pergamon-Brassey's International Defense Publishers,
8000 Westpark Drive, 4th floor, McLean, Virginia 22102

(Orders & Inquiries)

Pergamon Press, Maxwell House, Fairview Park,
Elmsford, New York 10523, U.S.A.

U.K.
(Editorial)

Brassey's Defence Publishers,
24 Gray's Inn Road, London WC1X 8HR

(Orders & Enquiries)

Brassey's Defence Publishers,
Headington Hill Hall, Oxford OX3 0BW, England

**PEOPLE'S REPUBLIC
OF CHINA**

Pergamon Press, Qianmen Hotel Beijing,
People's Republic of China

**FEDERAL REPUBLIC
OF GERMANY**

Pergamon Press, Hammerweg 6,
D-6242 Kronberg, Federal Republic of Germany

BRAZIL

Pergamon Editora, Rua Eça de Queiros, 346,
CEP 04011, São Paulo, Brazil

AUSTRALIA

Pergamon Press (Aust.) Pty., P.O. Box 544
Potts Point, NSW 2011, Australia

JAPAN

Pergamon Press, 8th Floor, Matsuoka Central Building,
1-7-1 Nishishinjuku, Shinjuku-ku, Tokyo 160, Japan

CANADA

Pergamon Press Canada, Suite 104, 150 Consumers Road,
Willowdale, Ontario M2J 1P9, Canada

Copyright© 1987 Pergamon-Brassey's International Defense Publishers, Inc.

Library of Congress Cataloging-in-Publication Data

Turner, Robert F.
Nicaragua v. United States

(Special report/Institute for Foreign Policy Analysis, Inc.)
Includes bibliographies.
1. United States—Foreign relations—Nicaragua.
2. Nicaragua—Foreign relations—United States.
3 Nicaragua—Politics and government—1979–
4. United States—Foreign relations—1981–
I. Title. II. Title: Nicaragua versus United States.
III. Series: Special report (Institute for Foreign Policy Analysis)

E183.8.N5T87   1987   327.7307285   87-16867

ISBN 0-08-034499-2 (Pergamon-Brassey's)

First Printing 1987
Printed by Corporate Press, Inc., Washington, D.C.

Contents

To the mothers of America
—who have a special appreciation of peace—
in the hope that armed aggression in
Latin America will end without
the sacrifice of another generation
of their children

Acknowledgments

This study is an expanded and somewhat updated version of work I did in the summer of 1985 under contract to the Office of the Legal Adviser to the Department of State, and I am deeply indebted to the Department for the outstanding cooperation I received at that time. In researching the subject I was provided access to boxes upon boxes of classified and unclassified cables and memoranda, and at my request meetings were set up with several groups of Foreign Service Officers who had served in Central America during the critical years 1979-1981.

Mr. Peter Olson, the Assistant Legal Adviser responsible for Inter-American affairs, not only assisted me in obtaining documents from the Department of State, but also arranged for me to see certain classified materials from the Department of Defense and the Central Intelligence Agency. At my request, he worked with other agencies to have some of the less sensitive materials reviewed and declassified for inclusion in this study. I am grateful to Mr. Olson for his help and encouragement, without which this study would not have become a reality. I would also be remiss if I did not express my appreciation to the other people at the State Department who were of assistance, including Assistant Legal Adviser Ted Borak and Ambassador Otto Reich.

In December 1985 the State Department gave permission for me to expand, update, and publish the study so it could be made available to individuals outside the government who might wish to have more information about the dispute. Because of other commitments, updating was sporadic. Several parts of the manuscript appear here virtually without change from the study I did for the Office of the Legal Adviser. Thus, the documentation of events in the conflict during the period up to the end of 1985 is more extensive than that provided for the last year and a half.

During the updating phase I sought suggestions and other assistance from several individuals, and in that connection I would like to acknowledge the

I would, above all, like to express a special appreciation to Professor John Norton Moore, Director of the Center for Law and National Security at the University of Virginia School of Law, for the tremendous contribution he has made over many years in helping me to better understand the importance of international law in promoting peace and protecting such fundamental national and international values as freedom, self-determination, and non-aggression. Those portions of my legal analysis which were not taken directly from his superb writings were developed following many years of study under his able guidance.

Finally, I wish to acknowledge my debt to Dr. Franklin D. Margiotta, President of Pergamon-Brassey's International Defense Publishers, and to Robert C. Herber, Director of Publications at the Institute for Foreign Policy Analysis. Both played instrumental roles in transforming my draft into the final product. I am also grateful to Valerie L. Shand, who typed and coded the revised manuscript and provided helpful suggestions and welcomed encouragement.

Despite all of the assistance I have received, there are undoubtedly errors in the final product. Responsibility for these, and for all views expressed herein, is mine alone. I would emphasize in particular that the views expressed should not be attributed to the Department of State, which made no effort to interfere with my professional judgments or scholarly conclusions; nor to the United States Institute of Peace, which does not take positions on such issues and with which I became associated long after this study was written and accepted for publication.

Robert F. Turner
Alexandria, Virginia
July 25, 1987

The Debate Over Nicaraguan Aggression: Searching for the Truth

"[T]he [Salvadoran] guerrillas acknowledge that, in the past, they received arms from Cuba through Nicaragua, as the Reagan Administration maintains."

—Alan Riding, "Salvador Rebels: Five-Sided Alliance Searching for New, Moderate Image," *New York Times*, March 18, 1982, p.A-1.

"A radio-equipped warehouse and boat facility, disguised as a fishing cooperative on an island in northwestern Nicaragua, has served for three years as a transshipment point for smuggling arms to El Salvador, numerous residents here say."

—Sam Dillon, "Base for Ferrying Arms to El Salvador Found in Nicaragua," *Washington Post*, September 21, 1983, p.A-29.

"At the time of the filing of this report, the Committee believes that the intelligence available to it continues to support the following judgments with certainty:
A major portion of the arms and other material sent by Cuba and other communist countries to the Salvadoran insurgents transits Nicaragua with the permission and assistance of the Sandinistas."

—U.S. Congress, House, Permanent Select Committee on Intelligence, House Report 98-122, pt.1, 98th Congress, 1st Session, May 13, 1983, p.6.

"In truth, my government is not engaged, and has not been engaged, in the provision of arms or other supplies to either of the factions engaged in the civil war in El Salvador."

—Miguel D'Escoto Brockmann, Foreign Minister of Nicaragua, Affidavit filed before the International Court of Justice, April 21, 1984.

"You don't understand revolutionary truth. What is true is what serves the ends of the revolution."

—Nicaraguan Minister of Social Welfare Lea Guido de López to United States officials, explaining inaccuracies and distortions in Nicaraguan propaganda; quoted in Lawrence E. Harrison, "We Tried to Accept the Sandinista Revolution," *Washington Post*,

Executive Summary

In 1961 a small group of Nicaraguan followers of Fidel Castro broke away from the Moscow-line communist party and established the Sandinista National Liberation Front (FSLN) to lead an armed revolution against the highly unpopular government of Anastasio Somoza Debayle. For many years the FSLN was openly Marxist-Leninist and was committed to supporting revolutionary warfare throughout Central America, but because of its radicalism it achieved little success in attracting popular support. By 1977 it was split into three feuding factions with a combined strength of perhaps 200 guerrillas.

Cuban Premier Fidel Castro played a critical role in the important period 1977-1979. He persuaded the FSLN to downplay its commitment to Marxism-Leninism and to adopt a broad program aimed at appealing to the masses of the people and bringing respected noncommunists into a broad united front. In addition, he used the promise of large quantities of military weapons to unite the feuding FSLN factions, to make them a credible military force, and to ensure ultimate Marxist-Leninist control over the very popular anti-Somoza revolution.

On July 19, 1979, the FSLN seized power in Nicaragua. Despite concerns about its Marxist-Leninist past, the new regime was welcomed by the United States government. Indeed, during the first eighteen months of its existence the Sandinista government received more foreign assistance from the United States than it did from any other country.

In approving assistance for Nicaragua, however, Congress included a requirement that before aid could be dispensed the President must certify that the Sandinistas were not engaged in terrorism or efforts to overthrow governments in neighboring states. Although the Sandinistas began such efforts almost immediately upon seizing power, President Carter continued the aid while sending a senior State Department official to Managua to inform the Sandinistas that assistance would be halted if they did not cease

the communist world through Nicaragua to the Salvadoran insurgents prior to the January 1981 "final offensive," Vietnam in one shipment alone provided 60 tons of M-16 rifles, ammunition, explosives, and other equipment left behind by the United States in 1975. This external assistance—which was accompanied by training, communications support, command-and-control assistance, money, and other forms of aid—totally transformed the nature of the struggle in El Salvador and threatened to bring about the overthrow of that country's government.

The Carter Administration responded to Nicaragua's unlawful armed aggression against El Salvador by terminating the Nicaraguan aid programs and beginning military assistance to El Salvador. A few days later President Reagan took office. In the months which followed, numerous meetings were held between U.S. and Nicaraguan officials in an effort to promote a peaceful resolution of the conflict. When these efforts proved unsuccessful, in December 1981—nearly two years after the Nicaraguan aggression against its neighbors had begun—the U.S. government began supplying limited assistance to antigovernment Nicaraguan guerrillas as a means of pressuring the Sandinista government to cease its aggression against its neighbors.

The nine comandantes who rule Nicaragua are all long-time Marxist-Leninists, and they have learned well the lessons of other revolutionary struggles. They understand, for example, that the Vietnamese communists succeeded in defeating the United States not through armed struggle on the battlefield but by political struggle inside the United States. Aware that Ho Chi Minh and Fidel Castro were able to neutralize the United States government and obtain significant support from the American public with assurances that they were not communists and that they sought only democracy and human rights, the current leaders of Nicaragua have taken an identical approach. It worked in Vietnam and it is working today in Central America.

Despite their historic commitment to supporting revolutionary movements in neighboring states, the Sandinistas have been very successful in concealing their aggression against their neighbors. Indeed, to further their image as the "victim" in the current controversy, the Sandinistas went so far as to file suit before the International Court of Justice alleging that the United

ists and scholars, and a wealth of other unclassified sources. These accounts are supplemented by statements made by senior Salvadoran guerrilla leaders, who have been taken prisoner or defected, which have been declassified for inclusion in this report. In addition, the conclusions of groups which—like the author—have had access over the years to highly classified intelligence information are also included.

Taken together, the evidence of Nicaraguan armed aggression against its neighbors, provided in chapters 3, 4, and 5, is overwhelming. The final chapter examines the complementary principles of contemporary international law regarding the permissibility of the use of armed force—the prohibition against aggressive use of force contained in article 2(4) of the UN Charter, and the right of states to use proportional force in self-defense and collective self-defense under article 51 when necessary to bring an end to unlawful armed aggression—and concludes that U.S. support for the Contras is lawful. It notes that U.S. support for the Contras is a virtual mirror-image of Nicaraguan support for the Salvadoran insurgents—albeit on a smaller scale and with greater regard for human rights—and that the primary objective of this program is to persuade Nicaragua to abandon its efforts to engineer the overthrow of neighboring governments by armed force.

The greatest impediment to U.S. success in this endeavor is the perception by the Sandinistas that the United States lacks the will to sustain its commitments. Congress was viewed as having "pulled the plug" in Indochina following an effective political warfare offensive, and the Sandinistas have followed a similar strategy. In addition to professing support for democracy and human rights, the Sandinistas have achieved at least limited success in branding the Contras as former Somoza national guardsmen and as flagrant violators of human rights. Yet the Contras, in fact, have included in their leadership many of the most distinguished noncommunist opponents of the old Somoza regime—many of whom served at first in key positions in the Sandinista regime.

The last chapter looks in some detail at one particularly effective Sandinista charge—that the Central Intelligence Agency had prepared a training manual to teach the Contras terrorism, assassination, and other techniques

have been a Sandinista "dirty trick" aimed at discrediting the Contras. It is worth noting that most of the objectionable language was discovered by other Contra leaders and removed from the manual before copies were distributed.

The future largely depends upon Congress and the American people. If the Sandinistas succeed in their propaganda campaign to persuade American students, the press, opinion makers, and the Congress that Nicaragua is simply a poor victim of President Reagan's "inordinate" fear of communism, U.S. aid to the Contras will likely be terminated and Nicaragua will step up its aggression against neighboring states.

Ironically, Central and Latin America during the past eight years have seen an unprecedented growth of democratic government. Today Nicaragua's Daniel Ortega is the only head of state in Central America who routinely wears a military uniform. Unfortunately, this trend toward freedom and democracy is threatened by the massive Nicaraguan arms buildup. Since 1979 the Sandinista army has grown about 2400 percent, to a point where it is now nearly ten times larger than the military force maintained by the dictator Somoza in 1978.

As the U.S. Congress has vacillated on aid to the Contras, the Soviet Union has dramatically stepped up its military aid to Nicaragua. Between 1985 and 1986, for example, Soviet bloc military deliveries to Nicaragua increased from 13,900 metric tons worth $115 million, to 23,000 metric tons worth approximately $600 million—a trend which continued in 1987. Among other equipment, the Soviets have provided Nicaragua with Mi-24/Hind-D helicopter gunships—the most modern such weapons in the Soviet arsenal and the holder of the world helicopter speed record. Today, in terms of military manpower, tanks, and armored vehicles, Nicaragua surpasses all of the other countries of Central America combined.

Thus, if the U.S. Congress decides once again to deny support to groups in Central America who wish to resist the Sandinistas, Nicaragua—with the continued support of Cuba and the Soviet Union—can be expected to succeed in its efforts to overthrow neighboring democratic governments. As this process continues, it is likely that the American people eventually will

1. Background to Conflict in Central America

Regional Trends

Long a region of poverty, social injustice, and international neglect, Latin America has in recent years been a region in transition.

Some of the changes have been very encouraging. For example, in the past decade there has been an unprecedented trend toward democracy in the region. Central America—indeed, Latin America—has seen more elections since 1981 than during any comparable period in the region's history.[1] In 1979, the year the Sandinistas[2] came to power in Nicaragua, only about one-third of the people of Latin America lived under democratic governments. By 1986, that figure had risen to greater than 90 percent. In recent years military governments have been replaced by elected civilian presidents in Argentina, Bolivia, Ecuador, El Salvador, Guatemala, Honduras, Panama, and Peru. Today, for the first time in history, every country in Central America—except Nicaragua[3]—is ruled by governments chosen in elections widely judged to be free and fair.[4] The only head of state in Central America who wears a military uniform today is Nicaragua's President Daniel Ortega.

Tragically, the past quarter century has also witnessed a concerted campaign to effect political change in Latin America by bullets rather than ballots—and for the purpose of replacing authoritarian and democratic governments alike with Marxist-Leninist dictatorships. Immediately after seizing power in 1959, the Cuban government of Fidel Castro began initiating or supporting armed revolutionary movements in many Latin American countries, including Panama, Nicaragua, the Dominican Republic, Haiti, Peru, Colombia, Venezuela, Guatemala, and Bolivia.[5]

---

[1] Department of State and Department of Defense, *The Challenge to Democracy in Central America* (Washington, D.C.: U.S. Government Printing Office, June 1986), p. 1. (Hereinafter cited as State/Defense, *Challenge to Democracy in Central America*.)

[2] The Sandinista National Liberation Front (Frente Sandinista de Liberación Nacional—FSLN) led the popular resistance that overthrew the government of Anastasio S_____ D_____

During this same period, the Soviet Union dramatically altered its policy toward the region. After decades of relative caution, perceived shifts in the correlation of forces and other considerations led the Soviet Union to conclude that certain countries in Latin America were ripe for armed revolution.[6] The enhanced Soviet interest in the area was reflected both by an increased Soviet presence and by the underwriting of Cuban, and more recently Nicaraguan, activities. To give just a few examples:

- In 1970 Soviet naval vessels spent 200 ship-days in the South Atlantic. A decade later Soviet naval ships spent approximately 2,600 ship-days in these waters—a thirteen-fold increase.

- During the seven-year period starting in 1970, Soviet trade with Latin America, excluding Cuba, grew ten-fold.

- Between 1970 and 1981 the number of U.S. military advisors throughout Latin America dropped from 516 to 70—at which time they were outnumbered fifty-to-one by Soviet military advisors.

- Latin America is now the largest recipient of Soviet foreign military and economic aid—with Cuba alone receiving 60 percent of regional aid, including four times more economic assistance than the United States gives to all of Latin America.

- Between 1981 and 1984 the Soviet Union gave Cuba more than $2.5 billion in military aid—nearly six times more than the United States gave to all of Latin America. Total Soviet aid to Cuba during this period averaged more than $3 billion annually—or more than $8 million each day. This represented about one-fourth of Cuba's gross national product.

- Since the Sandinista victory, Nicaragua too has become a major recipient of Soviet assistance. Indeed, during 1984 Nicaragua received more military aid from Moscow than the United States gave to all of Central America combined.

With substantial assistance from the Soviet Union, Cuba has engaged in a massive military buildup, and now has 160,000 active duty military personnel and 235,000 experienced reservists. By way of comparison, Cuba's 35,000-man expeditionary force in Africa is more than five times larger than the entire military force of the Batista regime Castro defeated in coming to power in 1959.[7] The Soviets have given Cuba more than 950 tanks and more than 200 jet fighters—including the modern MiG-23 that remains a mainstay of the Soviet Air Force.[8] Since the early 1960s Cuba has not paid for any of the military assistance it has received from the Soviet Union.[9] Cuba has, however, allowed the Soviets to station a 2,800-man combat

---

[6] See p. 25, fn. 16, and accompanying text.
[7] State/Defense, *Soviet-Cuban Connection*, op.cit., p.8.
[8] Ibid., p.6.
[9] Ibid., p.3.

brigade on its territory, and serves as host to approximately 7,000 civilian advisors, 2,800 military advisors (not counting the combat brigade), plus about 2,100 technicians engaged in intelligence activities.[10]

As will be discussed in more detail below, Castro played an instrumental role in the establishment of Nicaragua's FSLN in 1961,[11] and in the unification of the three FSLN factions in 1979.[12] In so doing, he helped to ensure Marxist-Leninist control of the very popular revolution to overthrow the dictatorship that ruled Nicaragua prior to July 1979.[13] After the Sandinista victory, and with the assistance of the new Nicaraguan regime, Castro engineered the unification of the feuding anti-government factions in El Salvador as well.[14]

The Overthrow of Somoza

If there is anything about recent Nicaraguan history upon which there is almost universal agreement, it is that Anastasio Somoza Debayle was a tyrant who exploited Nicaragua for his personal gain. He was widely hated by a large portion of the Nicaraguan people representing a broad range of political viewpoints. By January 1978, when the assassination of Somoza's leading critic, *La Prensa* editor Pedro Joaquín Chamorro, led to public demonstrations and a lengthy general strike, it was clear to most observers that the days of Somoza rule were limited—despite the fact that the armed opposition amounted to fewer than 1,000 guerrillas.[15] Indeed, on February 26, Somoza promised publicly not to seek reelection when his "term" expired in 1981, and to retire from the military as well at that time.

On August 22, 1978, Sandinista guerrillas led by Edén Pastora Gómez— known by the nom de guerre "Comandante Cero"—captured the National Palace in Managua, taking more than 1,500 hostages whom they traded for the freedom of 58 political prisoners (including FSLN co-founder Tomás Borge Martinez) and $500,000 in ransom. As a result of this daring operation, Pastora became perhaps the greatest hero of the revolution.[16] One scholarly study of the Nicaraguan revolution explains:

---

[10] Ibid.

[11] See pp. 24–27.

[12] See pp. 36–37.

[13] See p. 38.

[14] See pp. 49–50.

[15] Department of State and Department of Defense, *The Sandinista Military Buildup* (Washington, D.C.: U.S. Government Printing Office, Department of State Publication 9432, revised edition, May 1985), p.3.

[16] See, e.g., "Profiling the Sandinista guerrillas," *Christian Science Monitor*, June 22, 1979 ("The most prominent figure in the Sandinista camp is Edén Pastora. . . ."); "Cuba and the Sandinistas . . .," *Chicago Tribune*, June 29, 1979 (referring to "the near-legendary" Pastora); "Nicaragua: A Revolution Stumbles," *Economist*, May 10, 1980, p.21; and Martin Arostegui, "Revolutionary Violence in Central America," *International Security Review*, Spring 1979, p.89.

The Palace operation captured the imagination of the Nicaraguan people and gave the FSLN the popular legitimacy it had been seeking. It also gave the revolution a charismatic personification, in the form of Edén Pastora, the dashing Commander Zero. . . . As the guerrillas made their way from the Palace to the Managua airport, thousands of well-wishers gathered to cheer the Sandinistas in general, and Pastora in particular. . . . The National Directorate further focused attention on Pastora in late October 1978, when, with great fanfare, they named him "chief of the Sandinista Army." . . . The assault on the Palace catalyzed the Nicaraguan people. The . . . business-labor national strike began the day after [Pastora] and the commandos flew to foreign asylum, and another wave of rioting swept the country.[17]

International support for the Somoza regime continued to decline, and several states—including Venezuela, Panama, and Costa Rica—were actively aiding the insurgents.[18] On December 15, 1978, the United Nations General Assembly voted 85 to 2 (with 45 abstentions) for a resolution censuring the Somoza regime for the "repression of the civilian population of Nicaragua and the violation of the sovereignty of Costa Rica by Nicaraguan military aircraft"[19] (which were attacking Sandinista forces operating from bases in Costa Rica).

The United States was widely perceived as a supporter of the Somoza regimes over the decades, and much of the criticism was well founded. Although paternalistic at best, the motives behind most of U.S. policy toward the region were not evil. In principle the United States believed in democracy, self-determination, and anticolonialism; but in practice the driving force behind many U.S. actions seemed to fluctuate between benign neglect and an emphasis on political stability at virtually any cost.

The primary U.S. security concern was the preservation of the Monroe Doctrine—a unilateral warning in 1823 that the new nation would not tolerate European colonial intervention in the Western hemisphere[20]—and

---

[17] David Nolan, *The Ideology of the Sandinistas and the Nicaraguan Revolution* (Coral Gables, Florida: University of Miami, North/South Center, 1984), pp.92-93.

[18] Pulitzer Prize-winning journalist Shirley Christian writes that "By December 1978 the Costa Rican government had made the decision to go all out in support of the Sandinistas." Shirley Christian, *Nicaragua: Revolution in the Family* (New York: Random House, 1985), p. 80. She adds: "Johnny Echeverría, the Costa Rican public security minister, said a total of five hundred M-14 rifles and more than a million rounds of ammunition arrived from Venezuela in February 1979, some of which was turned over to the Sandinistas. This was just half of what had been promised." Ibid., pp. 89-90. For information on Panamanian assistance to the Sandinistas, see ibid., pp. 80, 90, 95-96. See also Department of State, *Cuba's Renewed Support for Violence in Latin America* (Washington, D.C.: U.S. Government Printing Office, Special Report No. 90, December 14, 1981), p.5. (Hereinafter cited as State, *Cuba's Renewed Support for Violence.*)

[19] UN General Assembly, 33rd Session, 85th Plenary Meeting, Resolution 33/76. In a paragraph of considerable relevance today, the resolution also "*Demand[ed]* that the Nicaraguan authorities stop military and other activities that endanger the security of the region, in particular those that threaten the sovereignty and territorial inviolability of neighbouring countries. . . ."

[20] As set forth by President James Monroe in his Seventh Annual Message to the Congress on December 2, 1823, the Doctrine proclaimed "as a principle in which the rights and interests of the United States are involved, that the American continents, by the free and independent

political instability and disorder were viewed as more conducive than law and order to extra-continental intervention in the region. Acting often as something of a ham-handed "big brother," the United States routinely intervened—with armed force when deemed necessary—to keep the peace and reduce the temptation for intervention by European powers.

In trying to bring stability to Nicaragua in the early decades of the twentieth century the United States virtually turned the country into a U.S. colony— occupying it for nearly 20 years with U.S. Marines. A byproduct of restoring peace was expected to be an eventual transition to responsible and representative government with political justice, but the end result was continued authoritarianism. The United States, once respected for its own revolutionary tradition and commitment to democratic principles, soon became identified in the eyes of many Latin Americans as a force of reaction and a protector of tyrants.

Christopher Dickey writes:

The "establishment of nonpartisan constabularies in the Caribbean states" has been "one of the chief objectives" of U.S. policy at least since the 1920s. But as fast as the United States has "professionalized" an army, it has been converted to political ends. The most conspicuous example was Nicaragua's *Guardia Nacional*. Through the almost 20 years it occupied Nicaragua, the United States attempted to depoliticize its armed forces, first through training, then by building a new force, the Guardia Nacional, from the ground up. But even as Secretary of State Henry Stimson was warning Nicaraguan president José Mariá Moncada in 1929 that Nicaragua's future was riding on "the establishment of an absolutely nonpartisan, nonpolitical Guardia which will devote its entire attention to the preservation of peace, law and order," Moncada was using it to round up his political enemies in the Conservative Party. By the time the U.S. Marines finally pulled out of Nicaragua in 1932, the force they had intended to be politically neutral served as the power base on which Guardia Commander Anastasio Somoza Garcïa constructed a family dictatorship lasting more than 43 years.[21]

United States support for authoritarian incumbents in Latin America increased with the coming to power of Fidel Castro in 1959 and the subsequent growth of Cuban-supported revolutionary movements in Central and South America. Ironically, the identification of the United States with authoritarian tyrants promoted the growth of anti-Americanism in the region and contributed to the "revolutionary situation" necessary for Leninist movements to grow. But the motives underlying U.S. policy in the region were never as evil as critics of U.S. policy portrayed them. The objective of U.S. policy was to introduce stable, democratic governments to the region.

---

condition which they have assumed and maintain, are henceforth not to be considered as subject for future colonization by any European powers." Reprinted in James D. Richardson, editor, *Messages and Papers of the Presidents* (Washington, D.C.: U.S. Government Printing Office, 1896), Vol. 2, p.209.
[21] Christopher Dickey, "I Obey But I Do Not Comply," in Robert S. Leiken and Barry Rubin, *The Central American Crisis Reader* (New York: Summit Books, 1987), pp.330-331.

5

U.S. disdain for the excesses and corruption of the Somoza regime increased dramatically following the abuses associated with the 1972 Managua earthquake; and even before the development of serious military opposition to Somoza, the United States had used its influence to moderate the regime's practices. For example, U.S. pressure was instrumental in bringing about a lifting of martial law in September 1977.[22] On February 8, 1979, the United States terminated its already suspended[23] military assistance program to Somoza and halted all nonmilitary aid except for programs already in an advanced stage and designed specifically to help the poor. At the same time, it withdrew 47 U.S. personnel from Nicaragua as an indication of its displeasure with the Somoza regime.[24] Two months later, at the request of the Sandinistas, Washington put pressure on Israel to cease supplying weapons to Somoza—resulting in the recall of an Israeli ammunition ship already en route to Nicaragua.[25] On June 23 the United States joined with other members of the Organization of American States (OAS) in adopting a resolution which declared in part:

That in the view of the Seventeenth Meeting of Consultation of Ministers of Foreign Affairs this solution should be arrived at on the basis of the following:

1. Immediate and definitive replacement of the Somoza regime.

2. Installation in Nicaraguan territory of a democratic government, the composition of which should include the principal representative groups which oppose the Somoza regime and which reflect the free will of the people of Nicaragua.

3. Guarantee of the respect for human rights of all Nicaraguans without exception.

4. The holding of free elections as soon as possible, that will lead to the establishment of a truly democratic government that guarantees peace, freedom, and justice.[26]

Four days later, the United States urged Somoza to step aside and permit the establishment of an interim government.

The military situation inside Nicaragua continued to deteriorate. The relatively small FSLN guerrilla army had grown more than three-fold to a strength of slightly more than 3,000, and although it was still outnumbered at least three-to-one by the Somoza National Guard it had the overwhelming support of the Nicaraguan people—support based almost entirely, it might

---

[22] Alan Riding, New York Times, August 24, 1978, p.25.

[23] See "Somoza Charges United States Has Cut Off All Aid to Nicaragua," New York Times, November 10, 1978, p.9.

[24] John M. Goshko, "U.S. Retaliates Against Somoza, Cuts Back Aid," Washington Post, February 9, 1979, p.1; Graham Hovey, "U.S., Rebuffed by Nicaragua, Will Sever Military Ties," New York Times, February 9, 1979, p.7. See also, "Somoza is given U.S. ultimatum," Baltimore Sun, January 17, 1979, p.4.

[25] Christian, op.cit., p.92. See also, p.10, fn.48 below.

[26] Resolution II, June 23, 1979, adopted by the 17th Meeting of Consultation of Foreign Ministers by a vote of 17 for, 2 against, and 5 abstentions (OAS doc. 40/79 rev. 2), reprinted in Department of State Bulletin, August 1979, p.58.

be added, on the Front's promise to replace Somoza with a freely-elected democratic government.[27] On May 29 a Sandinista column led by Coman-dante Cero entered Nicaragua from a base in Costa Rica and launched the final offensive that led to Somoza's resignation and flight from Nicaragua on July 17. On July 19, 1979, the Sandinistas marched victoriously into Managua to the cheers of large crowds.

U.S. Policy Toward the Sandinistas

The replacement of the Somoza regime was generally well received by the United States, which, despite certain indications that the FSLN was led by Marxist-Leninists,[28] sought to establish a cordial relationship with the new government. For example, following a July 15, 1979, meeting between a U.S. State Department representative and Sandinista leaders in which the Sandinistas were promised U.S. support, junta member Sergio Ramírez Mercado announced: "At this moment I think there is no point of disagree-ment between us."[29]

During the first two years of the new regime, the United States provided $118 million in economic assistance to Nicaragua—the largest economic assistance program given to any Central American country by the United States at the time,[30] and more than five times the aid of all categories that the U.S. government had given the Somoza regime in the preceding two years.[31] On July 10, nine days before the final Sandinista victory, the United States announced plans to start a 45-ton-a-day emergency airlift of food to Managua to be turned over to the Red Cross.[32] On July 22—two days before the United States formally recognized the Sandinista government[33]—the new U.S. Agency for International Development director for Nicaragua, Lawrence E. Harrison, arrived in Managua on a Flying Tigers DC-8

---

[27] See pp.32-33.

[28] See pp.33-36.

[29] "Nicaragua Rebels Say U.S. Is Ready to Back Regime Led By Them," *New York Times*, July 16, 1979, p.1.

[30] Department of State and Department of Defense, *Background Paper: Nicaragua's Military Buildup and Support for Central American Subversion* (Washington, D.C.: U.S. Government Printing Office, July 18, 1984), p.1. (Hereinafter cited as State/Defense, *Nicaragua's Military Buildup.*) See also, Karen DeYoung, "House Unit Votes $9 Million in Aid For Nicaragua," *Washington Post*, September 12, 1979, p.1 ("The State Department apparently has become convinced, that, as [Deputy Secretary Warren] Christopher said, the best way to promote democracy in Nicaragua is to 'work with the new government.'"); "Zorinsky Says U.S. Plans to Double Nicaraguan Aid," *Washington Star*, August 8, 1979, p.A-5; and "House Version of Nicaraguan Aid Bill Accepted by Senate," *Congressional Quarterly*, May 24, 1980, p.1395.

[31] For a breakdown of U.S. aid to Nicaragua during the early years of the Sandinista regime, see annex 72 to U.S. Counter-Memorial submitted to the International Court of Justice in the Case Concerning Military and Paramilitary Activities in and against Nicaragua (*Nicaragua v. United States of America*). (Hereinafter, references to this ICJ case will be cited as *Nicaragua v. United States.*)

[32] Gilbert A. Lewthwaite, "U.S. plans Nicaraguan food airlift," *Baltimore Sun*, July 11, 1979, p.1.

[33] "U.S. formally recognizes new Nicaraguan regime," *Chicago Tribune*, July 25, 1979, p.10.

stretch-jet loaded with food.[34] Six days later, U.S. Ambassador Lawrence A. Pezzullo—who had been recalled from Managua earlier that month to put additional pressure on the Somoza regime[35]—returned to Nicaragua on a plane carrying another 25 tons of food and medical supplies.[36] Indeed, in early August 1979 the Nicaraguan Red Cross stated that the United States had provided Nicaragua with more food and medicine than had any other country in the world.[37]

Only in the area of military assistance was there obvious disagreement between Washington and the new Nicaraguan government. In late August the United States decided against selling arms to Nicaragua—arguing that after two years of civil war, there were enough weapons already in the country to equip any reasonably sized armed force.[38] The United States did offer military advisors and a modest grant to train a small number of Sandinista soldiers at U.S. bases in Panama and to fund a tour of military bases in the United States by higher-level Sandinista officials.[39] Nicaragua, however, rejected these offers.[40]

In approving $75 million of aid to Nicaragua in May 1980, Congress tacked on a requirement that the President certify that Nicaragua was not supporting terrorism or violence in other countries before appropriated funds could be disbursed.[41] By September, evidence of Nicaraguan assistance to anti-government guerrillas in El Salvador was significant enough to prompt a visit to Managua by Deputy Assistant Secretary of State James Cheek, who warned the Sandinistas that continued assistance to Salvadoran guerrillas could force the United States to terminate its aid program and

---

[34] Lawrence E. Harrison, "We Tried to Accept the Sandinista Revolution," *Encounter*, December 1983, p.74. This article is a reprint of Harrison's "We Tried to Accept the Nicaraguan Revolution: The Sandinistas Couldn't Live With a Positive Image of the United States," *Washington Post*, June 30, 1983, p.27.

[35] Pezzullo had never formally presented his credentials to the Somoza government.

[36] *Washington Post*, July 28, 1979, p.6; "Today Show" news, July 30, 1979, 8:30 A.M.

[37] Charles A. Krause, "Nicaragua Unmoved by U.S. Overtures," *Washington Post*, August 7, 1979, p.1. Shirley Christian, op.cit., p. 194, notes that "the United States had been the major aid donor to Nicaragua in the first two years of the new government."

[38] "U.S. Resists Arms Sale to Nicaragua," *Washington Post*, August 30, 1979, p.20. For background on the Nicaraguan request, see Charles A. Krause, "New Leaders of Nicaragua Ask U.S. for Arms Aid," *Washington Post*, July 30, 1979, p.1.; and Roberto Suro, "Nicaragua Wants U.S. Arms to Avoid Any Hint of Soviet Ties, Sandinista Says," *Washington Star*, August 13, 1979, p.3. For another possible explanation of the desire for Western military equipment, see pp. 57–58.

[39] Karen DeYoung, "House Unit Votes $9 Million in Aid for Nicaragua," *Washington Post*, September 12, 1979, p.1. See also James D. Rudolph, editor, *Nicaragua: A Country Study* (Washington, D.C.: U.S. Government Printing Office, 1982), p.180.

[40] Beth Nissen, "Nicaragua's Junta Has Visit with Carter then Runs into Tension on Capitol Hill," *Wall Street Journal*, September 25, 1979, p.18.

[41] Special Central American Assistance Act of 1979, § 536(g), Pub.L. 96-257, approved May 31, 1980. This section was later redesignated as § 533(f) of the Foreign Assistance Act of 1961, as amended.

generally damage U.S.-Nicaraguan relations.[42] Captured documents indicate that this warning was taken seriously, and that further shipments of arms were temporarily suspended while the Sandinistas attempted to identify and eliminate the source of the U.S. intelligence information.[43] Despite intelligence reports indicating growing Nicaraguan support for Salvadoran guerrillas, the President, in a desire to maintain a good relationship with the Government of Nicaragua, certified to Congress in September 1980 that there was no conclusive evidence of the Nicaraguan government's aiding and supporting acts of terrorism and violence in other countries.[44] As will be discussed below,[45] at about this time massive amounts of arms, ammunition, and military equipment began arriving in Nicaragua from Vietnam and other communist states for delivery to Salvadoran insurgents, and it became increasingly clear in Washington that the Sandinistas were seriously intervening in El Salvador's internal affairs.

In January 1981, at the instigation of Nicaraguan officials, the Marxist-Leninist guerrillas in El Salvador launched a "final offensive" across the country in an effort to seize power prior to the inauguration of President Reagan in the United States. The offensive caught most observers by surprise, and showed the guerrillas to be far better armed, organized, and trained than had been the case before the Nicaraguan involvement. During the final days of the Carter Administration the State Department informally suspended certain aid deliveries,[46] and on April 1 the Department an-

[42] Christian, op.cit., p.194.

[43] This incident is discussed in more detail on pp. 40, 140-141.

[44] Presidential Determination No. 80-26, September 12, 1980, *Federal Register*, Vol. 45 (September 22, 1980), pp.62,799. This document is also reprinted in Leiken and Rubin, *Central American Crisis Reader*, op.cit., p.502. By its own terms, it relies in part on "the Government of Nicaragua's repeated assurances that it is not involved with international terrorism or supporting violence or terrorism in other countries," and notes that the "diverse . . . opinions" from "intelligence agencies as well as our Embassies in Nicaragua and neighboring countries" were "carefully weighed." That the certification was a close call was emphasized by the conclusion "that the available evidence *permits* the President to make the certification. . . ." (Emphasis added.) Ibid., pp.502-503. The author's discussions with State Department officials who were involved in the decision reaffirm that the Carter Administration sought to give Nicaragua the benefit of any doubt in order to continue assistance.

[45] See pp. 53–68.

[46] Juan de Onis, "U.S. Halts Nicaragua Aid Over Help for Guerrillas," *New York Times*, January 23, 1981, p.A-3. This article, datelined Thursday, January 22, reported that "The United States suspended payments to Nicaragua from a $75 million economic support fund last week because of evidence that left-wing guerrillas in El Salvador have been supplied with arms from Nicaragua, an official source said today." Christopher Dickey writes: "The Carter Administration, in the last days of its term, had suspended what was left of the $75 million in aid it won for the Sandinistas a year before. There had been little choice. Certainly there would have been no way to certify, after the Salvadoran 'final offensive,' that the Sandinistas were not abetting other rebel movements. The Nicaraguans had acted with incredible indiscretion. Years later Salvadoran dissidents and rebel leaders who were in Managua and Havana at the time would shake their heads when they recalled how they even trained acrobats for the victory parade through San

nounced it was formally suspending disbursement of aid to Nicaragua because of that government's support for the Salvadoran guerrillas. Even then, however, State Department officials stressed to Nicaraguan leaders that the United States would resume aid if Managua ceased its efforts to undermine other states in the region and limited its alarming military buildup.[47] Despite the aid cutoff, when Nicaragua suffered serious crop and housing damage from torrential rains in May 1982, the United States provided food aid and other humanitarian assistance.

Nicaraguan Hostility Toward the United States

Despite the significant efforts by the United States during 1979 to promote the transfer of political power from the Somoza government to a more representative and democratic group—efforts which included discouraging other countries from providing military aid to Somoza,[48] and which led to Somoza later naming the United States as having been responsible for his downfall[49]—and the massive influx of U.S. economic and medical assistance to the new regime, the Sandinistas made little effort to establish good relations with Washington.

Following are just a few examples of the way in which the new Nicaraguan government dealt with the United States:

- Shortly after the Nicaraguan Red Cross identified the United States as the largest donor of food and medical supplies to Nicaragua, the revolutionary government's minister of social welfare failed even to mention the United States when identifying the donors of emergency aid.[50]

- Under the new regime, Nicaraguan school children were taught to sing the FSLN Anthem which included the line: "We shall fight against the Yankee, for he is the enemy of humanity."[51] Repeated objections by the American Embassy to this characterization were ignored.[52]

Salvador. Edén Pastora would remember the Salvadoran guerrilla commanders decked out in well-pressed uniforms directing their triumph—then watching their defeat—from a command center at the house of Somoza's mistress." Christopher Dickey, *With the Contras: A Reporter in the Wilds of Nicaragua* (New York: Simon and Schuster, 1986), p.105.

[47] Nicaragua's arms buildup is discussed on pp.11–17.

[48] See, e.g., Rowland Evans and Robert Novak, "Latin Dominoes," *Washington Post*, August 1, 1979, p.21 (reporting that the United States had pressured Israel and Guatemala to halt aid to Somoza). See also, p.6, fn.25.

[49] "Somoza Accuses Carter of Trickery in His Ouster," *Washington Post*, August 23, 1979, p.29.

[50] Charles A. Krause, "Nicaragua Unmoved by U.S. Overtures," *Washington Post*, August 7, 1979, p.1.

[51] For the full text of the FSLN Anthem, see Leiken and Rubin, op.cit., p.235.

[52] See, e.g., Harrison, op.cit., p.74; and Christopher Dickey, "U.S.-Nicaraguan Relations Show Signs of Improvement," *Washington Post*, June 12, 1980, p.A-33.

- Less than a month after the Sandinistas came to power, an American journalist observed from Managua:

Despite U.S. efforts to cultivate Nicaragua's new revolutionary government, the guerrilla-backed administration has continued to denounce "Yankee imperialism" as the root of all Third World evil and to display strong anti-U.S. sentiment. . . .

While the United States maintains it is attempting to start the new relationship off on a different footing, Nicaragua's new leaders have found it difficult, or at least inexpedient, to accept any change publicly.

Barricada, the Sandinista newspaper that is currently the only one published here, . . . referred to the Organization of American States as the "Department of State's Ministry of Colonies.". . .

The only foreign news printed in *Barricada* is based on Prensa Latina, the Cuban wire service that freely interchanges references to the United States with synonyms such as "the imperialists" or "the reactionary forces."[53]

Arms Buildup in Nicaragua

During the weeks surrounding the Sandinista seizure of power in Nicaragua, there were indications that the new regime would exercise moderation in establishing a military force. For example, in a Panama City news conference on June 28, 1979, three of the five junta members said they expected the new government to maintain only "modest" armed forces.[54] Six weeks later, Sandinista leader Tomás Borge told a news conference that Nicaragua needed "a small number" of tanks, artillery pieces, and aircraft. "We want to establish a little army. We can't afford anything more than that. We would prefer to buy tractors instead of tanks."[55]

Shortly thereafter, however, the Sandinistas began a massive campaign to build the largest military establishment in the history of Central America. It began with the introduction of thousands of foreign military and technical advisors. For example, within a week of the fall of Somoza, Cuba had sent about 100 military and security advisors to Nicaragua[56]—adding to the 50 or so who actually participated in the "liberation" of Managua.[57] This figure

---

[53] Charles A. Krause, "Nicaragua Unmoved by U.S. Overtures," *Washington Post*, August 7, 1979, p.1. These denunciations have continued. For example, in addressing the United Nations General Assembly on September 27, 1983, Daniel Ortega called the United States "the greatest enemy of our peoples" in Central America. Jon Sawyer, "Nicaragua's Talk is Soviet Line, U.S. Says," *St. Louis Post-Dispatch*, September 28, 1983, p.A-7.

[54] Karen DeYoung, "U.S. Envoy Talks with Nicaraguan Junta Leaders," *Washington Post*, June 29, 1979, p.17.

[55] Roberto Suro, "Nicaragua Wants U.S. Arms to Avoid Any Hint of Soviet Ties, Sandinista Says," *Washington Star*, August 13, 1979, p.3.

[56] State/Defense, *Sandinista Military Buildup*, op.cit., p.29.

[57] Jiri Valenta and Virginia Valenta, "Sandinistas in Power," *Problems of Communism*, September-October 1985, p.23. This excellent article notes: "There appears to be a rough division of labor among the communist states that give security assistance to Nicaragua—a pattern also observed in Soviet-bloc dealings with such 'socialist-oriented' countries as Angola, Ethiopia, and (formerly) Grenada. The Soviets appear to be responsible for overall command and control; the Cubans provide manpower and serve as military and counter-

continued to grow, so that by 1984, of the more than 9,000 Cubans in Nicaragua, about 3,000 were military or security advisors attached to the Nicaraguan armed forces or to internal security and intelligence organizations.[58] There were in addition approximately 100 Soviet and East German military and security advisors, as well as a contingent of Bulgarians.[59]

According to Miguel Bolaños Hunter, a defector who once worked in Nicaraguan counterintelligence, in 1983 the 2,800 to 3,000 Nicaraguans in the Department of State Security were supplemented by about 70 Soviets, 400 Cubans, 40 to 50 East Germans, and 20 to 25 Bulgarians. He stated further that many of the Cuban military advisors were posing as teachers.[60]

When asked about the presence of "thousands of Cuban advisors" in Nicaragua, Interior Minister Tomás Borge Martinez admitted to *Playboy* magazine that the Cubans were there, but suggested that most were "doctors and teachers." He stated:

> The Reagan Administration would have everyone believe that they are all spies and military men who pretend to be doctors and teachers. . . . It would be absurd if Nicaragua were offered thousands of North American doctors and teachers and we refused them. We inherited a country where we have no doctors or teachers, and the Cuban government has generously sent some.[61]

The irony of this explanation is that the United States did, in fact, offer this type of assistance through the Peace Corps program—and the aid was *refused* by the Sandinistas.[62] The Nicaraguans did accept some Panamanian military advisors and trainers following the fall of Somoza; however, as the Cubans consolidated their predominance in this field the Panamanians returned home after a few months, leaving behind "friendly warnings" against over-reliance on Cuba.[63]

---

intelligence advisers; the East Germans provide trucks, policy specialists, and highly qualified communications technicians; the Bulgarians aid the processing of information in security matters; and Bulgaria and (to a lesser degree) Czechoslovakia provide weapons, explosives, and ammunition." Ibid., p.25.

[58] State/Defense, *Soviet-Cuban Connection*, op.cit., p.27. By comparison, the United States has a total of 55 military advisors in El Salvador.

[59] State/Defense, *Sandinista Military Buildup*, op.cit., p.29.

[60] Don Oberdorfer and Joanne Omang, "Nicaraguan Bares Plan to Discredit Foes," *Washington Post*, June 19, 1983, p.A-1.

[61] Claudia Dreifus, "Playboy Interview: The Sandinistas," *Playboy*, September 1983, p.190.

[62] When the Sandinistas came to power in Nicaragua, in addition to large amounts of economic assistance, the United States offered to send Peace Corps personnel to Nicaragua—including school teachers. Although in explaining the arrival of the first 600 Cuban teachers the Nicaraguan Minister of Education had stated that Nicaragua would welcome qualified teachers from any country, he rejected the U.S. Peace Corps offer as "inappropriate." Harrison, op.cit., p.74. An offer by Costa Rica to provide teachers was also reportedly rejected by the Sandinistas.

[63] Robert S. Leiken, "Eastern Winds in Latin America," *Foreign Policy*, Spring 1981, p.102.

In addition to providing large numbers of military and security advisors, Soviet bloc countries provided Nicaragua with well over 40,000 metric tons of military equipment and supplies between 1979 and early 1985, with a total value of nearly $500 million.[64] The estimated value of Soviet and East European military deliveries to Nicaragua increased more than five-fold during 1986, rising from 13,900 metric tons worth $115 million to 23,000 metric tons worth approximately $600 million.[65]

Nicaragua also received substantial military equipment from other sources. For example, in April 1983 the Government of Brazil inspected the cargoes of four large Libyan cargo aircraft—a U.S.-made C-130, and three Soviet-made Ilyushin aircraft—that were en route to Nicaragua. Although the planes' manifests indicated that they were carrying "medical supplies," the inspections disclosed that they were loaded with weapons and military equipment. A Brazilian Foreign Ministry spokesman said the American-made plane was capable of carrying 20 tons of cargo, and the three Soviet-made planes a combined cargo of 120 tons.[66] When the planes were unloaded they were found to be carrying arms of both U.S. and Soviet manufacture, "including heavy arms, missiles, Czechoslovak rifles, a dismantled Soviet training plane, and at least five tons of bombs and grenades."[67] When asked about this incident a few months later, Nicaraguan junta member (and later Vice President) Sergio Ramírez Mercado stated: "We feel proud that a country such as Libya would support us in a moment like this."[68]

A few days later, Costa Rican authorities examined the cargo of a Panamanian freighter bound for Nicaragua which was towed into the port of Punta Arenas after developing engine trouble. Although the ship's crew alleged the vessel was carrying "Swiss-made agricultural chemicals," an inspection disclosed a hidden compartment containing 100 tons of explosives and detonators.[69]

These incidents reminded some observers of a similar situation which occurred in July 1979, when a PLO-chartered aircraft allegedly carrying

---

[64] State/Defense, *Sandinista Military Buildup*, op.cit., p.29.

[65] Department of Defense, *Soviet Military Power 1987* (Washington, D.C.: U.S. Government Printing Office, March 1987), p.143. More than $300 million worth of Soviet weapons were delivered to the Sandinistas in the first half of 1987. "Asides: Arming Ortega," *Wall Street Journal*, July 22, 1987, p.20.

[66] "Brazil Stops Libyan Arms for Nicaragua," *Washington Post*, April 20, 1983, p.26.

[67] Warren Hoge, "Old U.S. Weapons Among Arms Found on a Libyan Plane," *New York Times*, April 25, 1983, p.1.

[68] Dreifus, op.cit., p.191. The *London Sunday Times* reported in early 1986 that Libya was continuing to provide aid to Nicaragua at a rate of about $100 million per year. Quoted in "Libya Aids Sandinistas to Tune of $400 Million," *Washington Times*, February 24, 1986, p.A-8.

[69] "Costa Ricans Intercept Arms for Nicaragua," *New York Times*, April 28, 1983, p.12.

"medical supplies" for the relief of Nicaraguan war refugees in Costa Rica was inspected in Tunis and found to be carrying 50 tons of arms for the Sandinistas—including an anti-aircraft gun.[70]

With this generous external assistance, Nicaragua has managed to transform its victorious guerrilla army of a little more than 3,000 men at the end of 1979[71] into an extremely well-equipped military force estimated by the prestigious London-based International Institute for Strategic Studies to include 72,000 active-duty soldiers[72] (an increase of twenty-four-fold) and an additional 250,000 reservists.[73] The active duty forces alone are nearly ten times greater than the military force generally maintained by the dictator Somoza during his tenure, and nearly four-and-one-half times the peak of the Somoza military during the height of the Sandinista revolution.[74] The number of major military installations in Nicaragua has more than doubled to keep up with the increase in personnel.[75]

Thanks to the generous support of the Soviet Union, Cuba, and other sympathetic governments and organizations, Nicaragua has been able to arm and equip its massive new army with little difficulty. Former Sandinista intelligence officer Miguel Bolaños Hunter—who possessed special knowl-

---

[70] Christopher Dickey, "PLO's Nicaragua office dealing in military expertise," *Houston Chronicle*, June 4, 1982, p.12. Dickey writes: "The PLO has since helped train and arm other Latin American guerrilla groups, including El Salvador's insurgents, but the extent of this activity remains murky." (Ibid.) Shortly after the overthrow of Somoza, Sandinista sources in Europe were quoted as having admitted that some of their guerrillas had been trained as early as the 1960s at PLO bases, had fought with the PLO against Jordan in 1970, and had taken part in PLO hijackings of commercial airliners in Europe and the Middle East. See *U.S. News and World Report*, August 27, 1979, p.10. At about the same time, PLO sources affirmed that the PLO had given "concrete material and political support" to the Sandinistas since 1977. Helena Cobban, "PLO hopes tie to Nicaragua will leave Israel out in cold," *Christian Science Monitor*, July 26, 1979. See also, "Nicaragua, Host to Arafat, Opens Relations with PLO," *Washington Post*, June 23, 1980, p.16.

[71] "The Sandinista forces by the end of 1979—the Sandinista armed forces—were somewhere in between 3,000 and 4,000 armed men. There was a much greater number of Sandinista sympathizers, but the armed men were around 3,000 or a little bit more." Statement by Nicaraguan Vice Minister of Interior, Comandante Luis Carrión, before the International Court of Justice, *Nicaragua v. United States*, Uncorrected Verbatim Record, CR 85/20, September 13, 1985, p.45.

[72] International Institute for Strategic Studies, *The Military Balance 1986-1987* (London: Garden City Press, 1986), pp.191, 215. (Hereinafter cited as IISS, *Military Balance 1986-1987*.) According to this source, Sandinista active duty forces increased from 62,900 in 1985 to 72,000 in 1986—an increase of greater than 14 percent.

[73] Ibid. It should be noted that this is a dramatic increase in the numbers usually associated with the Sandinista "militia" of about 57,000. See e.g., State/Defense, *Sandinista Military Buildup*, op.cit., pp.3, 4, 7, and *Soviet/Cuban Connection*, op.cit., p.22. According to plans announced by the Managua government in February 1981, the militia was planned eventually to reach 200,000 members. Alan Riding, "Fearful Nicaraguans Building 200,000-Strong Militia," *New York Times*, February 20, 1981.

[74] Less than a year before his defeat Somoza was protected by a National Guard of only 7,500 men. Alan Riding, *New York Times*, August 24, 1978, p.24.

[75] State/Defense, *Nicaragua's Military Buildup*, op.cit., p.8.

edge in this area not only because of his position in the security service, but also because one of his relatives was in charge of arms warehouses, and of shipping, billing, and repairing arms for the Nicaraguan government—said that in 1980 the Soviet Union told Nicaragua "not to worry" about weakening its own defenses when it supplied weapons to Salvadoran guerrillas, because the Soviets "would provide two AK-47s [modern automatic assault rifles] for every gun given to the Salvadoran guerrillas."[76] Bolaños claimed that Nicaragua by 1983 already had "200,000 brand new AK-47 machine guns," and that he had been told by his cousin that "there are three times the amount of arms necessary."[77]

During the war against Somoza the Sandinistas had no tanks or other armored vehicles, no artillery, and no helicopters. Somoza's forces had only three tanks, 25 armored cars, and three artillery pieces. Thanks to external aid, the Sandinistas have dramatically improved their capabilities in each of these areas. For example, they now have at least 340 tanks and other armored vehicles, including well over 100 Soviet T-55 medium tanks (formerly the main Soviet battle tank, and still a major component of many Warsaw Pact armies). In terms of capabilities, the T-55 can outgun any tank previously seen in Central America. Nicaraguan armor also includes about 25-30 PT-76 light tanks—capable of easily fording rivers and designed to maneuver in the kind of terrain found in much of Nicaragua.

A similar picture emerges when one examines Nicaraguan artillery. It inherited only three 105mm howitzers from the Somoza National Guard, but Soviet aid quickly transformed Nicaragua into the strongest artillery power Central America has ever seen. Today the Nicaraguans have at least 30 122mm D-30 howitzers (which have greater range and firepower than any other artillery in the region), two dozen Soviet-made 152mm BM-21 rocket launchers (each capable of firing a barrage of 40 rockets), scores of antitank guns, and hundreds of mortars.[78]

The Soviet Union and its allies have also substantially upgraded Nicaragua's helicopter force. Although pre-Sandinista Nicaragua had no military helicopters,[79] the Soviets have provided at least 18 Mi-8 HIP medium-lift helicopters, and the Sandinistas have also received six Polish-built Mi-2/

---

[76] On June 16-17, 1983, Miguel Bolaños Hunter was interviewed by two *Washington Post* journalists at the Heritage Foundation in Washington, D.C. A 42-page typewritten transcript of that interview was prepared by the Heritage Foundation and given limited circulation. The statement quoted here appears on page 20 of that transcript (hereinafter cited as *Miguel Bolaños Transcripts*). Excerpts from this interview were also published by the Heritage Foundation as "Inside Communist Nicaragua: The Miguel Bolaños Transcripts," *Backgrounder* No. 294, September 30, 1983, and many of the passages cited in this study also appear in that publication.

[77] *Miguel Bolaños Transcripts,* op.cit., p.36.

[78] State/Defense, *Soviet-Cuban Connection,* op.cit., p.22.

[79] Ibid.

Hoplite cargo helicopters. More alarming, in 1984 Moscow began supplying Managua with Mi-24/Hind-D helicopter gunships—the most modern such weapon in the Soviet arsenal and the holder of the world helicopter speed record. Often referred to as "flying tanks" because of their armor and armament, these sophisticated weapons are capable of carrying multiple-barrel machine guns, guided missiles, rocket pods, and bombs. They have been a mainstay of Soviet intervention in Afghanistan, and are capable of attacking key targets in Honduras, El Salvador, and Costa Rica.[80] By July 1, 1986, the Sandinistas were thought to have at least 10 Mi-24 gunships,[81] and in late October it was reported that its inventory had been increased by new shipments from the Soviet Union to as many as 16.[82]

President Daniel Ortega has acknowledged that Nicaragua is spending 40 percent of its budget on the military.[83] One of the great ironies of this massive military buildup—particularly given the widespread poverty in the country and the serious economic and social needs of its people—is that the buildup was announced and begun at a time when Nicaragua faced no significant internal or external threat which might justify such a policy. In February 1981, when Nicaragua announced that it would build a 200,000-man militia, the *New York Times* noted there was "surprisingly little counter-revolutionary activity" against the Nicaraguan government.[84] Indeed, after Somoza was defeated it was clear from their own internal documents that the Sandinistas did not believe they faced serious internal or external military threats. For example, a document, *Analysis of the Situation and Tasks of the Sandinist People's Revolution*, produced after a late-September 1979 Managua meeting of the Sandinist National Liberation Front (FSLN), said in part:

Imperialism lost its armed vehicle in Nicaragua and lacks solid avenues for putting together any sort of reactionary plan in the near future. Because of the kind of military victory that we achieved over the dictatorship, the defeated National Guard cannot possibly organize an attack on us for the time being, especially since it would have to have strong backing from a bordering or neighboring country. None of our neighbors could embark on such a chancy adventure, Honduras because it must remain neutral while in the midst of a quite complex domestic situation, and El Salvador and Guatemala because they have social upheavals to

---

[80] State/Defense, *Sandinista Military Buildup*, op.cit., p.17.

[81] IISS, *Military Balance 1986-1987*, op. cit., p.192.

[82] Marjorie Miller, "Nicaragua Gets More Soviet Arms," *Los Angeles Times*, October 28, 1986, p.1. See also, John Cushman, "Nicaragua Said to Get More Gunships," *New York Times*, October 29, 1986, p.3.

[83] Ibid., p.37. See also, "Nicaragua: Here We Are Again," *Economist*, August 17, 1985, p.31 ("Defence spending now accounts for 40-50% of the budget."). Nicaraguan Finance Minister William Hupper told the International Court of Justice on September 17, 1985, that in 1985 military spending "is going to be between 38 and 40 percent of our total budget." International Court of Justice, *Nicaragua v. United States*, Uncorrected Verbatim Record, September 17, 1985, CR 85/23, p.13.

[84] Alan Riding, "Fearful Nicaraguans Building 200,000-Strong Militia," *New York Times*, February 20, 1981, p.A-2.

deal with. . . .Though we do not wish to downplay the need for a strong army to take care of national defense, we would point out that at present there is no clear indication that an armed counterrevolution by Somozist forces beyond our borders is going to take place and jeopardize our stability. What merits our attention, instead, is domestic factors. Counterrevolutionary action from overseas will for some time most likely take the form of financial pressures by imperialism to undermine the economic and social foundation of the Sandinist Revolution.[85]

Elsewhere, the document stated: "Imperialism's military base in Nicaragua has clearly been destroyed; interventionist aggression is not knocking on our door for now. The reactionary bourgeoisie is defenseless. . . ."[86]

During the early period, when the massive arms buildup was planned and initiated, the United States—as already discussed[87]—was making a major effort to promote a friendly relationship with Nicaragua. Indeed, even Cuban President Fidel Castro commented on the "wise" policy of the United States in sending "food instead of bombers and Marines" to Nicaragua following the overthrow of Somoza.[88] The decision to fund a "Contra" operation was not made until December 1981, and the first Contra actions against the Government of Nicaragua occurred in March 1982.[89]

Given the substantial needs of the Nicaraguan people, one must question why the new Nicaraguan regime chose to direct its priorities in this direction. One possible answer is that Sandinista leaders knew that in the long run their efforts to destabilize and overthrow their neighbors would be met with anger and resistance, and they concluded that it was necessary to transform Nicaragua into an armed fortress in order to be able to implement their interventionist agenda without fear of future retaliation by their far weaker victims.

Reaction of Nicaragua's Neighbors

Nicaragua's massive arms buildup has had a dramatic impact upon the regional military balance. According to the International Institute for Strategic Studies, by mid-1986, measured in total active duty military manpower alone, Nicaragua had nearly four times as many soldiers (but less than one-half the population) as the combined armed forces of the neighboring states of Honduras and Costa Rica.[90] The same source estimates the ratio of reserve forces to be almost five-to-one in Nicaragua's favor.

---

[85] FSLN, *Analysis of the Situation and Tasks of the Sandinist People's Revolution*, October 5, 1979, p.14. (Captured document.) This document, often called the "Seventy-Two-Hour Document," is reprinted in part in Leiken and Rubin, op.cit., p.220.

[86] Ibid., p.18.

[87] See pp.7–10.

[88] National Day speech in Havana, July 26, 1979, quoted in *Washington Post*, July 28, 1979, p.6.

[89] See pp.123–124.

[90] IISS, *Military Balance 1986-1987*, op.cit., pp.184, 191, 198.

Another means of assessing the emphasis on militarism in the region is to examine the "force ratio"—that is, the number of full-time regular military personnel per 1,000 population[91]—in each country. This comparison is particularly revealing when one compares the *trends* of the past half-decade. In mid-1981 El Salvador, Guatemala, Honduras, and Nicaragua all had between 2 and 3 soldiers for every 1,000 people.[92] By mid-1986 Guatemala and Honduras had increased their forces to slightly more than 4 soldiers per 1,000 citizens, and El Salvador was up to more than 7. Costa Rica, which by law has no armed forces, increased its lightly-armed civil guard and police forces from a force ratio of 2.2 to one of 3.6.[93] During the same period, however, Nicaragua's "force ratio" had risen from 2.7 to 21.7.[94]

In terms of military manpower, tanks, and armored vehicles, by 1985 Nicaragua surpassed all of the other countries in Central America *combined*.[95] Costa Rica has neither tanks nor artillery, and until recently Honduras had only a small force of about a dozen British-made Scorpion armored reconnaissance vehicles. Faced with the reality of both an arms race and growing Nicaraguan intervention in its internal affairs,[96] Honduras has recently acquired 72 reconditioned armored cars.

This dramatic shift in the regional military balance—particularly in the context of Nicaraguan intervention in the internal affairs of all of its neighboring states[97]—has been a source of considerable alarm in other countries in Central America. For example, El Salvador's Ambassador to the United Nations told the UN General Assembly in 1983:

How can armies of the neighboring countries remain indifferent to the huge arms build-up in Nicaragua, in conjunction with the presence of thousands of military advisers from the Communist bloc?

In approximately three years, under the pretext of national defense, Nicaragua has acquired offensive weapons whose combined power is greater than that of all the other Central American States, with the sole aim of implanting Marxism-Leninism in the region on a

---

[91] For a general discussion of this comparative technique, see James L. Payne, "Are Soviets Serious About Peace? Look at 'Force Ratio,'" *Baltimore Sun*, March 1, 1987, p.K-5.

[92] IISS, *Military Balance 1981-1982* (Colchester, U.K.: Spottiswoode Ballantyne Ltd., 1981), pp.97, 101. In this edition the Costa Rican "military" was considered so insignificant that it was only dealt with in a footnote, and no population estimates were given. For this comparison, therefore, 1981 Costa Rican population estimates were taken from Central Intelligence Agency, *The World Factbook 1981* (Washington, D.C.: U.S. Government Printing Office, April 1981), p.42.

[93] IISS, *Military Balance 1986-1987*, op.cit., p.184.

[94] Ibid., p.191. By way of comparison, Canada has a force ratio of 3.3, Mexico of 1.6, Libya of 16.7, South Africa of 2.6, Japan of 2.1, and the United States of 9.5. The average for the 27 Marxist-Leninist regimes around the world is 13.0. See Payne, *Baltimore Sun*, op.cit., p.K-5.

[95] State/Defense, *Sandinista Military Buildup*, op.cit., p.37.

[96] See Chapter 4.

[97] See Chapters 3, 4, and 5.

permanent basis, through violence, and with impunity, knowing that with such an imbalance of forces the other Central American countries, if they have to rely solely on their own resources, cannot stand up to this machinery of war and expansion.[98]

Similarly, Honduran Ambassador to the Organization of American States Roberto Martinez Ordonez told a special session of the Permanent Council of the OAS on July 14, 1983:

[I]t is of highest priority for the rest of the Central American countries to discuss the regional problems created by Nicaragua because of its worrisome arms buildup, its direct participation in the destabilization of the other Central American governments, and its clandestine arms trafficking. . . . Nicaragua has upset the Central American region's military balance. In only 4 years its armed forces have grown by 1,300 percent. . . .The size of the Sandinist Armed Forces is much greater than the total of the military troops in the rest of the Central American countries.[99]

Other expressions of deep concern have come from Nicaragua's neighbors to the south. Former Costa Rican President Luis Alberto Monge said on November 7, 1982, that the Nicaraguan arms buildup was leading other countries in the region to conclude that they, too, must expand their military forces. When asked about U.S. actions in the region, President Monge indicated "that guerrilla actions supported by Havana and Managua may be the reason for the U.S. actions."[100]

While visiting Panama in late July 1983, Costa Rican Foreign Minister Fernando Volio commented:

I am extremely puzzled about the great international commotion over U.S. fleet maneuvers in Central American waters, since nothing is being said by the same international community about these 14 [Soviet] ships and other ships that have arrived in Nicaragua over many years—4 years— with war material. This has altered the region's military balance and created an international communist threat to the entire region. It has clearly and irrefutably established the presence of the USSR and Cuba in Central America. This presence is very dangerous. . . to all Latin America.[101]

While visiting Costa Rica in October 1984, General Manuel Noriega, Commander of Panama's Defense Force, told the San José newspaper *La Nación* that the Sandinista arms escalation posed a danger to the entire region.[102] In an editorial commenting on this statement, *La Nación* argued: "[T]he Nicaraguan arms escalation has reached such alarming levels that Noriega could not avoid referring to it as one of the most important developments of the moment. He affirmed that it is not just Nicaraguan communism that worries that country's neighbors, but rather the arms race it has begun. . . ."[103] The editorial added: "Sandinista

---

[98] Speech by Mr. Rosales Rivera of El Salvador to General Assembly, A/38/PV.49, p.26 [455/21].

[99] Tegucigalpa Domestic Service in Spanish, 1957 GMT, July 14, 1983; translated and reprinted in Foreign Broadcast Information Service (FBIS), Latin America, July 20, 1983, p.A-1.

[100] Radio Reloj (San José), in Spanish, 1200 GMT, November 8, 1982.

[101] RPC television, Panama, July 30, 1983, in Spanish.

[102] State/Defense, *Soviet-Cuban Connection*, op.cit., p.24.

[103] Editorial, "Noriega's Statement," *La Nación* (San José), October 16, 1984.

militarism has to be halted before it produces a holocaust in the entire Caribbean region."[104]

Concern over the Nicaraguan arms buildup—and other Nicaraguan actions as well—is not limited to government officials of neighboring countries. Between February and October 1983 an affiliate of the Gallup organization conducted a series of interviews in Central America under the sponsorship of the United States Information Agency. Using representative sampling techniques, the Gallup affiliate interviewed between 500 and 700 adults who had completed at least one year of secondary school and were living in major urban areas of four Central American states.[105]

When asked "Which country (if any) is a military threat to our country?," 80 percent of the respondents in Honduras identified Nicaragua, 38 percent said Cuba, 14 percent the USSR, and 1 percent the United States. In Costa Rica, this question resulted in 69 percent of respondents naming Nicaragua, 37 percent Cuba, 24 percent the USSR, and 7 percent the United States. In El Salvador, 45 percent said Nicaragua, 37 percent Cuba, 24 percent the USSR, and 10 percent the United States.[106]

An updated version of this poll was conducted in 1985, with even more dramatic results. For example, 92 percent of Costa Ricans and 89 percent of Hondurans polled identified Nicaragua as the "most serious threat" to their own countries.[107] According to the Gallup organization, a majority of the respondents in polls taken in El Salvador, Guatemala, Honduras, and Costa Rica approved of U.S. assistance to El Salvador, and also of U.S. aid to the so-called Contras who are fighting against the Sandinista government in Nicaragua.[108] Support for the Contras, for example, was voiced by 69 percent of those polled in Costa Rica, with 24 percent expressing disapproval and 7 percent expressing "no opinion" or being unaware of the issue.[109] A January 1987 Gallup Poll, incorporating a margin of error of plus or minus 3 percent, registered approval of U.S. military aid to the Contras by 70 percent in Costa Rica, 81 percent in Honduras, 69 percent in El Salvador, and 68 percent in Guatemala.[110]

---

[104] State/Defense, *Soviet-Cuban Connection*, op.cit., p.24.

[105] A comparable sampling in the United States would have involved tens of thousands of interviews—an unusually broad sampling.

[106] United States Information Agency, *Public Opinion in Four Countries of Central America, 1983*, Research Report R-1-84, pp.9, 11.

[107] Cord Meyer, "A Temptation for Democrats," *Washington Times*, January 3, 1986, p.D-1.

[108] Thomas D. Brandt, "Latins Favor Contra Aid From U.S., Poll Shows," *Washington Times*, February 24, 1986, p.A-1.

[109] State/Defense, *Challenge to Democracy in Central America*, op.cit., p.45. See also *Congressional Record*, February 20, 1986 (daily edition), Vol. 132, p.H-533.

[110] "Central Americans Support Aid to Contras," *Congressional Record*, Vol. 133, March 17, 1987, p.S-3199 (Mr. Dole); and Glenn Garvin, "Poll finds neighbors back aid to Contras," *Washington Times*, May 26, 1987, p.A-1.

The United States Congress has dramatically shifted, even reversed, its position on Nicaragua and the Contras on something like half-a-dozen occasions in as many years; as a result, governments in the region have become more circumspect in their public expressions of support for U.S. policy. No doubt they recall the fate of other relatively weak governments in recent years who accepted U.S. assurances of support against aggression only to be left swinging in the wind when the American Congress changed its mind—governments like South Vietnam, Laos, and Cambodia, and the non-Marxist-Leninist factions in Angola. But in private, off-the-record conversations the message is still there. As the *New Republic* noted in an editorial in March 1986:

Does one expect Costa Rica publicly to come out in support of overthrowing its neighbor, given the odds now that its neighbor will be in power permanently? Of course, such countries will make muted public statements. But, as many of the leaders of these weak democracies told the Kissinger Commission and others since, they are desperate to see the United States get rid of the Sandinistas for them.[111]

---

[111] "The Case for the Contras," *New Republic*, March 24, 1986, p.8.

2. Marxism-Leninism and Revolution in Central America

Virtually all revolutions have social, economic, or political roots unrelated to great power politics. Certainly this is true in much of Central America, where democracy has historically faced an uphill struggle against despotism, corruption, and exploitation. To ignore these factors is almost to guarantee misunderstanding the struggle. However, it would be equally in error to seek to explain what has transpired in Central America in the past quarter century without recognizing the influence of Marxism-Leninism and the involvement of the Soviet Union, Cuba, and other Marxist-Leninist states.

The Cuban Factor

In his successful struggle against Fulgencio Batista, Fidel Castro effectively hid his Marxist-Leninist beliefs from both the Cuban people and the international community.[1] Indeed, so successful was he at this deception that even today many people believe Castro was "driven into Moscow's arms" because the United States did not embrace his new regime—this despite the fact that Castro has subsequently acknowledged publicly that he was a dedicated Marxist-Leninist long before seizing power in Cuba in 1959.[2]

Almost immediately upon taking power, Castro embarked upon a series of adventures aimed at destabilizing other Latin American governments[3] and

---

[1] See, for example, Dana Adams Schmidt, "Castro Rules Out Role as Neutral: Opposes the Reds," *New York Times*, April 20, 1959, p.1. Reporting on Castro's appearance on "Meet the Press," Schmidt wrote: "The bearded soldier said that his heart lay with the democracies and that he did not agree with communism. Dr. Castro was questioned about earlier statements that had been interpreted to mean that Cuba would be neutral in a conflict between the West and the Soviet Union. He denied this inference and implied that Cuba would support the West. . . . 'If there happen to be any Communists in my Government,' he said, 'their influence is nothing.'" See also, R. Hart Phillips, "Castro Rules Out Any Foreign Hand in Cuban Activities," *New York Times*, July 4, 1959, p.1. ("Dr. Castro rejected all accusations of communism made by the former chief of the Cuban air force. . . . Dr. Castro said the Cuban revolution was purely Cuban.")

[2] For example, during a television interview in Spain in January 1984, Castro confirmed that U.S. hostility was not a major factor in his decision to take Cuba into the Soviet camp, adding that "inexorably, we considered ourselves to be Marxist-Leninists." Madrid Domestic Service, January 5, 1984; Foreign Broadcast Information Service (FBIS), Latin America, January 9, 1984, p.Q-4.

[3] For a discussion of early Cuban intervention in the Dominican Republic, Nicaragua, Peru, Venezuela, Bolivia, Panama, Haiti, Colombia, Guatemala, and Bolivia, see R. Hart Phillips, "Castro Rules Out Any Foreign Hand in Cuban Affairs," *New York Times*, July 4, 1959, p.1. See also, three articles by Benjamin Welles in the *New York Times*: "O.A.S. Views Photos

promoting "wars of national liberation"—including the sending of an armed guerrilla band from Cuba into Nicaragua in 1959. The Nicaraguan intervention is noteworthy, among other reasons, because it provides useful insight into Castro's attitude toward non-Marxist-Leninist revolutionary movements. The first public indication in the West that Nicaraguan guerrillas were being trained in Cuba came via a Cuban announcement on April 19, 1959 that "More than 100 persons were arrested . . . when the Cuban Army raided a Nicaraguan rebel training camp near San Diego de los Baños in Pinar del Rio Province." A Cuban official "explained that the action against them was taken because Premier Fidel Castro had declared that no armed expeditions could leave Cuban territory for other countries."[4]

However, just three months later a group including 28 Cubans was captured in Honduras "in an abortive attempt to invade Nicaragua."[5] The Organization of American States investigated the incident and linked the insurgents with the Castro government—and in particular with Major Ernesto "Ché" Guevara.[6] The apparent inconsistency was clarified in August 1959, when the band of Nicaraguan guerrillas "arrested" by the Castro government had been released and was apprehended by Honduran forces while trying to launch an attack on Nicaragua. The insurgents explained that they were noncommunists, and when they had approached Cuban Defense Minister Raul Castro for assistance they were told that they

Said to Show Guevara," September 23, 1967, p.1; "O.A.S. Ministers Adopt New Anti-Cuban Policies," September 25, 1967, p.1; and "Diplomats Doubt that O.A.S. Moves Can Check Subversion," September 28, 1967, p.20. (In the last article, Welles notes that since 1960 Castro's "subversion schools have turned out at least 2,500 Latin-American Communist agents.") See also, State, *Cuba's Renewed Support for Violence*, op. cit., p. 2; and Howard J. Wiarda, editor, *Rift and Revolution: The Central America Imbroglio* (Washington, D.C.: American Enterprise Institute, 1984), pp.168–169.

The Organization of American States frequently investigated and denounced Cuban aggression in the region. For example, at the meeting of the Council of the Organization of American States on June 15, 1967, a resolution was adopted which noted in part that "the present Government of Cuba . . . is carrying out a policy of persistent intervention in [the] internal affairs [of member states] with violation of their sovereignty and integrity, by fostering and organizing subversive and terrorist activities in the territory of various states, with the deliberate aim of destroying the principles of the inter-American system." See Arthur M. Schlesinger, Jr., editor, *The Dynamics of World Power: A Documentary History of U.S. Foreign Policy, 1945-1973* (Edgemont, Pa: Chelsea Hse. Pubs., 10 volumes, 1983), Vol. 3, p.701. A little more than three months later, on September 24, 1967, the Twelfth Meeting of Consultation of Ministers of Foreign Relations resolved: "To condemn forcefully the present Government of Cuba for its repeated acts of aggression and intervention against Venezuela and for its persistent policy of intervention in the internal affairs of Bolivia and of other American states, through incitement and active and admitted support of armed bands and other subversive activities directed against the governments of those states." Ibid., p.705.

[4] "Nicaragua Rebels Arrested in Cuba," *New York Times*, April 20, 1959, p.1. The article observed: "Revolutionary organizations aimed at overthrowing the governments in four Caribbean countries—Panama, the Dominican Republic, Nicaragua, and Haiti—have been formed here. Exiles continued to arrive from these countries, and are arming."

[5] "Honduras Returns 28: Sends Home Cubans Caught Trying to Invade Nicaragua," *New York Times*, July 4, 1959, p.5.

[6] "Castro Aide Linked to Nicaraguan Raid," *New York Times*, July 28, 1959, p.2.

could receive help only if they would join in a "popular front" under the leadership of the Marxist-Leninist group. When they refused to join the communist-led guerrillas being trained in La Cabaña by Major Guevara, Ché had them arrested. They were released after the failure of the Marxist insurgency group, and were subsequently apprehended near the Nicaraguan border in Honduras.[7]

When the 1959 effort to infiltrate an insurgent group into Nicaragua proved unsuccessful, the Cuban Ambassador to Nicaragua, Quintin Piño Machado, reportedly helped to found an organization called "Patriotic Youth," which was a precursor to the Sandinist Front.[8] As will be discussed below, the Cubans were instrumental in the establishment of the FSLN, and when tactical disagreements split the Front and threatened its effectiveness, Castro used his personal prestige and the promise of arms to reestablish unity. One former senior FSLN official has alleged that during this period the Soviet KGB was providing funds for the Sandinist Front via Cuba.[9] From the earliest days of the FSLN, Nicaraguan guerrillas were given extensive military training at bases in Cuba.[10] According to the Department of State, by 1985 Cuban soldiers were actually engaged in combat alongside their Sandinista allies in Nicaragua.[11]

The 1976 Cuban Constitution openly asserts a right and duty to support revolutionary and national liberation movements,[12] and Cuban support for revolutionary movements in Latin America has continued into the 1980s.[13]

---

[7] "Cuba Said to Aid Nicaragua Reds," New York Times, August 23, 1959.

[8] Humberto Belli (former FSLN member and La Prensa editorial writer) in Three Nicaraguans on the Betrayal of Their Revolution, Heritage Lectures 41, October 11, 1984, p.4.

[9] See Valenta, op.cit., p.5.

[10] See State, Cuba's Renewed Support for Violence, op.cit., pp.5-6. An FSLN member who was arrested in January 1969 told Nicaraguan authorities that he had been in Cuba since 1967 undergoing guerrilla training. See Lynn Ratliff, "Nicaragua," in Richard F. Staar, editor, 1970 Yearbook on International Communist Affairs (Stanford, Calif.: Hoover Institution Press, 1971), p.453. A Mexican intelligence report released in July 1978 reported that 500 to 600 FSLN guerrillas underwent training in Cuba prior to the August 1978 offensive against Somoza. See Arostegui, op.cit., p.90. See also, Karen DeYoung, "Another Cuba Under Sandinistas?," Washington Post, July 24, 1979, p.1 ("Sandinista ties with Cuba go back to the 1960s when leaders of the then small guerrilla band went there for refuge, training and support. . . . In the early 1970s there was more Cuban training."); and "Profiling the Sandinista guerrillas," Christian Science Monitor, June 22, 1979 ("Quite a few of the Sandinista commanders are avowedly Marxist, trained in Cuba. . . .").

[11] "Cubans Fighting in Nicaragua, U.S. Says," Washington Times, December 6, 1985, p.A-1.

[12] "The Republic of Cuba . . . recognizes the legitimacy of the wars of national liberation . . . [and] considers that its help. . . to the peoples that struggle for their liberation constitutes its international right and duty." Constitution of the Republic of Cuba, Art. 12(c)(1976).

[13] See, e.g., Warren Hoge, "Colombians Combat Cuban Interference," New York Times, August 13, 1981, p.3 ("'It is evident,' said President Turbay, 'that Cuba has turned more active in exporting revolution.'"); and Department of State, Cuban Support for Terrorism and Insurgency in the Western Hemisphere, Statement by Assistant Secretary of State Thomas O. Enders before the Subcommittee on Security and Terrorism of the Senate Committee on the Judiciary, March 12, 1982, Current Policy No. 376, p.2. (Enders quotes Colombian President Turbay as saying, "when we found that Cuba, a country with which we had diplomatic relations, was using those relations to prepare a group of guerrillas, it was a kind of Pearl Harbor for us.") See also, "Castro's threat

Indeed, Cuban President Fidel Castro and other government officials have confirmed their role in providing arms to guerrillas in El Salvador, Guatemala, and Honduras.[14]

The FSLN

Like every other country in Latin America, Nicaragua had had a tiny communist party for many years prior to Castro's victory in Cuba. The Nicaraguan party—called the Socialist Party of Nicaragua (Partido Socialista de Nicaragua—PSN) but openly Marxist-Leninist—was founded in 1937. Except for a brief period surrounding World War II, the PSN was always illegal and generally ineffective under the Somoza regimes. At its peak in the pre-Sandinista period its membership probably reached about 200. Like other Moscow-line parties at the time, the PSN rejected revolutionary violence—arguing that conditions were not yet ripe for "armed struggle" in Nicaragua.[15]

Although the official Soviet position on armed struggle in Latin America would not change until two decades later,[16] the success of the Cuban

to Venezuela: MiGs and troops," *Business Week*, July 6, 1981, p.42; and State, *Cuba's Renewed Support for Violence*, op.cit., p.12. The latter reports diplomatic protests against Cuba by Venezuela (withdrew ambassador in 1980), Jamaica (broke diplomatic relations in 1981), and Ecuador (withdrew ambassador in 1981). More recent evidence of Cuban (and Soviet) aid to revolutionaries in Latin America is cited in Joanne Omang, "Arms Cache in Chile is Linked to Cubans," *Washington Post*, October 22, 1986, p.30. She reports that "Ten tons of arms found hidden in Chile two months ago provide evidence that Cuba and the Soviet Union are making a new effort to destabilize the government of President Augusto Pinochet and eventually foment a civil war, according to U.S. intelligence analysts. . . . The discovery at 10 sites in northern Chile yielded 3,383 used M16 rifles [from Vietnam] . . . , 2 million rounds of ammunition, nearly 2,000 Soviet rocket-propelled grenades and other explosives, the report said. The arms were valued at more than $10 million." On this subject, see also, Richard Halloran, "Latin Guerrillas Joining Forces, U.S. Officers Say," *New York Times*, March 3, 1987, p.8.

[14] Daniel Southerland, "Mexico, Venezuela try to end Salvador fighting," *Christian Science Monitor*, April 27, 1981; Sol W. Sanders, "How Snipers are Shooting Down a Salvadoran Solution," *Business Week*, May 18, 1981; "Text of a U.S. Report on Cuban and Nicaraguan Role in Salvador," *New York Times*, March 21, 1982, p.13; Rowland Evans and Robert Novak, "Latin Dominoes," *Washington Post*, August 1, 1979, p.21.

[15] "Meanwhile, the PSN's underground central committee had declared in December 1959 that, since the vanguard party of the working-class (the PSN) lacked the resources to lead the armed struggle, military action was premature." Nolan, op.cit., p.23.

[16] Valenta, op.cit., p.21. The shift in the Soviet position occurred in 1979. The new position was reflected in January 1981, when the Soviet English-language publication *New Times* focused on the situation in El Salvador and asserted that the "illusion" that the crisis could be "overcome by peaceful means" had been "dispelled by the course of events." (Baryshev, "The Rising Tide of Revolt," *New Times*, No. 3-81, January 1981, p.9.) Even the "petty bourgeoisie" were said to be "joining those who are ready to wage an armed struggle for the much-needed change." (Ibid., p.10.) Later that same month, a front-page editorial in another issue of the same publication asserted that the struggle in El Salvador was a test case: "In the present situation the Salvadorans have advanced to the forefront of the anti-imperialist movement in Latin America. The development of this movement in the 1980s will depend in no small measure on the success of their struggle." Editorial, "Solidarity with the People of El Salvador," *New Times*, No. 5-81, January 1981, p.1. See generally, John Norton Moore and Robert F. Turner, *International Law and the Brezhnev Doctrine* (Lanham, Md.: University Press of America, 1987).

revolution in 1959 led some Nicaraguan Marxist-Leninists to question this nonviolent approach. With the cooperation and encouragement of Cuba's President Castro,[17] three Marxist-Leninist radicals—Carlos Fonseca Amador, Tomás Borge Martinez, and Silvio Mayorga[18]—established the Sandinista National Liberation Front in Honduras on July 23, 1961.[19] The Front was named after one of Nicaragua's greatest heroes, General Augusto César Sandino, who led an active and effective guerrilla resistance campaign against U.S. Marine occupation during the 1920s. Sandino was accompanied during part of this period by Augustín Farabundo Martí, a Salvadoran Marxist-Leninist who served as the envoy of the Communist International to the Sandinista forces. Sandino was a nationalist, not a communist, and his refusal to follow instructions from Moscow led him eventually to sever relations with Martí.[20]

For most of its history the FSLN was a small group, with perhaps 100 active members by the end of its first decade.[21] Its activities were limited largely to sporadic bombings, bank robberies, and assassinations of government officials. It experienced several major setbacks at the hands of the Somoza government, and was nearly destroyed on more than one occasion. During one lengthy Fonseca stay in Cuba beginning in 1970, the FSLN appeared almost to cease to exist inside Nicaragua.[22] Its membership reportedly dropped from

---

[17] Fonseca, who had been a member of the PSN since 1955 and was its representative in 1957 at the Sixth World Youth and Student Festival in Moscow (see p.28, fn.32), participated in the Cuban-backed guerrilla column (discussed on pp. 23, 28) and was wounded in combat in June 1959. He escaped to Cuba, where he became personally acquainted with Castro and Ché Guevara. FSLN co-founder Tomás Borge Martinez traveled to Cuba in 1960 seeking Castro's support for the Nicaraguan revolution, and once remarked that "Fidel was for us the resurrection of Sandino, the answer to our reservations. . . ." Nolan, op.cit., pp.22-23, 139, 144-145.

[18] Fonseca, the FSLN Secretary General, was killed in combat in the mountains of Zinica during November 1976. Borge is currently Nicaraguan Interior Minister and the only FSLN founder to live to see the overthrow of Somoza. Mayorga and most of his guerrilla column were killed in battle in August 1967 at Pancasan.

[19] Nolan, op.cit., p.1. The organization was initially called simply the "National Liberation Front," but a few months later the name "Sandinista" was added—in a clever move to attract broader public support. See Rudolph, op.cit., pp.146-147. Rudolph asserts that the FSLN was "officially founded . . . on the symbolic date of July 26, 1961 (the eighth anniversary of Castro's attack on Moncada Barracks that launched the Cuban revolution)." Ibid., p.189.

[20] Nolan, op.cit., pp.16-17. Nolan states that "Sandino was never a Marxist, and his insular nationalism contributed to his rejection of the Salvadorean Marxist Augustín Farabundo Martí's efforts to tie Sandinismo to the Third (Communist) International." See also, Belli, op.cit., p.2 fn.*. The guerrilla national liberation movement in El Salvador is named after Farabundo Martí. See Valenta, op.cit., p.2; and Douglas Payne, "Sandinistas Bid 'Farewell to the West,'"*Freedom at Issue*, November-December 1985, p.14. Payne asserts that Sandino—a member of Nicaragua's Liberal Party—actually requested that the United States set up a military government to avoid Nicaragua being ruled by the rival Conservative Party.

[21] See, e.g., Lynn Ratliff, "Nicaragua," in Richard F. Staar, editor, *1972 Yearbook on International Communist Affairs* (Stanford, Calif.: Hoover Institution Press, 1971), p.399.

[22] "After the exile of Fonseca to Cuba in 1970, the FSLN went completely underground, confining its operations to propaganda statements issued by its leader." John J. Tierney, Jr., "Nicaragua," in Richard F. Staar, editor, *1976 Yearbook on International Communist Affairs* (Stanford, Calif.: Hoover Institution Press, 1976), p.505.

about 100 in 1970 to about 50-60 two years later, and the only outward signs of its existence were the occasional propaganda statements issued out of Havana.[23]

The general lack of success of the FSLN led to ideological and tactical disputes among its leaders. In October 1975 the so-called GPP group[24]—led by Tomás Borge, Henry Ruiz, and Bayardo Arce, and closely identified with Cuba—expelled the TP group[25]—led by Jaime Wheelock, Luis Carrión, and Carlos Núñez—for advocating urban mass organizing over rural guerrilla warfare.[26] A year later, a third group—called the TI[27] or *Tercerista* (third force) faction, and led by Humberto Ortega, Daniel Ortega, and Victor Tirado—split from the GPP. The Terceristas argued that it was unnecessary to build a revolutionary base among either the campesinos or the urban proletariat, and that it was possible to move immediately to civil war by relying on a "third social force" composed of the petite bourgeoisie and other urban middle sectors.[28] The Terceristas became the dominant faction on the FSLN national directorate in the 1977-1979 period, and so were often identified as the "national leadership" of the Front.[29] During this period, the FSLN grew rapidly, increasing from an estimated 200 guerrillas in 1977 to 2,500 by late 1978 and as many as 5,000 by the time the Somoza regime was overthrown in July 1979.[30]

Marxism-Leninism and the FSLN

For pragmatic political reasons—which will be discussed below—current Sandinista leaders occasionally find it expedient to deny the Front's Marxist-Leninist orientation.[31] Lest there be any confusion on this point, it will be useful to examine the political credentials of the FSLN and its key leaders.

---

[23] Ibid. Membership figures are from the 1969-1972 editions of the *Yearbook*.

[24] Guerra Popular Prolongada (Prolonged Popular War), a group favoring the strategy of classical rural guerrilla warfare.

[25] Tendencia Proletaria (Proletarian Tendency), a group advocating focusing the revolution on politicizing the urban masses rather than relying on the rural campesinos.

[26] Nolan, op.cit., pp.57-58, 133, 136.

[27] Tendencia Insurreccional (Insurrectional Tendency).

[28] Nolan, op.cit., p.62, and Arostegui, op.cit., p.91.

[29] Nolan, op.cit., p.62.

[30] Ibid., p.133. Most U.S. government sources give the figure of 5,000 for FSLN military strength at the time of the overthrow of Somoza; however, Nicaragua's Vice Minister of the Interior, Comandante Luis Carrión, testified before the International Court of Justice on September 13, 1985, that Nicaraguan armed forces at the end of 1979 "were around 3,000 or a little bit more." International Court of Justice, *Nicaragua v. United States*, Oral Argument, Uncorrected Verbatim Record, CR 85/20, September 13, 1985, p.45.

[31] See, e.g., Alan Riding, "Nicaraguan Rebels Deny Marxist Aim," *New York Times*, October 26, 1977, p.9; and Karen DeYoung, "Sandinistas Disclaim Marxism: Nicaraguan Rebels Reject Cuban Model," *Washington Post*, October 16, 1978, p.1.

The Front's most prominent founder (often listed as "the founder") and chief ideologist was Carlos Fonseca Amador, a hard-core member of the Marxist-Leninist PSN since his student days, who founded a Marxist cell on campus. He had visited the Soviet Union, and in 1958 had written a laudatory booklet entitled *A Nicaraguan in Moscow* which praised the USSR for its religious and press freedoms.[32] The FSLN was from its inception openly Marxist-Leninist and Castroite in its orientation, and Fonseca—who had become friends with Castro and Ché Guevara after having been wounded in combat as a member of the Cuban-sponsored column of "internationalists" that invaded Nicaragua in 1959—spent considerable time in Cuba. Indeed, he inaugurated a campaign of sporadic terrorist actions (bank robberies, bombings, assassinations of government officials, etc.) by "declaring war" on the Nicaraguan government during the Latin American Solidarity Organization conference in Havana in 1967. In May 1969, Fonseca issued a clandestine message to Nicaraguan students in which he said: "Any people's action that is not backed by the rifles of the guerrilla is doomed to failure."[33]

In August 1969 Fonseca was arrested by the Costa Rican government for bank robbery. He was quickly freed from prison after Costa Rican guerrillas hijacked a Costa Rican airliner on October 21, 1970, forced it to fly to Cuba, and offered to exchange four U.S. businessmen on the plane for Fonseca and three other Central American revolutionaries.

In 1971 Fonseca sent a message to the Twenty-Fourth Congress of the Communist Party of the Soviet Union (CPSU) in which he said: "The ideals of the immortal Lenin, founder of the CPSU, are a guiding star in the struggle which the revolutionaries of our country are waging with the aim of overthrowing the reactionary regime." The FSLN, he continued, was proud to be bringing to the "popular masses. . .socialist ideals which were victoriously implemented for the first time in history in the great Soviet Union." He concluded by stating that "with complete justification" the FSLN considered itself the "successor of the Bolshevist October Revolution."[34]

During an interview with *Playboy* magazine, FSLN co-founder Tomás Borge stated: "I grew up in the kind of family where my mother once told me, when I was just beginning to have my political awakening, 'The day you become a Communist, I will fall over dead.' . . . I told her that I would not be

[32] *A Nicaraguan in Moscow* was first published in 1958 and was reprinted in *Barricada*, the FSLN newspaper, on November 8, 1980. Excerpts are included in Leiken and Rubin, op.cit., p.147. Fonseca "assented to the Soviet line when he attended, under the auspices of the PSN, the Sixth World Youth Festival in Moscow in 1957; he remained in the USSR for four additional months after the festival. . . ." Valenta, op.cit., p.4. See also, Nolan, op.cit., pp.16, 20, 144.

[33] *1970 Yearbook on International Communist Affairs*, op.cit., p.453.

[34] *1972 Yearbook on International Communist Affairs*, op.cit., p.401.

blackmailed by her gentleness and her naivete and that I *was* a Communist."[35] Shortly thereafter, this exchange occurred:

Playboy: Perhaps we can shift to Father Ernesto Cardenal. Father, you're the minister of culture, and the first question that comes to mind is How can a Catholic priest also be a Marxist revolutionary?

Father Cardenal: As Christians, we don't think that there should be any incompatibility with Marxism. One can be a Marxist without being an atheist.[36]

Nicaraguan Defense Minister Humberto Ortega has stated that "Marxism-Leninism is the scientific doctrine that guides our revolution, our vanguard's analytical tool for understanding its historical process and carrying out the revolution. . . . [O]ur doctrine is Marxism-Leninism."[37]

Another of the nine comandantes of the supreme National Directorate of the FSLN to add insight to this subject is Bayardo Arce—the Coordinator of the FSLN's Political Committee. Arce's comments are particularly valuable since they were not intended for public consumption. In a secret speech to the Marxist PSN—the authenticity of which was later confirmed by Junta Coordinator (and now Nicaraguan President) Daniel Ortega[38]—Comandante Arce explained in May 1984 that under normal circumstances an "election" would be "totally out of place in terms of its usefulness," because "What a revolution really needs is the power to act." However, although elections were "a nuisance" they were necessary because of U.S. pressure. He argued:

Imperialism says that Sandinismo means totalitarianism, Sandinismo means Marxism-Leninism, Sandinismo means the spread of Soviet-Cuban influence, Sandinismo is an imposition on the Nicaraguan people. We believe that the elections should be used in order to vote for Sandinismo, which is being challenged and stigmatized by imperialism, in order to be able to demonstrate that, in any event, the Nicaraguan people are for that totalitarianism, the Nicaraguan people are for Marxism-Leninism.[39]

---

[35] Dreifus, op.cit., p.60. During a visit to Havana in 1984, Borge said: "We have come to share in the jubilation of the Cuban people, to be next to the Cuban people and next to Fidel, next to our brothers of the Communist Party of Cuba, to tell them once again what we already said once when we spoke to the Cuban people: that Cuba's friends are Nicaragua's friends, and Cuba's enemies are Nicaragua's enemies." Havana Domestic Service radio, June 25, 1984; translated in FBIS, Daily Report, Latin America, July 27, 1984.

[36] Ibid. Elsewhere, Father Cardenal has "proclaimed that the 'true Kingdom of God is a Communist society, and Marxism is the only solution for the world.'" (Llosa, op.cit., p.46); and he has expressed the view "that not only can a Christian be a Marxist, but that in order for him to be authentically Christian, he must be a Marxist, with emphasis on 'must.'" Interview with Luis Baez, *Bohemia*, November 18, 1977, pp.48-49, quoted in Nolan, op.cit., p.75.

[37] See, for example, his speech to the closing session of the Meeting of Specialists, reprinted in *La Prensa* (Managua), October 27, 1981, pp.16-19. An almost identical statement was made in an August 25, 1981, speech to Sandinista military personnel.

[38] "Ortega. . .said that recently disclosed comments by Sandinista Political Commission head Bayardo Arce 'do not represent the official position of the Sandinista front.'. . .Ortega did not deny that Arce. . .had made the comments. . . ." Robert J. McCartney, "Nicaraguan Hails 'Fluid' Talks with U.S. on Security," *Washington Post*, August 12, 1984, p.A-1.

[39] U.S. Department of State, *Comandante Bayardo Arce's Secret Speech Before the Nicaraguan Socialist Party (PSN)*, Department of State Publication 9422, Inter-American Series 118, pp.5-6. (Hereinafter cited as State, *Bayardo Arce's Secret Speech*. This speech was tape-recorded without Comandante Arce's knowledge, and later published by several sources outside

These are but a few examples of the kind of evidence that makes it clear that, while many people within the FSLN—and an overwhelming majority of their supporters—back the Front because of its struggle against the hated dictator Somoza and because of its democratic promises, the top leadership of the Front (including all nine members of its governing National Directorate) are Marxist-Leninists.

In order to obtain the greatest possible support both inside Nicaragua and from the international community during the anti-Somoza struggle, the Sandinistas were advised by Castro in 1978 to follow the tactic he had used successfully in Cuba nearly two decades earlier and to try to conceal their Marxist-Leninist orientation.[40] In August 1978 an American journalist who visited the FSLN troops inside Nicaragua reported that the guerrillas were busy removing all of the communist literature and insignia from their hideouts. One guerrilla was quoted as saying, "We have been instructed to say nothing about Marxism-Leninism or the Cuban help we have received all these years."[41]

Shortly thereafter, during a Mexico City news conference on December 4, 1978, Tomás Borge told the press: "Somoza painted us as Marxists. . . . We are neither Marxist nor liberal, we are Sandinistas."[42] Five days after the overthrow of Somoza, he was again quoted as telling reporters: "I've never said I'm a Marxist. We are Sandinistas."[43]

One American journalist who followed developments in Nicaragua closely observed:

The greatest myth about Nicaragua is that the Sandinistas' turn to the left is the result of American hostility. There are many people outside Nicaragua, and particularly in the United States, who believe that Ronald Reagan is to blame for the regime's avowed Marxism-Leninism. Nothing could be farther from the truth. Unlike Cuba, where Fidel Castro kept his real intentions hidden until well after he overthrew Batista, the Sandinistas—for anyone who cared to read—have always been up-front about their orientation.[44]

Nicaragua.) See also, Payne, op.cit., p.12, in which Payne quotes from the March 4, 1985, Tass interview with Socorro Galan, Secretary General of the Nicaraguan Association for Friendship with the Socialist Countries, who said: "The USSR's successes in building communism, in bringing up a new man, have always been and will remain an inspiring example for the Nicaraguan people building a democratic society." On August 23, 1980, Comandante Humberto Ortega said "the elections that we are talking about are very different from the elections sought by the oligarchs and traitors, the conservatives and liberals, the reactionaries and the imperialists, the 'gang of villains,' as Sandino called them. . . . *they are elections to improve the power of the revolution, but they are not a raffle to see who has power, because the people have the power through their vanguard, the Sandinista National Liberation Front and its National Directorate. . . .*" (Emphasis in original.) Reprinted in Leiken and Rubin, op.cit., p.229.

[40] State/Defense, *Soviet-Cuban Connection*, op.cit., p.6.

[41] Quoted in Constantine C. Menges, "Echoes of Cuba in Nicaragua," *Chicago Tribune*, June 29, 1979.

[42] Nolan, op.cit., p.97.

[43] Karen DeYoung, "Another Cuba Under Sandinistas?," *Washington Post*, July 24, 1979, p.1.

[44] Michael Kramer, "The Not-Quite War," *New York*, September 12, 1983, p.38. If there was any doubt about the Marxist-Leninist nature of the comandantes, it should have been dispelled by their conduct since taking power. Three key comandantes (Daniel Ortega, Ernesto

United Front Strategy

Writing in *"Left Wing" Communism: An Infantile Disorder* in 1920, Lenin taught his followers the importance of isolating one's enemies and making expedient alliances with temporary friends in order to create a correlation of forces conducive to success. He wrote:

The more powerful enemy can be vanquished only by exerting the utmost effort, and *without fail* by most thoroughly, carefully, attentively, and skillfully using every, even the smallest, opportunity of gaining a mass ally, even though this ally be temporary, vacillating, unstable, unreliable and conditional. Those who fail to understand this, fail to understand even a particle of Marxism, or of scientific, modern Socialism *in general.*[45]

Fidel Castro has learned this lesson well, and above almost all else he emphasizes the importance of unity within revolutionary movements. As one American government expert recently noted: "Cuba's approach to revolutionaries who are not in power is consistently to urge the formation of the widest possible alliance of the left, not excluding alienated persons in the moderate center, with the purpose of building a successful revolutionary force."[46]

Not surprisingly, given Castro's role in its founding, the FSLN embraced this doctrine. More than fifteen years ago the Front described itself as a "political-military organization whose objective is the seizure of political power through the destruction of the bureaucratic and military apparatus of the dictatorship and the establishment of a Revolutionary Government based on a worker-peasant alliance and the support of all the anti-imperialist patriotic forces of the country."[47] In a similar vein, in 1975 the

---

Cardenal, and Moises Hassan) flew to Havana to "thank" President Castro less than a week after taking power, and Tomás Borge made a secret visit to Cuba a few weeks later. (Charles A. Krause, "Top Nicaraguan Minister on Undisclosed Mission to Cuba," *Washington Post,* August 16, 1979, p.16.) In March of the following year Borge led one of many Nicaraguan delegations to Moscow, during which he signed an agreement of cooperation with the Soviet Communist Party. As the *Los Angeles Times* (May 20, 1980) observed, such "party-to-party" accords are "normally reserved for out-and-out Communist parties." See also, Brophy O'Donnell, "Nicaragua, hat in hand in Washington, joins Moscow in anti-American blast," *Baltimore Evening Sun,* April 3, 1980, p. 15. ("The joint communique issued at the end of the visit appears to put Nicaragua squarely in the Soviet camp.") Consider this account: "The harder Sandinista political line was illustrated in recent weeks by observances marking the centenary of Karl Marx's death, including speeches by Sandinista Commander Victor Tirado that contained some of the most explicit references to Marxism as a goal for Nicaragua in the 3-½ years of Sandinista rule. Underlining the point, a banner has gone up on the fence surrounding the Defense Ministry compound reading, 'Marx, the greatest living thinker,' and the official Radio Sandino told breakfast-time listeners the other day about how the father of communism was also a devoted father to his children." Edward Cody, "Tension Grows in Nicaragua," *Washington Post,* April 5, 1983, p.1.

[45] V. I. Lenin, *"Left-Wing" Communism: An Infantile Disorder* (Moscow: Books for Socialism, n.d.), p.65. (Emphasis in original.)

[46] "The United States and Cuba," address by Kenneth N. Skoug, Jr., Director of the Office of Cuban Affairs, December 17, 1984, U.S. Department of State Current Policy Series No. 646, p.3.

[47] *Tricontinental* (Havana), No. 17, March-April 1970, quoted in Lynn Ratliff, "Nicaragua," in Richard F. Staar, editor, *1971 Yearbook on International Communist Affairs* (Stanford, Calif.: Hoover Institution Press, 1971), p.468.

FSLN indicated that it would achieve victory by isolating the Somoza government and by uniting all "progressive" sectors of society—from the proletariat to members of the Catholic Church.[48]

The decision to downplay the Marxist-Leninist nature of the FSLN was an element of this united front strategy. The Front was not abandoning its Marxist-Leninist beliefs in order to broaden its popular support—it was concealing those beliefs while endeavoring to maintain full control of the revolution. Thus, the FSLN's May 4, 1977, "Political-Military Platform" stressed that the Front's goals were "inseparably linked" to, and guided by, the "Marxist-Leninist cause," and described the Sandinista movement as part of the same worldwide "proletarian cause" that had created the Soviet Union and Cuba. The Platform emphasized that "The dialectical development of human society leads to the transformation from capitalism to communism."[49] However, this document was not for circulation among the masses. To win the support of the people, the Platform called for the development of "a minimum program of government aimed at attracting broad support for action against the Somoza regime *through the avoidance of leftist rhetoric.*" (Emphasis added.) The 1977 Sandinista Platform provided for the creation of "a broad anti-Somoza front," including bourgeois/democratic opposition groups; but because there would be "a strong Sandinista army," this would "guarantee FSLN control of the post-war government."[50]

The "minimum program" envisioned by the 1977 Platform was announced early the following summer. It was non-ideological, called for "a government composed of all of us," and "consisted mostly of promises to meet specific economic aspirations such as higher wages, better working conditions, and more social services. Freedom of speech, organization, and religion were guaranteed . . . ."[51]

The benefits of avoiding Marxist-Leninist rhetoric during the final stages of the anti-Somoza struggle were noted by Comandante Humberto Ortega in a January 7, 1979 letter:

---

[48] *1976 Yearbook on International Communist Affairs,* op.cit., p.506.

[49] Nolan, op.cit., pp.66-67.

[50] Ibid., p.78.

[51] Ibid., pp.89-90. The FSLN program reflected a strategy used effectively by Marxist-Leninist forces in Vietnam decades earlier. Discussing a similar program offered by the Indochinese Communist Party in 1930, Ho Chi Minh wrote: "This programme was fully in keeping with the aspirations of the peasants, who comprised the majority of the people. In this way our Party succeeded in uniting the large revolutionary forces . . . and its prestige grew." Ho Chi Minh, "Thirty Years of Activity of the Viet Nam Worker's Party," *Selected Works* (Hanoi: Foreign Languages Publishing House, 1962), Vol. 4, p.432. As will be discussed, in the late 1960s "the Sandinistas studied the Chinese, Vietnamese, Israeli, and Algerian insurgencies" and "began to emulate Asian people's war by reincorporating mass organizing into the process." Nolan, op.cit., p.38.

Without slogans of "Marxist orthodoxy," without ultra-leftist phrases such as "power only for the workers," "toward the dictatorship of the Proletariat," etc., we have been able—without losing at any time our revolutionary Marxist-Leninist identity—to rally all our people around the FSLN . . . .

It is right that we demand in our ranks . . . more class consciousness and more Marxist ideological clarity, but let us not do this on an open and mass level, since we run the danger of becoming sectarian and isolating ourselves from the masses.[52]

Humberto Belli, a former FSLN member and *La Prensa* newspaper editorial writer who split with the ruling junta in 1982 over the question of press censorship, explains how this doctrine contributed to the decision to downplay the Front's Marxist-Leninist orientation:

Throughout the sixties and early seventies, Tomás Borge, Henri Ruiz, the Ortega brothers, Fonseca Amador himself, all communists and the key leaders of the revolution, spent several months and years in communist countries (especially Cuba and the Soviet Union) being trained and studying. So their leanings were very obvious. . . . It was very clear that they were Marxist-Leninists. . . . It was not until 1978, when the struggle against Somoza started to heat up, that the Sandinistas started to adopt a more democratic facade. They became interested in uniting themselves with other forces, and they began to talk about establishing a Nicaraguan pluralistic regime, a democracy, nonalignment.

A key strategy they used was to create a front of decent democratic people called the Group of Twelve, a group of Nicaraguan personalities including many truly democratic people like Dr. Arturo Cruz, who became the spokesmen for Sandinistas everywhere. There were some priests in this group, Father Ernesto Cardenal and Father Miguel D'Escoto, a Maryknoll priest, and that they were Marxist priests was not very well known. People would say, "Look there are priests in the Twelve. There are people like Cruz. There are people like Casimiro Sotelo and others who are democratic. This has got to be something different."[53]

Because the Sandinistas were in reality unwilling to share power with the non-Marxists they brought into the government, they had difficulty keeping principled moderates in the regime. For example, when policy differences arose between the Sandinista leadership and the junta that theoretically held supreme authority in the government, the FSLN usually prevailed. As the London *Economist* observed:

The junta has long been treated with contempt by Sandinist leaders. . . . When, for example, the junta decided to back the United Nations resolution condemning the Russian invasion of Afghanistan, its leading Sandinist, Commander Daniel Ortega, asked for time to refer the question to the nine-man Sandinist directorate. To their astonishment, junta members were later told that Nicaragua's ambassador to the UN had abstained on the vote—on the instructions of the directorate.[54]

The original understanding with the moderates, reached in July 1979 at Punta Arenas, Costa Rica, was that only 13 of the 33 members of the Council of State would be Sandinistas. But in April of the following year—before the Council of State had held a single meeting—the Sandinistas

---

[52] Quoted in Nolan, op.cit., p.68.

[53] Belli, op.cit., p.4. For a discussion of the role of "the Twelve," see Nolan, op.cit., pp.72-73.

[54] "Nicaragua: A Revolution Stumbles," *Economist*, May 10, 1980, p.22. See also, Valenta, op.cit., p.21.

announced plans to expand the Council to 47 seats, of which the Sandinistas would be given 24. This had the effect of increasing Sandinista representation from 39 percent to a 51 percent majority.[55]

Comandante Daniel Ortega was in Africa when the issue came before the junta, leaving a potential tie vote between the two remaining Sandinistas (Sergio Ramírez Mercado and Moisés Hassan Morales) on the one hand, and the two non-Sandinistas (Alfonso Robelo Callejas and Violeta Chamorro)[56] on the other. When the time arrived for the vote, however, "three Sandinista leaders turned up to tilt the vote 5:2."[57]

Following these and other incidents, both Mrs. Chamorro and Alfonso Robelo resigned from the junta.[58] Although Mrs. Chamorro at first remained silent about her displeasure with Sandinista policies—explaining her departure as a "personal" matter—she eventually denounced the FSLN for leading the country "down the path of Marxism-Leninism" and for "abus-[ing] the trust we gave them by violating democratic principles."[59] After denouncing the "totalitarian direction" in which the regime was moving, Robelo went into exile in Costa Rica and eventually joined the Contras. Twenty-five other members of the government resigned with him.[60]

The Sandinistas obtained their absolute majority on the Council of State, and appointed as one of three vice presidents long-time Somoza critic José Francisco Cardenal, who was first imprisoned by the Somoza regime in 1959. Six days later, Cardenal fled the country, charging that the Sandinistas were imposing a "totalitarian dictatorship" in Nicaragua. He, too, eventually joined the Contras.[61]

The damage done to the Sandinistas by the resignation of Alfonso Robelo and Violeta Chamorro was somewhat mitigated when in May they were replaced by Arturo José Cruz Porras (who had cofounded the Nicaraguan

---

[55] See, e.g., Valenta, op.cit., pp.16-17; Rudolph, op.cit., p.163.

[56] Robelo was a leader of the January 1978 anti-Somoza general strike, and founded the Nicaraguan Democratic Movement. A 1978 New York Times article on five key Nicaraguan opposition leaders who might eventually replace Somoza listed Robelo first, describing him as "the boy wonder" who was "considered to have a following that is growing within the opposition" to Somoza. The main criticism voiced about Robelo was that he might be "too much in with leftist groups." Gordon D. Mott, New York Times, October 23, 1978, p.27. Mrs. Chamorro is the widow of Pedro Joaquín Chamorro Cardenal, the La Prensa editor whose murder—believed to have been on Somoza's orders—set off the January 1978 strike and united much of Nicaragua against the dictator.

[57] "Nicaragua: A Revolution Stumbles," Economist, May 10, 1980, p.22.

[58] The Sandinistas explained the reduction in the size of the junta from five to three as a way to guarantee "more cohesion, effectiveness and efficiency." "Junta in Nicaragua Consolidates, Dropping Two of Five Members," New York Times, March 5, 1981.

[59] "Ex-Managua official rakes Sandinistas," Washington Times, August 22, 1985, p.A-5.

[60] Ibid., p.21. See also, Henry L. Trewhitt, "Administration cites need for swift aid to Nicaragua," Baltimore Sun, May 17, 1980, p.4.

[61] "House Version of Nicaraguan Aid Bill Accepted by Senate," Congressional Quarterly, May 24, 1980, p.1396; Nolan, op.cit., p.140.

Christian Democratic movement in 1948 with Pedro Joaquín Chamorro) and Rafael Cordova Rivas (a conservative lawyer who had also been close to Chamorro).[62] The following month, during a visit to Washington, Cruz was instrumental in securing overwhelming Congressional approval of additional economic aid for Nicaragua.[63] However, Cruz, too, proved unwilling to remain in the junta. He subsequently served from March to November 1981 as Nicaraguan Ambassador to the United States before resigning and joining the Contras. He was replaced as Ambassador by Francisco Fiallos—who defected a year later.[64]

As has already been observed,[65] if one individual could be called the "hero" of the anti-Somoza revolution in the eyes of the Nicaraguan people, it would be Edén Pastora Gómez (Comandante Cero). Pastora's father was killed by Somoza's National Guard in the 1940s, and Pastora had been engaged in armed opposition to the dictatorship since before the FSLN was established. He worked with the Marxists between 1967 and 1972, but then quit in frustration at the slow pace and ideological narrowness of the Front. With the establishment of the more aggressive Tercerista strategy, Pastora returned to the FSLN in August 1977. He served as the Front's point of contact with both the Venezuelan and Panamanian governments (which provided significant support to the Sandinistas),[66] led the successful seizure of the National Palace in August 1978, and commanded the Southern Front invasion forces as "Chief of the Sandinista Army" during the May-July 1979 final offensive.[67]

Because he was never a Marxist, Pastora was never fully trusted by the other FSLN leaders. David Nolan has written: "The real Tercerista leadership, especially Humberto Ortega, stayed out of the limelight, capitalizing on Pastora's military skill, democratic rhetoric, charisma with the masses, and status as an international media hero, while obscuring the true ideological nature of the FSLN."[68]

---

[62] Nolan, op.cit., pp.142-143.

[63] "In an extraordinary turnaround, in part because of pleas from a new member of the ruling group in Nicaragua [Cruz], the House yesterday cast a resounding vote of 243 to 144 against cutting $25 million in economic aid to that country. . . . Last winter a bill authorizing $75 million in aid to help Nicaragua recover from civil war squeaked through the House by only five votes." "House Rejects Cut in Nicaraguan Aid," Washington Post, June 6, 1980.

[64] Harrison, op.cit., p.76.

[65] See p.3. An article on Nicaragua in the New York Times in late 1978 featured photographs of Somoza and Pastora—apparently as symbols of the two opposing groups. Alan Riding, "U.S. Strategy in Nicaragua Keeps the Time Bomb Ticking," New York Times, December 17, 1978, p.E-3.

[66] Venezuelan and Panamanian assistance to the FSLN is discussed on p.4, fn.18.

[67] Nolan, op.cit., pp.148-149. See also, Christian, op.cit., pp.60, 65, 89. Discussing the siege of the national palace, Christian writes: "Thousands of people lined the streets and cheered as Pastora and his raiders left the palace on buses. . . . Almost unnoticed amidst the appreciation for Pastora was the presence of Tomás Borge, the surviving founder of the FSLN and one of those freed from prison." Ibid., p.65.

[68] Ibid., p.92.

After the revolution was victorious, Pastora served first as Vice Minister of Interior, and then as Vice Minister of Defense in charge of the militia. He resigned from the government in July 1981 and left Nicaragua. Nine months later, he denounced the FSLN National Directorate for betraying the revolution—for "transforming a dictatorship of the right into one of the left"[69]—and he joined with Alfonso Robelo to create the Democratic Revolutionary Alliance (Alianza Revolucionaria Democratica—ARDE), a Contra group which began armed operations against the FSLN along Nicaragua's southern border in May 1983.[70]

Alfredo César Aguirre began working with the FSLN in 1977, and was arrested by Somoza's National Guard after fighting in the September 1978 insurrection. After the Sandinista victory, he renegotiated Nicaragua's foreign debt and later served as head of the Central Bank. In May 1982 he defected.[71]

Reuniting the FSLN

If a united front with individuals and organizations outside the revolutionary movement was important, it was even more critical that there be unity within the FSLN itself. Castro was insistent upon this, and he used his control of arms and equipment to pressure revolutionary forces in Nicaragua—and later in El Salvador,[72] Honduras,[73] and Guatemala[74]—to set aside their differences and work together for the success of the revolution.[75]

---

[69] Valenta, op.cit., p.17.

[70] Nolan, op.cit., p.130.

[71] Ibid., p.141; Harrison, op.cit., p.74.

[72] In December 1979, Castro brought together in Havana the leaders of three rival Salvadoran insurgent groups. For details, see p.50.

[73] "As it did in El Salvador and Nicaragua, Cuba (now working with Nicaragua) has tried to develop a unified guerrilla movement in Honduras. Training of Honduran guerrillas was already under way in 1979. In March 1983, Honduran guerrilla organizations merged into the National Unity Directorate of the Revolutionary Movement of Honduras (DNU-MRH), just as the Nicaraguan and Salvadoran guerrilla groups had formed unified commands to receive Cuban backing." State/Defense, *Nicaragua's Military Buildup*, op.cit., p.28.

[74] Beth Nissen, "Nicaraguan Echo: Overthrow of Somoza Spurs Other Guerrillas in Central America," *Wall Street Journal*, July 27, 1979; Graham Hovey, "U.S. Fears Unrest in Central America," *New York Times*, July 22, 1979, p.13. According to a captured Salvadoran guerrilla document, the Guatemalan unity agreement was actually signed in Nicaragua. See Department of State, *Communist Interference in El Salvador: Documents Demonstrating Communist Support for the Salvadoran Insurgency*, February 23, 1981, Document K, p.6. (Hereinafter cited as State, *Communist Interference in El Salvador*.) See also, State, *Cuban Support for Terrorism*, op.cit., p.2.

[75] Castro mediated disputes among the Sandinista factions for several years prior to the overthrow of Somoza. See Leiken, op.cit., p.102. Pulitzer Prize-winning *New York Times* journalist Shirley Christian writes that the day after Christmas 1978, "Cuban radio announced that the three factions of the Sandinista Front. . .had agreed to merge their forces both politically and militarily. . . . Though details of Castro's role in the unification discussion are unknown, various would-be Sandinista combatants who had come into Costa Rica during late 1978 and early 1979 said it was widely understood that Cuba had made military assistance conditional on this unification." Christian, op.cit., pp.82-83.

In July 1978 the unification of the three factions making up the FSLN was announced by Cuba at the World Youth Festival.[76] Shortly thereafter, Cuban advisors were sent to Costa Rica to train FSLN guerrillas with arms that had been infiltrated from Cuba.[77] The three FSLN factions also issued a joint communique in December announcing their provisional unification.[78] When further friction threatened to divide the Front, Castro called Borge and the Ortega brothers back to Havana, and the unity pact was renewed. On March 7, 1979, leaders of the three FSLN factions announced the formation of a Combined National Directorate (Dirección Nacional Conjunto—DNC), composed of three representatives from each of the three factions.[79] Redesignated the "National Directorate" following a major FSLN conference between September 21 and 23, 1979, this nine-man body remains the highest body of the FSLN,[80] and the de facto supreme political authority in Nicaragua.

Although increasingly popular with the Nicaraguan people, the Sandinistas lacked the military capacity to seriously challenge the National Guard because of a shortage of weapons.[81] Their difficulties increased with the December 3, 1978, electoral defeat of Venezuelan President Carlos Andres Perez, who had been providing the Sandinistas with a large part of their military equipment and was their main foreign ally.[82] By the spring of 1979 Cuba had become the primary source of military assistance for the Sandinistas—acting through a logistics network in Liberia, Costa Rica.[83] A subsequent investigation by the Costa Rican National Assembly estimated that at least one million pounds of war materials entered Costa Rica from

---

[76] State, *Cuba's Renewed Support for Violence*, op.cit., p.6.

[77] Ibid.

[78] Nolan, op.cit., p.97.

[79] The Terceristas were represented by Daniel and Humberto Ortega and Victor Tirado. The GPP was represented by Tomás Borge, Henry Ruiz, and Bayardo Arce. Jaime Wheelock, Luis Carrión, and Carlos Núñez represented the Proletarios. See ibid., pp.97-98.

[80] FSLN, *Analysis. . .of the Sandinist People's Revolution*, op. cit., p.2.

[81] Alan Riding, *New York Times*, August 24, 1978, p.25.

[82] State/Defense, *Nicaragua's Military Buildup*, op.cit., p.12; Alan Riding, "U.S. Strategy in Nicaragua Keeps the Time Bomb Ticking," *New York Times*, December 17, 1978, p.E-3. For a discussion of Venezuelan aid to the FSLN, see pp. 4, 35, 45.

[83] Shirley Christian writes that Costa Rican Public Security Minister Johnny Echeverría "said in an interview that, according to his recollection, the Cuban arms began to arrive in either December 1978 or January 1979, but the CIA reported that arms from Cuba were already being flown into Panama as early as September 1978 for transshipment to Costa Rica. The CIA report, prepared in May 1979 on the basis of information from a high-level informant in Panama, said eight crates of weapons, including .50-caliber machine guns, came from Cuba in September and that three additional flights came into Panama from Cuba during the week of November 5 to 11 and were flown to Costa Rica later the same month. The proof of these shipments soon showed up in Nicaragua, where the National Guard captured several hundred Belgian-made FALs, which had been the rifle of Marxist guerrilla groups around Latin America since Fidel Castro came to power in Cuba on January 1, 1959. Castro's forces inherited thousands of nearly new FALs from the Fulgencio Batista regime, but after the new Cuban army began to receive Soviet equipment the FALs were available for other uses." Christian, op.cit., p.80. See also, pp.95-96.

Cuba in the final six to eight weeks of the anti-Somoza struggle—not including materials shipped earlier.[84]

By insisting upon unity among the far Left as a condition for the supply of arms, Castro was able to increase the effectiveness of this element of the revolution. By channeling weapons only through this element, he was able virtually to ensure Marxist-Leninist control of the resistance struggle. Alfonso Robelo—a member of the first Sandinista junta and one of the highest ranking individuals to defect from the Nicaraguan government—observed:

A good many of us businessmen, moderates mostly, helped to make the 1979 revolution . . . . When we won, we were easily dismissed by the new government because we had always been only the political side of the struggle. We had no weapons, and when it came time to set things up, it was the Sandinistas, the party, the F.S.L.N. . . ., who had the monopoly on the guns and hence the power.[85]

A very important document, *Analysis of the Situation and Tasks of the Sandinist People's Revolution*, prepared following a 72-hour-long meeting in Managua in late September 1979 and not intended for circulation outside the party, indicated that one of the three "essential points" that had led to the Front's victory over Somoza was "[a] bold policy aimed at a nationwide combative alliance. . . ."[86] Under the heading, "the correlation of forces," the document stated:

The Reconstruction Government (which was born of an alliance of classes but which was mainly the political alternative that Sandinism had organized to neutralize Yankee intervention) entered Managua triumphant. . . . Sandinism had won the war, and the people acknowledged the total victory of Sandinism above all else. It is true that in 1977 the main purpose of the alliance with the democratic segments of the bourgeoisie was to isolate Somozism and to expand the forces of the Sandinist Front. It was an alliance aimed at a domestic neutralization. However, the alliance that took the form of the National Reconstruction Government, the cabinet and, to a major extent, the FSLN's basic program, under the circumstances of the new offensive by the uprising, was designed to neutralize Yankee interventionist policies in light of the imminent Sandinist military victory. Organizing the government was a relatively easy task; it did not involve negotiations with the parties of the bourgeois opposition. Instead, it involved appointing patriotic figures who were somewhat representative. . . . We can assert that since 19 July the FSLN has exercised power on behalf of the workers and other oppressed segments of society, or to put it in another way, the workers exercise power through the FSLN. In spite of its sweeping victory, however, Sandinism has not made radical moves to transform all of this power once and for all into the power of workers and peasants. This is because our political tactics are to develop conditions more favorable to the revolution and because our most urgent task at present is to consolidate the revolution politically, economically and militarily so that we can move on to greater revolutionary transformations.[87]

Much later, the study identified "organizational objectives that we are presently striving for," including "D. To begin building the revolutionary

---

[84] Ibid., p.96.
[85] Quoted in Kramer, op.cit., p.34.
[86] FSLN, *Analysis. . .of the Sandinist People's Revolution*, op. cit., p.3.
[87] Ibid., pp.7-9.

party, whose ideology is none other than that embodied in our Sandinist heritage and enriched by the contributions of the World Revolution."[88] Such candor in documents not intended for circulation outside the FSLN leaves little doubt about the future the Sandinistas have in store for Nicaragua.

Political Warfare

During the late 1960s the Sandinistas became enamored with the revolutionary writings of Chinese, Vietnamese, and other insurgencies, and they were particularly influenced by Mao Tse-Tung's *On Protracted War*.[89] Writing during the Sino-Japanese war in 1938, Mao explained:

"War is the continuation of politics." In this sense war is politics and war itself is a political action. . . . The anti-Japanese war is a revolutionary war waged by the whole nation, and victory is inseparable from the political aim of the war—. . .inseparable from the effective application of united front policy, . . . and from the efforts to win international support and the support of the people inside Japan.[90]

This lesson was also learned by the Vietnamese communists. During the early days of the war with France in 1947, party Secretary-General Truong Chinh wrote in *The Resistance Will Win*:

Many people think that resistance consists only in sending troops to the front to fight the enemy. In fact, to take up arms and kill the enemy is only the military aspect of the problem. The resistance of our people must be carried out in every field: military, economic, political, and cultural. . . .

Concerning our foreign policy, what must our people do? We must isolate the enemy, win more friends. We must act in such a way that the French people and the colonial peoples in the French colonies will actively support us and oppose the reactionary French colonialists, that all peace-loving forces in the world will defend us and favour the aims of our resistance. . . . The French people and soldiers should oppose the war by every means: oppose the sending of troops to Indochina, oppose military expenditure for the reconquest of Vietnam . . . [and] they should demand from the French Government peaceful negotiations with the Ho Chi Minh Government.[91]

After political warfare proved instrumental in the defeat of the French, a similar strategy was followed against the United States during the second Indochina war. A resolution adopted at the ninth plenum of the Vietnam Worker's [Communist] Party Central Committee in December 1963 provided:

Continue to intensify efforts for winning international sympathy and support:

---

[88] Ibid., p.42.

[89] See, e.g., Nolan, op.cit., pp.33, 38; Ernest Evans, "Revolutionary Movements in Central America: The Development of a New Strategy," in Wiarda, *Rift and Revolution*, op.cit., p.180.

[90] *Selected Works of Mao Tse-tung* (Peking: Foreign Languages Press, 1967), Vol. II, pp.152-153.

[91] Truong Chinh, *The Resistance Will Win* (Hanoi: Foreign Languages Publishing House, 1947), pp.35, 46, 47.

. . . . We must make every effort to motivate various peace organizations . . . and various organizations of the people of Africa, Asia and Latin America to take stronger actions in asking the U.S. imperialists to end their aggressive war, withdraw their troops, military personnel and weapons from South Viet-Nam, and let the South Vietnamese people settle their own problems. We must also win the sympathy and support of the people of the nationalist and imperialist countries (the U.S., France and England).

In our hard and complicated struggle against the U.S. imperialists, international support and solidarity are important factors in our victory. Along with the intensification of our armed and political struggles in South Viet-Nam, we must step up our diplomatic struggles for the purpose of isolating warmongers, gaining the sympathy of antiwar groups in the U.S. and taking full advantage of the dissensions among the imperialists to gain the sympathy and support of various countries which follow a peaceful and neutral policy.[92]

Given the success of political warfare by Vietnam in neutralizing the effectiveness of the United States and eventually contributing to a communist victory, it is hardly surprising that the strategy is also being used extensively by Marxist forces in Central America. Professor Ernest Evans has observed:

The Sandinistas made strenuous efforts to get a broad array of international backing. . . . [T]hey felt that a major constraint against U.S. intervention against them would be if they were supported by a broad range of countries in Latin America. . . . [T]hey believed that it was important to get as much support as possible from sympathetic groups in the United States; they felt that a badly divided American public would tend to immobilize U.S. policy toward Nicaragua.[93]

Indeed, in the aforementioned internal *Analysis of the Situation and Tasks of the Sandinist People's Revolution*, FSLN leaders listed as the first of three "essential points" that led to victory over Somoza "[t]he national and international isolation of the dictatorship. . . ."[94]

Nicaragua is engaged in a massive political warfare offensive against the United States, hoping to spread enough disinformation to leave public opinion divided and U.S. policy immobilized in the face of Nicaragua's military buildup and the export of revolution to neighboring states.[95] Just as in the final days of South Vietnam the U.S. Congress rejected pleas for additional aid, the Central American Marxists hope to use their propaganda offensive against the American people to pressure Congress to deny funds for aid to El Salvador, the Nicaraguan Contras, and other groups in the region. In an interview in Mexico City in June 1984, Comandante Tomás Borge said that President Reagan "is not standing on such firm ground in the United States himself." He explained:

---

[92] Quoted in Robert F. Turner, *Vietnamese Communism: Its Origins and Development* (Stanford, Calif.: Hoover Institution Press, 1975), p.248.

[93] Evans, op.cit., p.179.

[94] FSLN, *Analysis . . . of the Sandinist People's Revolution*, op.cit., p.3.

[95] Evans, op.cit., pp.177-180; State/Defense, *Nicaragua's Military Buildup*, op.cit., p.5.

There are important sectors of the American people, political and religious sectors and even sectors in Congress, that have become aware of the magnitude of the disrespect and injustice involved in the policy of aggression against us. . . . [W]e will have to wait and see what happens in Congress. We will have to see what balance of political forces emerges within Congress after the elections.[96]

The 1984 campaign was not the first U.S. election of interest to the Sandinista leaders. Indeed, according to a captured Salvadoran insurgent document, dated September 30, 1980, one reason that the Nicaraguan Front decided to suspend shipments of arms to El Salvador for a one-month period "ha[d] to do with a political decision related to the U.S. elections, that is a possible understanding in order not to cause problems to Carter before November." The document further explained that "a breather in the fighting must be considered in order to see how the Carter-Reagan problem is solved."[97]

Particularly when it comes to the conduct of political warfare, Marxist-Leninists have no moral compulsion to tell the "truth"—at least as that term is used by most of the world. They have their own special meaning for the word. For example, in 1956 Ho Chi Minh said: "Truth is what is beneficial to the Fatherland and to the people. What is detrimental to the interests of the Fatherland and the people is not truth. To strive to serve the Fatherland and the people is to obey the truth."[98] This exercise in "humpty dumpty semantics"[99] is endorsed by the Sandinista leadership. Consider, for example, this account by the former Director of the U.S. Agency for International Development in Nicaragua:

A few months later [U.S. Ambassador] Larry Pezzullo and I were in Washington to lobby in Congress for the much delayed $75 million special appropriation for Nicaragua. The Sandinista Minister of Health. . .ånd we had dinner together. During the conversation, I complained about inaccuracies and distortions in *Barricada*, the official Sandinista newspaper, and *El Nuevo Diario*, which closely followed the Sandinista line. Both sounded very much like Cuba's official newspaper, *Granma*, particularly in their treatment of the United States. The Minister's response: "You don't understand revolutionary truth. *What is true is what serves the ends of the revolution.*"[100]

To give an example of how this pragmatic approach to truth works in practice, consider the Nicaraguan attitude toward the United States. Nicaraguan students regularly sing a national anthem which includes the

---

[96] *Excelsior* (Mexico City), June 4, 1984, p.A-1; quoted in FBIS, Daily Report, Latin America, June 8, 1984, pp.P-11, -13.

[97] Excerpt of letter from 'Fernando' to 'Federico' (dated September 30, 1980), translated and reprinted in State, *Communist Interference in El Salvador*, op.cit., Document J, p.5. See also, Document K, pp.3-4, for another reference to the U.S. election.

[98] Ho Chi Minh, *Selected Works*, op.cit., Vol. 4, p.176.

[99] "'When I use a word,' Humpty Dumpty said in a rather scornful tone, 'it means just what I choose it to mean—neither more nor less.' 'The question is,' said Alice, 'whether you CAN make words mean so many different things.' 'The question is,' said Humpty Dumpty, 'which is to be master—that's all.'" Lewis Carroll, *Alice in Wonderland*.

[100] Harrison, op.cit., p.75. (Emphasis added.) See also, Kramer, op.cit., p.37.

sentence: "We're fighting against the Yankee, the enemy of humanity."[101] The aforementioned 1979 internal party "analysis" said that "American imperialism" was "the rabid enemy of all peoples who are struggling to achieve their definitive liberation or are in the process of achieving it. . . ."[102] At the September 1979 Non-Aligned Movement summit in Havana, Comandante (now President) Daniel Ortega delivered a fiery anti-American speech, and in 1981 Defense Minister Humberto Ortega told the closing session of a "Meeting of Specialists": "Our revolution is profoundly anti-imperialist, profoundly revolutionary, profoundly class-oriented. We are anti-Yankee. We are against the bourgeoisie. . . . We are guided by the scientific doctrine of revolution, by Marxism-Leninism."[103]

Despite this, when Nicaragua sent Ricardo Espinoza, an official from its Washington embassy, to address a convention of the United Church of Christ in support of a subsequently adopted resolution "to protest against any U.S. military intervention in Nicaragua," Señor Espinoza had no hesitation in assuring the delegates that his government was neither communist nor Marxist, but founded on political pluralism, a mixed economy, and political nonalignment. He added: "We are by historical traditions nearer to the United States than to the eastern countries, and we intend to keep it that way."[104]

On this same point, consider this excerpt from the October 1983 *Playboy* interview with Sandinista leaders:

Father Cardenal: But this war may never happen—and can be prevented if there is sufficient pressure from the people, the press and the Congress of the United States on Reagan. . . .

[Tomás] Borge: Let me add something . . . let me stress how much the North Americans are loved and appreciated by the Nicaraguan people. . . . So if it fits in this *Interview*, we want to express that affection and respect to a people who knew their great historical responsibility during the war in Vietnam.[105]

This concept of "revolutionary truth" also helps to explain how, after years of active dedication to Marxism-Leninism, Sandinista leaders could in 1979—when it was important to win over as many moderates as possible inside Nicaragua and around the world—deny that they were communists, and yet the following year Humberto Ortega could announce: "We have always declared that we are Sandinistas, but we have never denied that we are

---

[101] Kramer, op.cit., p.37.

[102] FSLN, *Analysis . . . of the Sandinist People's Revolution*, op.cit., p.22.

[103] Speech by Humberto Ortega Saavedra, Nicaraguan Minister of Defense, reprinted in *La Prensa* (Managua), October 27, 1981, pp.16-19.

[104] Kristen Burroughs, "Get out of Nicaragua, church group urges," *Washington Times*, July 1, 1985, p.A-1. For a similar statement by Fidel Castro during his "non-communist" period, see p. 22, fn.1.

[105] Dreifus, op.cit., p.195.

Marxist-Leninists."[106] More importantly, it also helps explain how the Government of Nicaragua could deny providing arms, equipment, training, and other support on massive levels to Salvadoran guerrillas in the face of overwhelming evidence to the contrary.[107]

Sandinista Commitment to "Liberation Wars"

Although for political reasons Nicaragua generally denies its role in assisting armed revolutionary movements seeking to overthrow democratically-elected governments in neighboring states,[108] support for "national liberation movements" has been a consistent element of FSLN strategy from its inception.

For example, the 1968 Oath which each FSLN guerrilla was required to pledge provided in part:

> Before the image of Augusto César Sandino and Ernesto Ché Guevara . . . I place my hand on the red and black banner . . . and swear. . . to fight for the redemption of the oppressed and exploited of Nicaragua *and the world*. If I fulfill this oath, the liberation of Nicaragua and all of the peoples will be my reward; if I betray this oath, death in dishonor and disgrace will be my punishment.[109]

The following year, the Front adopted the Program of the Sandinist Front of National Liberation, including the following provisions:

> 13) **Solidarity among peoples**. The people's Sandinist revolution will practice a true combative solidarity with the peoples fighting for their liberation.
>
> a) It will actively support the fight of the peoples of Latin America, Africa, and Asia against imperialism, colonialism, and neocolonialism. . . .
>
> 14) **Central American people's unity**. The people's Sandinist revolution will struggle for the true union of the Central American peoples within one country.
>
> a) It will support an authentic unity with its brother peoples in Central America. This unity will begin with the cooperation of forces to achieve national liberation. . . .[110]

In order to avoid unnecessary problems with their neighbors and with other states (since such intervention is a flagrant violation of international law), the Sandinista leadership downplayed this aspect of their philosophy upon

---

[106] R. Bruce McColm, "The Nicaraguan Revolution: Slouching Toward Oblivion," *Freedom at Issue*, September-October 1981, p.9.

[107] See Chapter 3.

[108] The Sandinistas are clearly aware that their public statements will be carefully scrutinized and that indiscretion could undermine the success of their political warfare efforts. In a speech to the Nonaligned Conference in Havana, Cuba, in September 1979, Daniel Ortega said: "We know that. . . the most reactionary sectors of the United States government and of Latin America are waiting to pounce on our declarations at this meeting." Reprinted in Leiken and Rubin, op.cit., p.208.

[109] Quoted in Nolan, op.cit., p.35. (Emphasis added.)

[110] "Notes for History: Program of the Sandinist Front of National Liberation," *Tricontinental* (Havana), No. 17, March/April 1970, p.68. This document is also reprinted in Leiken and Rubin, op.cit., pp.148-153.

coming to power in 1979; however, some of their more enthusiastic subordinates apparently did not get word of the new line. Consider, for example, this journalistic account written near the end of the first week of Sandinista rule in Nicaragua:

Even before the shouting and tumult over the Sandinista victory in Nicaragua had quieted, glances were being cast northward to El Salvador and Guatemala as the next targets in a guerrilla sweep of Central America.

In fact, some Sandinistas are making no secret of their desire to "liberate" the people of those two countries from what they view as governments of the same ilk as that of deposed Nicaraguan President Anastasio Somoza Debayle. . . .

The other evening, a Sandinista soldier who said he had "political duty" in Nicaragua, talked of the coming struggle elsewhere in Central America. In a parting comment he said, "I will see you in Salvador and Guatemala."[111]

Despite obvious efforts to avoid admitting their support for "liberation" struggles in other countries, Sandinista leaders occasionally provide evidence of such involvement.[112] On other occasions, they publicly reaffirm their historic commitment in principle to support such movements. For example, in March 1980 Comandante Daniel Ortega met in Grenada with Maurice Bishop (head of Grenada's People's Revolutionary Government) and Michael Manley (Prime Minister of Jamaica). According to press accounts of the meeting, "[t]he three leftist leaders all committed themselves to aiding other revolutionaries. . . ."[113] As if to ratify this undertaking, after condemning "Yankee imperialism" as the "common enemy," Ortega presented Bishop with a Soviet-made Kalashnikov automatic rifle at the conclusion of his remarks.[114]

The FSLN occasionally reaffirms its "internationalist duty" in its internal propaganda. In late 1983, for example, a pamphlet prepared by several FSLN organizations to commemorate the sixteenth anniversary of the death of Ché Guevara stated: "For us Sandinistas evoking Ché Guevara is to keep in mind the projection without frontiers of the revolution, of the internationalist. . . ."[115]

Nicaraguan leaders have suggested that the success of their own revolution cannot be assured until neighboring states follow a similar course. For

---

[111] James Nelson Goodsell, "Nicaragua: War for Export?," *Christian Science Monitor*, July 25, 1979.

[112] Admissions of involvement in the guerrilla effort to overthrow the Government of El Salvador are discussed on pp. 89–94.

[113] Gilbert A. Lewthwaite, "3 leftist chiefs pledge unity in Caribbean area," *Baltimore Sun*, March 14, 1980, p.6. See also, Karen DeYoung, "Nicaragua Gets Cheers at Nonaligned Summit," *Washington Post*, September 7, 1979, p.11. DeYoung reported that "Nicaragua brought the sixth nonaligned summit to its feet today with a speech [by Daniel Ortega] loudly defending 'liberation struggles,' denouncing historical 'U.S. imperialism' and asking for help in consolidating its own revolution."

[114] Ibid. (Lewthwaite).

[115] Quoted in *El Nuevo Diario* (Managua), October 8, 1983.

example, during an interview in *Cuadernos de Marcha* (Mexico) in January 1980, Sergio Ramírez stated:

It must be admitted that deeper social change cannot take place in one country without similar transformation in those that surround it. To be specific, a process of change in one Central American country requires that a similar process be in progress in the others. Naturally, this does not mean that we leave off pursuing our own course to its ultimate consequences, but we cannot neglect giving special attention to our immediate neighbors.[116]

Support for International Terrorism

Nicaraguan support for insurgency movements in El Salvador, Honduras, and Costa Rica will be dealt with in subsequent chapters. However, it is important to keep in mind that Sandinista support for terrorist groups is not limited to Central America. Indeed, Nicaragua has become a haven for terrorist organizations from around the world—including the Palestine Liberation Organization (PLO), the Irish Republican Army (IRA), the Basque ETA, the German Baader-Meinhoff gang, the Italian Red Brigade, and the Colombian M-19 group.[117]

A study prepared in 1982 for the Foreign Area Studies program of American University observed:

Influence of another sort on the Sandinista Armed Forces [EPS] came from the PLO, which had a long-standing relationship with the FSLN. Sandinista spokesmen acknowledged that they received training in PLO bases in Algeria and Jordan and participated in PLO terrorist operations such as hijackings. PLO leader Yasser Arafat was an honored guest at the July 19, 1980, celebration; shortly afterward it was reported that a senior PLO military commander led a delegation to Nicaragua to supervise the training of EPS soldiers in unspecified Soviet-bloc weapons.[118]

In February 1985 Italian Prime Minister Bettino Craxi charged that 44 Red Brigade terrorists were in Managua.[119]

Nicaragua was implicated by the Government of Colombia in the November 6, 1985 M-19 seizure of the Palace of Justice in Bogota, which resulted in nearly 100 deaths (including 11 Supreme Court justices). Among other evidence of Nicaraguan involvement was the fact that some of the weapons used in the assault were traced by their serial numbers to weapons given to the Sandinistas by Venezuela for use against Somoza. In part because of this incident, Colombia recalled its ambassador from Managua in December 1985.[120]

---

[116] Reprinted in Leiken and Rubin, op.cit., p.214.

[117] See, e.g., U.S. Department of State, *The Sandinistas and Middle Eastern Radicals* (Washington, D.C.: U.S. Government Printing Office, August 1985), p.13, and sources cited therein.

[118] Rudolph, op.cit., p. 215.

[119] "Terrorism's Western Branch," *Washington Times*, May 16, 1986, p.A-11.

[120] See, e.g., "Nicaraguan Arms Found in Colombia," *Washington Post*, January 5, 1986, p.A-22; "Sandinistas Reject Colombian Charge They Armed Rebels," *Washington Times*, January 6, 1986, p.B-5.

3. Nicaraguan Aggression Against El Salvador

The Sandinistas give total help, advice and direction on how to manage the war and internal politics. The guerrillas are trained in Managua, the Sandinistas help the air force, army and navy get arms through. Some arms come from Cuba via Nicaragua. They use the houses of Nicaraguan officers for safehouses and command posts. There is a heavy influx of communications giving orders. You can say the whole guerrilla effort is managed by Nicaragua. The Sandinistas told them unless the guerrillas got their factions together they wouldn't give them any help.

Miguel Bolaños Hunter,
former Sandinista intelligence officer[1]

The Government of Nicaragua has engaged in a substantial and continuing attempt since at least 1980 to destabilize and overthrow the Government of El Salvador.[2] Because the Sandinistas realize that evidence of their unlawful intervention in El Salvador would undermine their efforts to gain the political support of the people of the United States and other countries, they have endeavored to conceal the extent of their support for the Salvadoran insurgents.[3] Nevertheless, there is an abundance of evidence, both classi-

---

[1] *Miguel Bolaños Transcripts*, op.cit., p.37. Bolaños led a 60-man Sandinista guerrilla command (one of 12 in Managua) during the final battles of the anti-Somoza revolution. He subsequently served as an assistant to the Chief of Staff of the Nicaraguan Army, and between 1980 and his decision to seek asylum in Costa Rica on May 7, 1983, he worked as a member of the Sandinista intelligence service, the Direccíon General de Seguridad del Estado (DGSE). According to the *Washington Post*, whose writers conducted this interview, "Various independent sources here and in Central America confirm Bolaños' identity . . . ." (Don Oberdorfer and Joanne Omang, "Nicaraguan Bares Plan to Discredit Foes," *Washington Post*, June 19, 1983, p.A-1.)

[2] The FSLN was actually providing training and other assistance to Salvadoran guerrillas long before their own victory over Somoza. See p. 69, fn. 92. For an unclassified reference to U.S. intelligence reports concerning Nicaraguan arms shipments to "guerrillas in Central America," see Juan de Onis, "Congress Releases Aid to Nicaraguans," *New York Times*, September 13, 1980, p.2. See also, Christopher Dickey, "El Salvador's Shadowy War," *Washington Post*, June 30, 1980, p.1. ("Many of the guerrilla arms captured by the [Salvadoran] government originated in Venezuela. But they were never intended for El Salvador. They had been sent by the former government of Social Democrat Carlos Andres Perez last year to Nicaragua's Sandinistas.")

[3] Sandinista spokesmen have frequently flatly denied providing any assistance to Salvadoran guerrillas. For example, in a sworn affidavit dated April 21, 1984, accompanying the Nicaraguan Memorial to the International Court of Justice, Foreign Minister Miguel D'Escoto Brockmann stated: "I am aware of the allegations made by the government of the United States that my government is sending arms, ammunition, communications equipment and medical supplies to rebels conducting a civil war against the government of El Salvador. Such allegations are false. . . . In truth, my government is not engaged, and has not been engaged, in the provision of arms or other supplies to either of the factions engaged in the civil war in El Salvador." At the height of the arms buildup for the January 1981 "final offensive" (discussed below), Interior Minister Tomás Borge Martinez asserted: "Those who

46

fied and unclassified, which establishes beyond reasonable doubt substantial Nicaraguan involvement in the internal affairs of El Salvador in violation of fundamental rules of international law.[4]

Creation of the FMLN

Before examining the role of Nicaragua in the armed campaign to overthrow the Government of El Salvador, it is useful to review briefly the origin and organization of the Farabundo Marti National Liberation Front (FMLN)[5]—the umbrella organization directing the Marxist-Leninist insurgency in El Salvador—and its component military and political organizations.

The Communist Party of El Salvador (Partido Comunista de El Salvador— PCES) was founded in March 1930, and was accepted into the Third (Communist) International later that year. The PCES was virtually destroyed in January 1932, when most of its members were killed during an abortive uprising.[6] During the mid-1970s its membership was estimated at between 100 and 200.[7]

The PCES has always taken a pro-Soviet stand, and its relatively moderate position (based in part on the disastrous 1932 experience) prior to the 1979 shift in Moscow's policy on the use of force led to serious dissension within the party—especially after the victory of Fidel Castro in Cuba—and

---

say that the Salvadoran revolution is being promoted from other countries are deliberately lying. For example, although we support the Salvadoran people, we have not interfered in their internal affairs. . . . On the contrary, our position is that the Salvadorans should be permitted to resolve their own domestic national situation without interference from anyone." (Remarks at ceremony to promote several Interior Ministry officials, Radio Sandino, December 27, 1980.) When asked by a Venezuelan magazine about U.S. charges that "Nicaragua has become a bridgehead for the shipment of weapons to El Salvador by the Cubans and Soviets," Borge responded: "They say that we are sending weapons to El Salvador but they have not offered any real proof. But let us suppose that weapons have reached El Salvador from here. This is possible. More than that, it is possible that Nicaraguan combatants have gone to El Salvador, but this cannot be blamed on any decision of ours." (*Bohemia* [Caracas], April 20-26, 1981.) Shortly after coming to power, Borge had indicated "that the junta 'probably would not' stop volunteer Nicaraguans from fighting with guerrilla groups active in Guatemala and El Salvador. . . ." Charles A. Krause, "Nicaragua Unmoved by U.S. Overtures," *Washington Post*, August 7, 1979, p.1.

[4] For a brief discussion of the legality of Nicaragua's intervention in El Salvador and other countries, see pp. 112–116. A more detailed legal analysis may be found in John Norton Moore, "The Secret War in Central America and the Future of World Order," *American Journal of International Law*, Vol. 80, January 1986, p.43. See also John Norton Moore, *The Secret War in Central America* (Frederick, Md.: University Publications of America, 1987), p.71, n.13.

[5] The FMLN was named after Farabundo Marti, a prominent Salvadoran Marxist and Comintern agent who served for a while with General Augusto César Sandino in Nicaragua. Marti was eventually asked to leave Nicaragua by the nationalist Sandino because of ideological differences. See p. 26.

[6] For a discussion of this period, see Thomas P. Anderson, "The Roots of Revolution in Central America," in Wiarda, op.cit., pp.119-120. Anderson writes that during the abortive uprising, ten thousand or more rebels were shot. Ibid., p.120.

[7] See, e.g., *1976 Yearbook on International Communist Affairs*, op.cit., p.478.

eventually to the establishment of more militant radical groups.[8] The first of these rifts occurred in 1964, when PCES Secretary General Salvador Cayetano Carpio[9] split with other party leaders over their refusal to endorse armed struggle, and using the nom de guerre "Comandante Marcial" formed the Farabundo Marti Popular Liberation Forces (FPL)—the largest of the insurgent groups now in El Salvador.[10]

By 1972 another faction of Castroite, Maoist, and Trotskyite dissidents had abandoned the PCES and established the People's Revolutionary Army (Ejército Revolucionario del Pueblo—ERP) under the leadership of Roque Dalton García, Joaquin Villalobos, and Ana Maria Guadalupe Martinez.[11] In May 1975, Roque Dalton was assassinated by a dissident element of the group. This led to the establishment of the Armed Forces of National Resistance (FARN), a splinter group led by Ernesto Jovel and Fermán Cienfuegos. Each of these Marxist-Leninist organizations controlled a "popular front" group.[12] There was also a tiny Trotskyite group, the Revolutionary Party of Central American Workers (PRTC), reportedly headed by former University of El Salvador rector Fabio Castillo.

---

[8] See, e.g., Alan Riding, "Salvador Rebels: Five-Sided Alliance Searching for New, Moderate Image," *New York Times*, March 18, 1982, p.A-1.

[9] For useful background on the FPL and other FMLN groups, see Leiken and Rubin, op.cit., pp.322-323. This source notes that "the FMLN was far more explicitly Marxist-Leninist than were the Sandinistas." Ibid., p.322. Carpio, sometimes referred to as "El Salvador's Ho Chi Minh," joined the Communist Party in 1948 at the age of 28. (Ibid.) He was the leading Salvadoran guerrilla commander at the time of his death in Nicaragua (reportedly by suicide) in April 1983.

[10] Lest there be any doubt about the Marxist-Leninist orientation of these groups, the official flag of the FPL includes the Soviet hammer and sickle. State/Defense, *Nicaragua's Military Buildup*, op.cit., p.24, n.47. Cayetano Carpio has been quoted as having said: "The revolutionary process in Central America is a single process. The triumphs of one are the triumphs of the others. Guatemala will have its hour. Honduras its. Costa Rica, too, will have its hour of glory. The first note was heard in Nicaragua." Kramer, op.cit., p.41. Kramer writes: "What would a Villalobos-led government be like? 'Well,' says José Rodriguez Ruiz, a member of the rebel directorate, 'there are parts of Ho Chi Minh, parts of Mao, parts of Kim Il Sung [North Korea's premier] that appeal to us.'" (Ibid.) FMLN admiration for the Marxist-Leninist regime of Fidel Castro was emphasized in a speech by Comandante Fermán Cienfuegos of the FMLN general command, who said in early August 1985: "[W]e consider that the new Cuba is successful evidence of what the new Latin America and the Caribbean will be: our America." Speech at Foreign Debt Conference, Havana; reported in FBIS, Daily Report, Latin America, August 5, 1985, p.Q-12. See also, Joe Frazier, "El Salvador battle grows," *Philadelphia Inquirer*, September 16, 1979, p.A-16. Frazier reported that "Ideological disputes separate the groups, which have not formed a united front. All want to replace the regime of General Carlos Humberto Romero with a Marxist one, but ideology and method remain in dispute." There is some disagreement about the date of Carpio's break with the PCS and formation of the FPL. Robert Leiken, for example, asserts that it occurred in 1970. See Leiken, op.cit., p.115.

[11] See Alan Riding, "Salvador Rebels: Five-Sided Alliance Searching for New, Moderate Image," *New York Times*, March 18, 1982, p.A-1.

[12] The PCES for several decades has worked through the National Democratic Union (UDN), a legal political party which was invited to participate in recent Salvadoran elections but refused to do so. The FPL controls the Popular Revolutionary Bloc (BPR), the ERP controls the Popular Leagues of February 28(LP-28), and the FARN controls the Movement of Popular Liberation (MLP).

Prior to 1979 extremist guerrilla groups in El Salvador were generally ineffective. They not only refused to cooperate, but often fought with each other.[13] Their activities were limited primarily to occasional assassinations, bombings, and—for fund-raising purposes—bank robberies and kidnappings. All of this changed dramatically with the July 1979 Sandinista victory in Nicaragua.

In December 1979 leaders of the PCES,[14] FPL, and FARN were invited to Cuba for the first of several meetings with Fidel Castro. Although many details of this meeting are not available in unclassified form, senior Salvadoran guerrillas who participated in other such meetings have indicated that Nicaraguan officials are commonly present.[15] One thing that is known is that Castro offered to supply modern arms, other military equipment, and training[16] if the rival guerrilla groups would agree to work together for the common purpose of overthrowing the Government of El Salvador.[17] The three factions agreed to form the Revolutionary Coordinator of the Masses (CRM)—a federation to coordinate the activities of far left political fronts and armed groups—and the decision was made public the following month.

In April 1980—a month associated by some scholars with the start of El Salvador's civil war[18]—several small noncommunist organizations formed a "Democratic Front,"[19] which almost immediately merged with the Marxist

---

[13] See, e.g., Alan Riding, "Salvador Rebels: Five-Sided Alliance Searching for New, Moderate Image," *New York Times*, March 18, 1982, p.A-1: "By 1975, three guerrilla groups were active in El Salvador, although they were barely on speaking terms. The police would later distinguish them by referring to the Popular Forces of Liberation as the 'pistoleros,' or gunmen, the People's Revolutionary Army as the 'bomberos,' or bombers, and the National Resistance as the 'pisteros,' or money-chasers, because of the huge war chest they had built up from assaults and kidnappings."

[14] At its Seventh Party Congress in April 1979, the PCES had shifted to support for "armed struggle." See interview with PCES Secretary General Shafik Handal, *Granma* (Havana), June 1, 1980, cited in Warner Poelchau, editor, *White Paper Whitewash: Interviews with Philip Agee on the CIA and El Salvador* (New York: Deep Cover Books, 1981), p.79.

[15] For example, intelligence sources have confirmed high-level Nicaraguan participation in the founding in May 1980 of the Unified Revolutionary Directorate (DRU)—discussed below—and defector Moises López-Arriola has given details about a meeting in which he participated with Fidel Castro, other Cuban leaders, members of the Sandinista Liberation Front, and other FMLN representatives in July 1981.

[16] Even prior to the Sandinista victory Cuba had already trained more than 200 FPL guerrillas, and FARN's Fermán Cienfuegos was known to have met regularly with Cuban intelligence officers. See State/Defense, *Nicaragua's Military Buildup*, op.cit., p.15.

[17] See, e.g., State, *Cuba's Renewed Support for Violence*, op.cit., p.6; and Alan Riding, "Salvador Rebels: Five-Sided Alliance Searching for New, Moderate Image," *New York Times*, March 18, 1982, p.A-1.

[18] See, e.g., Thomas P. Anderson, "The Roots of Revolution in Central America," in Wiarda, op.cit., p.121.

[19] These organizations include the National Revolutionary Movement (MNR)—a member of the Socialist International—headed by Guillermo Manuel Ungo (who in December 1980 was selected to head the Revolutionary Democratic Front—FDR); and the Popular Socialist Christian Movement (MPSC), which was composed of a handful of former Christian Democrats who were either expelled from or abandoned the Salvadoran Christian Democratic Party in early 1980. See "El Salvador Tilts Further Toward Full Civil War," *New York Times*, April 6, 1980, p.E-2.

political groups to form the Revolutionary Democratic Front (FDR). The FDR has no control over military decisions, and operates largely outside El Salvador, serving as a noncommunist facade for dealing with democratic groups abroad.

In May 1980 CPES Secretary General Jorgé Roberto Shafik Handal,[20] the FPL's Carpio, and other Salvadoran Marxists again visited Cuba and met with Nicaraguan and Cuban leaders.[21] As a result of these discussions, the Unified Revolutionary Directorate (DRU) was formed, to serve as the high military and political command for the five Marxist-Leninist revolutionary groups.[22] The democratic elements of the FDR have no voice in the DRU, which coordinates both political and military strategy for the war.

The insurgent leaders again returned to Havana in October 1980, at which time they agreed to create a political/military umbrella front for all of the far left opposition groups. The Farabundo Marti National Liberation Front (FMLN) brought together the organizations of the DRU and the FDR; but, although most guerrilla activities are conducted in its name, it is in reality subordinate to the DRU, which actually decides military and political strategy.

The FMLN and Political Warfare

Just as the FSLN in Nicaragua learned from the experiences of earlier revolutionary movements in Cuba, China, Vietnam, and elsewhere, the Salvadoran FMLN has placed great emphasis on political warfare and has sought to emulate the successes of the Sandinistas. To gain the support of the Salvadoran people they have established a United Front, and they have promised that if victorious they will "ensure a just distribution of wealth and

---

[20] Handal joined the Communist Party in 1951 at the age of 20, and has been the PCES Secretary General since 1972. He has long maintained close ties with both Moscow and Havana. See, e.g., Alan Riding, "Salvador Rebels: Five-Sided Alliance Searching for New, Moderate Image," *New York Times*, March 18, 1982, p.A-1.

[21] This meeting is referred to in captured Salvadoran guerrilla documents. See, for example, "Report on meeting of guerrilla Joint General Staff (EMGC) of September 26, 1980," translated and reprinted in State, *Communist Interference in El Salvador*, op.cit., Document I, p.1. ("I am including these facts in the report because this has been more or less the operating situation of the Joint General Staff since it came from Cuba.")

[22] The PRTC did not join the DRU until later in the year. Although the FARN participated in the original December 1979 unification meeting in Havana, and joined the DRU when it was created in May of the following year, it later withdrew from the Directorate. As will be discussed, this led to deep concern within the DRU that Nicaraguan and Cuban arms supplies might be terminated, but Nicaraguan officials assured DRU representatives in Managua that the supplies would continue. After FARN leader Ernesto Jovel died in September 1980 (under confused circumstances, variously attributed to an automobile accident and an airplane crash), the group rejoined the DRU. According to Alan Riding, the leaders of all five groups "profess to be Marxists. . . ." See Riding, "Salvador Rebels: Five-Sided Alliance Searching for New, Moderate Image," *New York Times*, March 18, 1982, p.A-1. For a discussion of this meeting, see Bernard Weinraub, "Cuba Directs Salvador Insurgency, Former Guerrilla Lieutenant Says," *New York Times*, July 28, 1983, p.A-10.

health, and an international policy of peace and nonalignment." According to Carpio, a victorious FMLN "will guarantee the democratic representation of all people's democratic and revolutionary sectors which participated actively in the overthrow of the military dictatorship," and will "support all private businessmen who cooperate. . . ."[23]

Like the Sandinistas before them, a major FMLN priority has been to influence public opinion in the United States. As Philip Taubman wrote in the *New York Times* in 1982:

In recent months, with increasing sophistication, the leaders of the guerrilla movement in El Salvador have mounted a public relations campaign directed at world opinion in general, and at American public opinion in particular.

"We have to win the war inside the United States," said Hector Oqueli, one of the rebel leaders. . . . His colleague, Ruben Zamora, added: "We have tried to change our public image."

By drawing on advice from American and Mexican friends and employing the latest technology such as video recorders, the insurgents have brought a little bit of Madison Avenue to the violent business of waging revolution. . . .

Vietnam Example Cited
The guerrillas began with the example of Vietnam. "The American media, especially television, turned public opinion against the war," said Mr. Zamora.[24]

Recognizing that they lack the popular support to gain power through a free election,[25] the insurgents hope to strengthen their own military forces so as to gain at the conference table a role in the government they could not obtain through elections. Until the correlation of forces is more favorable, they do not expect negotiations to be substantively productive—but they are nevertheless important because of their political value. A June 1980 strategic plan devised in Cuba for the Salvadoran insurgency, which was later captured by Salvadoran government forces, included these points:

---

[23] *Le Monde* (Paris), January 9, 1981, p.7. See also, "Rebel Communique Issued," Tass (Moscow), in English, 0635 GMT, January 12, 1981; in FBIS, Soviet Union, January 12, 1981, p.K-1. (This broadcast, datelined Managua, transmitted a "communique" which promised to defend "the interests of the broad masses of the people," and said that "All the popular, revolutionary and democratic forces, which are taking an active part in crushing the anti-national dictatorship, will participate in the activity of the government.")

[24] Philip Taubman, "Salvadorans' U.S. Campaign: Selling of Revolution," *New York Times*, February 26, 1982. Napoleón Romero García, one of the most senior leaders to defect from the FMLN, explained that the insurgents' propaganda theme would be to tell the Salvadoran people that Duarte—who they recognized was very popular—had "promised much but actually accomplished very little. . . . This unfavorable view of the Duarte government would then be used by the FMLN's international supporters to gain the insurgents' second objective—the reduction or termination of U.S. support to El Salvador." . . . Declassified transcript of debriefing with Napoleón Romero García, former Secretary General of Metropolitan Front and Central Committee member, Popular Liberation Forces (FPL), provided to author by Department of State (hereinafter cited as "Romero debriefing"). See also, Department of State, *Background Paper: Central America*, May 27, 1983, p.14.

[25] See, for example, Kramer, op.cit., p.41, where he reports: "I asked if the guerrillas would participate in next year's elections in El Salvador. 'No way, man,' said Zamora. 'We'd lose.' "

U.S. Initiatives: Representatives should strengthen ties with sympathetic American organizations and seek support from American politicians.

Public Posture: From the outset, representatives should call for a dialogue to seek resolution of the conflict. "The policy of a dialogue is a tactical maneuver to broaden our alliances, while at the same time splitting up and isolating the enemy."[26]

In April 1985 the Salvadoran National Guard arrested Napoleón Romero García (alias Miguel Castellanos) in a raid on a safehouse in San Salvador. Romero was a member of the Central Committee of the Popular Liberation Forces (FPL) and Secretary General of the FPL's Metropolitan Front. A recently declassified summary of his debriefing reveals how the insurgent leaders view negotiations:

According to Romero, the insurgents see a clear distinction between dialogue, which they consider to be a preliminary stage, and actual negotiations when specific points are discussed. . . . In general, the FMLN regards the dialogue as simply another tactic, albeit a useful one. For them, the main purpose of any talks is to support the armed conflict—their primary concern. The basic view of insurgent leaders, said Romero, is that a true dialogue leading to meaningful negotiations will not be possible until the military strength of the FMLN is on a par with that of the Salvadoran Armed Forces. . . . Romero cited the FMLN belief that a refusal to meet with Duarte would give the United States an excuse to send more aid to El Salvador. They also see the dialogue as a chance to gain time in which to strengthen their military position.

Romero said that politically, the dialogue is seen by the FMLN high command as a propaganda bonanza for the insurgent cause, as it affords the FMLN with an opportunity to present a message to a great number of people and, hopefully, to gain support both domestically and internationally. . . . Even though there are some minor differences [between the FPL and the ERP], both groups generally regard the dialogue as a tactical maneuver, believing that the more intransigent they can make the government appear, the more they gain justification for continuing the armed conflict.[27]

---

[26] State, *Background Paper: Central America*, op.cit., p.14. Consider this exchange during an interview with an FDR representative: "Q.: What actions will the FDR and the [FMLN] take in the international field? A.: We have already announced the creation of an FMLN-FDR political/diplomatic committee to carry out the diplomatic tasks of the Salvadoran people's army abroad, especially in the American continent, but also in other countries in Europe, Africa and Asia. Therefore, we are immediately launching a diplomatic offensive to show that the FDR is the only possible alternative for power, government and peace in El Salvador. Naturally, this diplomatic offensive has as its objective to prevent intervention by other countries, such as . . . the U.S. Government. . . ." Fabio Castillo, Radio Noticias del Continente (San José), 1900 GMT, January 11, 1981; in FBIS, Central America, January 12, 1981, p.P-16. Under the heading, "Negotiations as Strategy," Robert S. Leiken writes: "After the failure of the 'final offensive' in February 1981, the political diplomatic commission of the FMLN-FDR approved an internal document which committed it for the first time to negotiations. Yet the document supported negotiations only as a 'tactic,' a 'maneuver' for 'gaining time and diplomatic initiative.' " Robert S. Leiken, "The Salvadoran Left," in Leiken, op.cit., p.121.

[27] Romero debriefing, op.cit.

52

Providing Arms and Equipment

In 1982 the Commander-in-Chief of the ERP's National Central Guerrilla Front (Frente Central Nacional Guerrillero), Alejandro Montenegro, was apprehended in Honduras while en route to a meeting with Salvadoran guerrilla leaders in Nicaragua.[28] In a subsequent interview with the *New York Times*, Montenegro stated "that virtually all of the arms received by the guerrilla units he led came from Nicaragua."[29] Such charges have been strongly denied both by Nicaraguan and Salvadoran insurgent spokesmen.

- **Supplying M-16 Rifles**

In January 1981, Nicaraguan Defense Minister Humberto Ortega stated:

We stand accused of being in solidarity with the just struggle of the Salvadoran people, and we are accused of intervening in El Salvador, of arming the Salvadoran people. What happens is that our enemy does not realize that when they decide to struggle, people find arms anywhere and turn everything into a weapon, just as the Nicaraguan people did when they turned paving stones into weapons, turned into weapons their will to die until they were victorious.[30]

While perhaps an inspirational statement, in reality Salvadoran guerrillas were not armed with "paving stones." Indeed, during the so-called final offensive of January 1981, many Salvadoran guerrillas carried modern U.S.-made M-16 automatic rifles. Some of these were captured by Salvadoran government forces and displayed to the international press.[31] This was readily explained by Salvadoran guerrilla leaders: "Imperialist spokesmen have reported that the FMLN has expensive and sophisticated weapons that were acquired in the Socialist countries and brought into the country through Nicaragua. . . . This misinformation campaign seeks to minimize the huge amount of weapons that our victorious army has seized in battle."[32] On another occasion, the FMLN explained: "We wish to tell the

---

[28] His importance to the guerrilla movement is illustrated by the fact that in mid-September 1982 guerrillas kidnapped four ministers and 200 Honduran civilians inside San Pedro Sula Chamber of Commerce and demanded Montenegro's release. When their demands were not met, they released the hostages on September 28 in return for transportation to Cuba.

[29] Hedrick Smith, "A Former Salvadoran Rebel Chief Tells of Arms from Nicaragua," *New York Times*, July 12, 1984, p.A-10.

[30] Remarks at the First International Meeting of Solidarity with Nicaragua, Managua domestic service, January 31, 1981.

[31] Salvadoran Defense Minister José Guillermo García held a press conference on January 19, 1981, at which time he displayed M-16 rifles along with other weapons captured from the insurgents. See FBIS, Latin America, January 21, 1981, p.P-4. See also, Jeffrey Antevil, "El Salvador rebels getting M-16s via Cuba, Nicaragua, U.S. says," *Philadelphia Inquirer*, January 29, 1981, p.D-1; and Gerald F. Seib, "Big Cuban Aid to Salvador Guerrillas Gives U.S. a Rationale to Turn Tough," *Wall Street Journal*, February 5, 1981, p.24. Seib reported that "Among the weapons captured from guerrillas were U.S. M-16 rifles, which may have come from the large stocks of American arms left behind in Vietnam."

[32] FMLN General Command statement of July 24, 1984, quoted in United States Department of State and Department of Defense, *News Briefing: Intelligence Information on External Support of the Guerrillas in El Salvador*, August 8, 1984, p.3. (Hereinafter cited as

United States administration that the weapons carried by the Salvadoran workers are the weapons we have recovered, in combat, from the army they train and direct."[33]

This explanation suffered from two serious flaws. First, Salvadoran anti-government insurgents were armed with M-16s at least as early as December 1980—over a month *before* such weapons were even issued to Salvadoran military forces fighting against the insurgents.[34] The United States did not make the decision to provide "lethal" assistance—including a limited quantity of M-16 rifles—to the Government of El Salvador until a week after the "final offensive."[35]

Second, M-16 rifles are individually marked with serial numbers, and a comparison of the serial numbers from the more than 200 M-16s captured by Salvadoran government soldiers from FMLN guerrillas as of June 1984 showed that only 40 weapons—19 percent of the total—were traceable to U.S. deliveries to the Salvadoran government.[36] A study done at the same time based on the serial numbers from 239 additional M-16s identified in captured guerrilla records produced only 12 weapons (5 percent) traceable to deliveries to Salvadoran armed forces. On the other hand, the study showed that nearly three-quarters (73 percent) of the captured M-16s were traceable by their serial numbers to stockpiles captured by the Vietnamese communists after the United States withdrew from Vietnam more than a decade ago.[37]

State/Defense, *External Support of Guerrillas in El Salvador*.) Actually, one of the noteworthy aspects of the "final offensive" was the amount of weapons and equipment captured by the government from guerrilla troops. See Christopher Dickey, "U.S. Adds 'Lethal' Aid to El Salvador," *Washington Post*, January 18, 1981, p.1: After noting how well armed the insurgents were, Dickey commented: "But they have also lost a good deal of this equipment in battle. . . ."

[33] FMLN General Command statement of July 6, 1984, quoted in State/Defense, *External Support of the Guerrillas in El Salvador*, op.cit., p.3.

[34] It is worth noting that M-16 rifles were not the only U.S.-made weapons captured from Salvadoran insurgents during the "final offensive" that were not yet in the Salvadoran army inventory. For example, the same was true of M-79 40mm grenade launchers. See, e.g., San Salvador Domestic Service in Spanish, 1853 GMT, January 20, 1981; translated in FBIS, Latin America, January 21, 1981, p.P-7.

[35] See, e.g., Christopher Dickey, "U.S. Adds 'Lethal' Aid to El Salvador," *Washington Post*, January 18, 1981, p.1 (noting that M-16 rifles would be included in a $5 million aid package); and Christopher Dickey, "Salvadoran Military Begins Training with U.S. Weapons, Advisers," *Washington Post*, January 25, 1981, p.15: "Salvadoran troops are breaking out their new American M-16 rifles, grenade launchers, flak jackets and steel helmets. . . . [F]or the first time since El Salvador was caught in the net of Carter administration refusal to provide guns and bullets to alleged human rights abusers in Latin America in 1977, that aid now includes 'lethal' military equipment."

[36] State/Defense, *External Support of the Guerrillas in El Salvador*, op.cit., p.15. As of August 1984, fewer than 2,000 of the 36,000 M-16s provided to Salvadoran armed forces had been lost in combat or were unaccounted for (ibid.), and Salvadoran military forces had captured (or in some cases recaptured) several hundred M-16s from insurgents.

[37] Ibid. The Vietnamese communists took possession of an estimated 700,000 M-16 rifles when they captured South Vietnam in 1975. See Edward C. Ezell, *Small Arms Today: Latest*

Given the secrecy which understandably surrounds such an operation, there is a surprisingly clear record of how thousands of U.S.-made M-16 rifles got from communist Vietnam to guerrillas fighting against the Government of El Salvador nine thousand miles away—even without resorting to the kind of sensitive intelligence sources and methods that are unavailable for inclusion in an unclassified study.[38]

Between June 9 and July 3, 1980, Salvadoran Communist Party Secretary General Shafik Handal visited the Soviet Union and a number of other "socialist" countries seeking arms and equipment for the anti-government insurgency in El Salvador. A detailed report based upon his trip was captured in November 1980 by Salvadoran government forces during a raid on a San Salvador art gallery belonging to Handal's brother. It indicates that virtually everywhere he stopped Handal found a receptive audience, although not every government could provide substantial quantities of the "Western-made" weapons he was particularly seeking in order to conceal the extent of his communist bloc external support.[39] For this purpose, however, the Vietnamese government was particularly helpful. Consider this excerpt from the Handal trip report:

1. Vietnam from 9 to 15 June. Received by Le Duan, secretary general of the Vietnamese C[ommunist] P[arty]; Xuan Thuy, member of the secretariat of the central committee and vice president of the National Assembly; and Tran Van Quang, lieutenant general, deputy minister of National Defense. Friendly and enthusiastic reception. They agreed to provide aid in weapons, the first shipment consisting of: 192 9mm pistols; 1,620 AR-15 rifles [M-16s[40]]; 162 M-30 medium machine guns; 36 M-60 heavy machine guns; 12 M-50 heavy machine guns (caliber 12.7mm); 36 6mm mortars; 12 81mm mortars; 12 DKZ-57 antitank rocket launchers. Ammunition: 15,000 cartridges for M-30 and M-60 machine guns (7.62mm); 130,000 cartridges for M-50 machine guns (12.7mm); 9,000 shells for 61mm mortars; 4,000 shells for 81mm mortars; 1,500 shells for DKZ-57 antitank weapon. Approximate weight of the entire shipment: 60 tons.

According to a message received at the embassy here on July 24 and read to the comrade, the above-mentioned material will be ready for shipment during the first five days of September.[41]

Reports on the World's Weapons and Ammunition (Harrisburg, Pa.: Stackpole Books, 1984), p.229.

[38] For a discussion of the problems associated with disclosing sensitive intelligence information, see infra pp. 82-83.

[39] For references in a captured document to obtaining "Western-made weapons," see the "Excerpt of a report on trip to the socialist countries, Asia, and Africa by Shafik Handal, Secretary General of the Salvadoran Communist Party, June 9-July 3, 1980," in State, *Communist Interference in El Salvador*, op.cit., Document E, pp.4-7, 9.

[40] The commercial, semi-automatic version of the M-16 rifle is designated the AR-15. It is not clear why this designation was used for military M-16s left behind by the United States in Vietnam. Whatever the reason, the distinction has been useful to at least one critic of the 1981 State Department white paper (*Communist Interference in El Salvador*), who, after reviewing the documents, concluded confidently that "no M-16's appear on the Vietnam weapons list (Documents E and F)." Poelchau, op.cit., p.100.

[41] "Excerpt of a report on trip to the socialist countries, Asia, and Africa by Shafik Handal, Secretary General of the Salvadoran Communist Party, June 9-July 3, 1980," in State, *Communist Interference in El Salvador*, op.cit., Document E, p.1.

The details of this account are largely verified by another important captured document, a report on a September 30, 1980, meeting of the Unified Revolutionary Directorate (DRU) in El Salvador. It gave this cryptic summary of the Handal visit to Vietnam:

IX. The PC secretary general's trip

Offer from Vietnam (they will be in Esmeralda [Cuba] on 5 September)

192 9mm pistols

1,620 AR 15

162 M30 machineguns

36 M60 heavy machineguns

12 12.7 caliber machineguns. . . .[42]

One noteworthy difference between the two accounts is the inclusion of a reference to 1,500,000 cartridges for AR-15 (M-16) rifles in the second report.[43]

Vietnamese support for the Salvadoran insurgents has been confirmed by both Nicaraguan and Vietnamese officials. For example, in March 1981 Nicaraguan Defense Minister Humberto Ortega visited Vietnam, and in a speech on March 11 said: "We sincerely thank the Vietnamese people and highly value their support for the heroic Salvadoran people. . . . [T]he fierce and bloody struggle in El Salvador requires the support of all progressive nations and forces throughout the world."[44] A few months later author William Shawcross visited Vietnam, and he later gave this account in the *New York Times Review of Books*: "Had Vietnam been distributing any of the vast pile of weapons left by the Americans? Col. Bui Tin acknowledged, in effect, that it had. In El Salvador? 'It's not fair to say the US can help the junta but we cannot help our friends. We do our best to support revolutionary movements in the world.'"[45]

Prisoners and defectors from the FMLN have also confirmed that large quantities of M-16s and other weapons left in Vietnam by the United States Army were shipped to Nicaragua for use by anti-government guerrillas in El Salvador. Montenegro (who, as already observed, was Commander-in-Chief of the National Central Guerrilla Front of the People's Revolutionary Army [ERP] prior to his capture in 1982) has stated:

What I knew first-hand was that beginning in October 1980 arms began to arrive [in El Salvador] for the January offensive. These arms arrived in transport trucks. They came through

---

[42] Translated and reproduced in ibid., Document F, p.7.

[43] Ibid. This suggests that the second document was probably not prepared exclusively from the Handal trip report, which made no reference to this ammunition.

[44] Unclassified State Telegram O230054Z March 1982, "Statement and Background Papers released by Department of State to Press on Saturday, March 20, 1982, p.16.

[45] *New York Times Review of Books*, September 14, 1981.

Honduras, some entered to Guatemala and came through the western part of the country to Santa Ana. . . .

As far as percentages, I estimate that 90% of the arms came from the outside. The arms came from Vietnam, a good part of them, they were arms captured from the American arsenal in Vietnam. The other share were given by the Sandinistas because they began to arm themselves with Soviet weapons. The arms taken from the Somoza army were taken to El Salvador.[46]

Another former senior insurgent leader captured by the Government of El Salvador was Moises López-Arriola, who once served as Western Regional Chief of the Armed Forces of National Resistance (FARN). He stated that in the month of January 1981 Vietnam had delivered 30 tons of weapons to Nicaragua to be forwarded to the FMLN. More recently, during debriefings senior defector Napoleón Romero Garcïa stated that "Vietnam has provided a large quantity of M-16 automatic rifles."

● Laundering Soviet-Bloc Weapons in Nicaragua

In addition to the Western-made weapons provided by Vietnam and certain other "socialist" states, Comandante Bayardo Arce proposed a mutually beneficial triangular deal to the Salvadoran insurgents—as recounted by a captured trip report which included a summary of a meeting on July 23, 1980, between Salvadoran insurgents and Bayardo Arce:

Bayardo and G. arrived. The most important of the things they stated were as follows:. . .

5. Since we were going to receive aid which all would pass through Nicaragua, they had thought of a "triangular deal"; that is, they would give us arms from the EPS [Sandinista People's Army] and then replace them with those which are coming, and also they would exchange those which are only used in the socialist world [particularly for the EPS] with others from the capitalist world.[47]

This Nicaraguan practice of providing Western-made weapons from its own supplies[48] and from those captured from the Somoza regime to Salvadoran guerrillas, while arming their own forces with newly received Soviet-bloc

---

[46] Republican Study Committee, U.S. House of Representatives, "Republican Study Committee Task Force on Central America Briefing with Alejandro Montenegro," Thursday, July 12, 1984, p.3.

[47] Translated and reprinted in State, Communist Interference in El Salvador, op.cit., Document G, pp.8-9.

[48] It is also worth noting that as early as the first half of 1980 Salvadoran government forces were capturing insurgent weapons that were traceable to shipments donated by Venezuela to the Sandinistas for use in overthrowing Somoza. Christopher Dickey, "El Salvador's Shadowy War," Washington Post, June 30, 1980, p.1. The desire for U.S.-made weapons as a way of concealing the extent of external Marxist intervention in neighboring states may have been a consideration in the Sandinistas' request to obtain such weapons from the United States in 1979—particularly given the Sandinistas' aversion to any other kind of military relationship with the United States. For information on the Sandinista request for U.S. arms, see Charles A. Krause, "New Leaders of Nicaragua Ask U.S. for Arms Aid," Washington Post, July 30, 1979, p.1; and Roberto Suro, "Nicaragua Wants U.S. Arms to Avoid Any Hint of Soviet Ties, Sandinista Says," Washington Star, August 13, 1979, p.3.

weapons, has been confirmed by many defectors and prisoners. It explodes the myth that the insurgents in El Salvador are armed predominantly with weapons captured from government troops.

- Captured Soviet-Bloc Weapons

Another problem with the theory that Salvadoran insurgents are armed with weapons they captured from government armed forces or somehow "found" in other ways is the existence within their ranks of communist bloc weapons and equipment that have never been seen before in El Salvador. Despite the generally successful effort to obtain Western-made weapons, as a way of concealing external assistance, a significant amount of Soviet, East European, and Vietnamese equipment was included in the massive arms shipments that came through Nicaragua.[49] Some of this equipment—including significant numbers of Soviet fragmentation grenades, Chinese rockets, anti-tank weapons, and recoilless rifles—has been captured by Salvadoran government forces, particularly during the heavy fighting surrounding the ill-fated "final offensive" of January 1981.[50] During a three-month period in 1984 Salvadoran military units captured a quantity of Bulgarian ammunition, a Chinese-made mortar sight with Vietnamese markings, and a supply of Soviet-made time fuzes for detonating explosives.

- Transshipment of Arms from Nicaragua to El Salvador

Including the massive shipments of arms from Vietnam already discussed, Handal's June 1980 visit to Soviet bloc states produced some 200 tons of

---

[49] During the June-July 1980 trip of Salvadoran Communist Party Secretary General Shafik Handal to the "socialist countries," the insurgents were promised a wide range of aid from countries other than Vietnam. For example, Ethiopia promised "several thousand weapons," including 150 Thompson submachine guns, 1,500 M-1 rifles, 1,000 M-14 rifles, and a total of more than 300,000 rounds of ammunition (note that all of these are U.S.-made weapons); Bulgaria promised, inter alia, 300 German Shpagin machine guns with 200,000 rounds of ammunition; Czechoslovakia promised to provide "a quantity" of Czech weapons (some of a type "circulating on the world market"), but "did not specify what this materiel consisted of, because it was up to the military to select it." Hungary offered communications equipment, but "said that they didn't have any [weapons] of Western, Chinese, or Yugoslav origin and they would be willing to participate in a deal with Ethiopia or Angola." East Germany also said they had no Western-made weapons, but "decided to continue seeking a solution to this problem although no time frame was set for this." The Soviet Union also told Handal that it lacked a large supply of Western-made weapons, but expressed a willingness in principle to provide "explosives, ammunition, materials for making explosives, and money for the purchase of arms." The Soviets suggested that Vietnam would be the best source of Western weapons, and volunteered to finance Handal's trip to Hanoi in search of aid. Although final approval would have to be obtained from "the leadership organs," the Soviet representative expressed a willingness "in principle" to provide transportation for weapons donated by Vietnam to the guerrillas. See "Excerpt of a report on trip to the socialist countries, Asia, and Africa by Shafik Handal, Secretary General of the Salvadoran Communist Party, June 9-July 3, 1980," in State, *Communist Interference in El Salvador*, op.cit., Document E, pp.2-9.

[50] See, e.g., Christopher Dickey, "Fighting Subsides in El Salvador; 3 Journalists Hurt," *Washington Post*, January 13, 1981, p.1; and Jeffrey Antevil, "El Salvador rebels get M-16s via Cuba, Nicaragua, U.S. says," *Philadelphia Inquirer*, January 29, 1981, p.D-1.

donated weapons by the start of the guerrillas' unsuccessful "final offensive" on January 10, 1981. Virtually all of these were first delivered to Cuba, then transported to Nicaragua, and finally smuggled into El Salvador via Honduras.[51]

The magnitude of the logistical campaign was illustrated by a report on a meeting of the Salvadoran guerrilla Joint General Staff (EMGC), dated September 26, 1980, and subsequently captured by government forces. It reported that only four tons of equipment had by that time been brought into El Salvador, but that another 130 tons were already "warehoused in Lagos [a frequently used guerrilla designation for Nicaragua]. . . ."[52] According to the captured report, "the material now in Lagos is only equivalent to one-sixth of all the material obtained that the DRU [Unified Revolutionary Directorate of Salvadoran insurgents] will have concentrated in Lagos." This suggests that as of late September 1980 Salvadoran guerrillas were anticipating receiving approximately 780 tons of military equipment via Nicaragua.

The sudden influx of materiel created logistical difficulties for the guerrillas, and these were reflected in various captured documents. For example, a captured typewritten letter addressed to "Federico," signed by "Fernando," and dated September 30, 1980, spoke of the need for the guerrillas to ensure that there were "adequate personnel, especially with regard to drivers . . .," and especially drivers "who have heavy equipment licenses." It notes that "we have been using only small vehicles," but reports a decision made in late September to use "some centavos that were obtained in solidarity" to purchase "a van at a cost of $25,000." The letter explained that this "solidarity" money included $100,000 from East Germany and $200,000 given by Iraq for "logistics." It noted further: "We are drawing up a plan for acquiring new methods of transport."[53]

Apparently the insurgents did not move quickly enough, because their representatives in Managua were soon under pressure from Nicaraguan officials to expedite the shipment of arms to El Salvador. One indication of

---

[51] According to the *New York Times*, in 1982 Salvadoran guerrillas admitted that Cuba supplied armaments through Nicaragua for the January 1981 "final offensive." Alan Riding, "Salvadoran Rebels: Five-Sided Alliance Searching for New, Moderate Image," *New York Times*, March 18, 1982, p.A-1.

[52] "Report on meeting of guerrilla Joint General Staff (EMGC) of September 26, 1980," translated and reprinted in State, *Communist Interference in El Salvador*, op.cit., Document I, p.2. *Lagos*—Spanish for "lakes"—is frequently used in guerrilla documents to refer to Nicaragua or to the FMLN command structure located in the Managua area—a designation which reflects the fact that the two largest lakes in Central America are both located within about 25 miles of Managua. Lago de Nicaragua is about 25 miles southeast of Managua, and Lago de Managua is immediately north of the capital city. This designation has been confirmed by senior Salvadoran insurgents who have either been captured by or have defected to the Government of El Salvador.

[53] Translated and reprinted in ibid., Document J, pp.2-4.

this was a captured handwritten document identified as "Report Number 4" and datelined "Lago, 1 November 1980." It was addressed to "Comrades Joaquin, Jacobo, Marcial," and was signed "Vladimir" (a name identified through other documents as the senior FMLN logistics representative in Managua). The report stated in part:

Here, as regard the shipments, they have been packing the bundles day and night. In fact, these people from Lago have stepped things up. It is such a hot potato for them that they are now pushing us, as this cannot be endured much longer. On the other hand, the warehouses in Esmeralda [Cuba] are filled to the brim with the shipment that arrived last week, over 150 tons. Also, they will have a backlog because more shipments will be arriving this week in Esmeralda reaching between 300 and 400 tons. So this has become a sort of chain, of which we are the last and most important link.[54]

The report also indicated active participation by the Nicaraguan FSLN in "approving" and modifying arms shipment plans proposed by the FMLN:

On 19 October we forwarded an enclosed plan subject to the confirmation of the points dealing with the reception submitted by the comrades from domestic logistics; this plan was approved by the [Sandinista] Front, but dates were changed on the 25th thereby scheduling the first shipments to begin on the fourth. They also said we would be getting the shipping schedule this week. Yesterday, 30 October, they handed me a schedule that practically doubles the previous projected amount, with a plan to smuggle into the country 109 tons this month alone, which represents 90% of the total stored here. They appear to be in a hurry and determined. . . . I believe it is almost impossible to smuggle 109 tons this month, but we must make every effort to bring in as much as we can.

Vladimir observed further: "It is impressive how all countries in the socialist bloc fully committed themselves to meet our every request and some have even doubled their promised aid. This is the first revolution in Latin America to which they have unconditionally turned to assist, before the taking of power."[55]

Smuggling Arms By Land. The Sandinistas have provided invaluable assistance to the guerrillas by concealing weapons in vehicles so that they can be driven through Honduran and Salvadoran checkpoints without detection. According to Montenegro, the Sandinistas have three repair shops for vehicle modifications under the direction of a special section of the Nicaraguan Ministry of Defense.[56] He gave this description of how a Spanish ETA terrorist would regularly smuggle arms from Managua to San Salvador: "He carried them hidden in the body of his van. In Managua they put them in the sides of the van and then welded and painted it so it looked new. When they reached San Salvador, we performed the same operation, only in reverse."[57] Following an interview with Montenegro in mid-1984, the *New York Times* wrote:

---

[54] Ibid., p.1.
[55] Ibid., p.4.
[56] State, *Central America*, op.cit., p.9.
[57] Interview with Montenegro at Department of State, Division of Language Services, transcript number 112533, p.36.

Mr. Canadas [Montenegro] said that in 1981 and 1982 [the year in which he was apprehended] urban commandos and 200 guerrillas under his command in Guazapa received monthly arms shipments from Nicaragua that were trucked across Honduras, hidden in false panels and floors. He said the trucks moved through the normal customs checkpoint of Las Manos at the Nicaraguan border with Honduras and the checkpoint of Amantillo at the Honduran border with El Salvador.

Each truck, he said, carried roughly 25 to 30 rifles and about 7,000 cartridges of ammunition. The rifles, he said, were American-made M-16s captured in Vietnam and FAL rifles formerly used by the Nicaraguan Army under Somoza.

Sometimes the trucks arrived without rifles and carried just ammunition and in that case, he said, a typical load would include up to 15,000 cartridges, Soviet-made grenades, and explosives like TNT for sabotage attacks against Government installations.[58]

One of the Salvadoran guerrillas captured with Montenegro in Honduras admitted to having made five trips to Managua in 1982 to pick up weapons for the insurgents. He stated that he transported the weapons to El Salvador in a truck modified by the Sandinistas to carry concealed weapons.[59]

Another key Salvadoran insurgent leader to provide information about arms shipments from Nicaragua was Napoleón Romero Garcïa. As Secretary General of the FPL's Metropolitan Front prior to his capture in April 1985, he had special responsibilities for overseeing logistical matters and thus possessed unusual expertise in this area. He told his debriefers:

The FPL brings in supplies by land from Nicaragua to Honduras. From Tegucigalpa, some supplies are trucked down near the Salvadoran border, where they are carried on foot into northern Chalatenango Department, passing the frontier in the area of San Fernando. Other supplies are sent on through Guatemala, entering western El Salvador at normal border-crossing points. Documentation and vehicles, which have special hidden compartments, are changed in Honduras to avoid the suspicion attached to any sort of shipment originating in Nicaragua.[60]

Although this means of arms smuggling has proven to be extremely effective, from time to time such specially prepared vehicles have been discovered and seized. Perhaps the most dramatic such seizure occurred in January 1981, when Honduran officials discovered a refrigerated trailer truck from Nicaragua en route to El Salvador with more than one hundred M-16 automatic rifles and thousands of rounds of ammunition, including mortar shells and rockets, hidden in its hollowed roof.[61] Over the years other vehicles with elaborate hidden compartments containing arms and equipment for Salvadoran guerrillas have also been captured.

In addition to being transported concealed in specially-modified trucks and automobiles—a practice which continues today[62]—arms from Nicaragua are

---

[58] Hedrick Smith, "A Former Salvadoran Rebel Chief Tells of Arms from Nicaragua," *New York Times*, July 12, 1984, p.A-10.

[59] State, *Central America*, op.cit., p.9.

[60] Romero debriefing, op.cit.

[61] State/Defense, *Nicaragua's Military Buildup*, op.cit., p.20.

[62] A pickup truck containing 84 boxes of ammunition concealed in hidden compartments was apprehended by Salvadoran authorities at the Honduran border on August 27, 1985.

also being transported to El Salvador by boat, airplane, and on foot. Former Nicaraguan intelligence officer Miguel Bolaños Hunter explained in 1983:

In the beginning there were a number of routes. Through the Gulf of Fonseca in high speed boats. On land, they used mules, walking or trucks and vehicles. . . . Lately they are using small aircraft that can land on highways.

Usually two planes a day and they drop 30-40 rifles. Also lately with radar intervention it's more delicate so they now use parachute drops with arms and ammunition.[63]

Honduran military forces have on occasion encountered bands of FMLN insurgents backpacking or using mules to transport arms picked up in Nicaragua. For example, on March 26, 1983, a squad of eleven armed Salvadoran insurgents was surprised by the Honduran National Police about 20 kilometers away from the El Salvador border. In the ensuing struggle, two FMLN guerrillas were killed and the others escaped. However, they were forced to leave behind a large quantity of communications equipment, weapons, and a notebook detailing an arms trafficking route from Nicaragua through Honduras to El Salvador. Among the abandoned supplies the Honduran police also found a supply of Sandinista propaganda material and a Sandinista flag.

Salvadoran soldiers have also captured boxes of Venezuelan ammunition which were identified by their lot numbers as having been sent by the Venezuelan government in the late 1970s to the Sandinistas for use in their effort to overthrow the Somoza government.[64]

It is clear that Nicaraguan involvement in the smuggling of weapons, ammunition, and military equipment continues. For example, on December 7, 1985, a Soviet-built Lada automobile en route from Nicaragua to El Salvador blew a tire and crashed in Honduras. Honduran authorities investigating the accident noticed wires protruding from the vehicle's air conditioning ducts, and upon investigation found some of the 86 blasting caps concealed in the vehicle. Further inspection turned up six hidden compartments, containing 450 pounds of military equipment. In addition to the blasting caps, the vehicle was carrying 7,000 rounds of ammunition, 12 radios (wrapped in copies of the Sandinista newspaper *Barricada*), 21 hand grenades, several one-time code pads, numerous letters (some in Russian), and other documents. The Nicaraguan driver admitted that he was smuggling supplies to the FMLN, he had been trained in Cuba, and this was not his first smuggling trip during 1985.[65]

---

[63] *Miguel Bolaños Transcripts*, op.cit., pp.37-38.

[64] See, e.g., supra p.46, fn.2; and Salvadoran President Duarte's press conference of January 17, 1981, in which he displayed a box of such ammunition, AFP (Paris), 0259 GMT, January 17, 1981; in FBIS, Daily Report, Latin America, January 19, 1981, p.P-5.

[65] See Joanne Omang, "Crash Said to Yield Rebel Aid Data," *Washington Post*, December 20, 1985, p.A-49; James Morrison, "Salvadoran Rebel Arms Linked to Sandinistas," *Washington Times*, December 20, 1985, p.6-A.

Smuggling Arms By Air. Airplanes have been used to smuggle arms from Nicaragua to El Salvador since at least 1980. Nicaragua was almost certainly involved in the flight of a stolen Panamanian Air Force plane which, while trying to deliver 22,000 rounds of ammunition to Salvadoran guerrillas, crashed about 160 kilometers east of San Salvador on June 15, 1980. According to eyewitnesses, the plane's pilot—along with an uniden-tified quantity of weapons—was rescued by a second aircraft before government forces could reach the crash site.[66] Evidence found at the scene included a flight plan showing the Aerocommander 560-A had come to El Salvador from Nicaragua, and several crates of Venezuelan ammuni-tion dated June 1977—reportedly with documents establishing that the ammunition had been sent to Nicaragua's Sandinista guerrillas on June 26, 1977.[67] While not mentioning Nicaragua by name, Salvadoran Defense Minister Garcïa said in a press conference:

As you will understand, this is not the first thing we have found that came from Venezuela. I don't recall the number of times we have found ammunition coming from Venezuela. I want to tell you that it is not that we are determining that it is being sent by Venezuela to El Salvador. But we all know that this ammunition was sent to another country. We also know the circumstances involved and it is supposed that this ammunition is coming from that country.[68]

Defense Minister Garcïa also stated that other arms-smuggling aircraft had in the past been detected by Salvadoran forces, but had successfully managed to avoid capture.[69]

Nicaragua also provided air shipments of arms to Salvadoran insurgents in preparation for the ill-fated "final offensive" of January 1981. At that time intelligence information established that Nicaragua's Papalonal airfield was being used for direct supply flights to El Salvador. In late July 1980, Papalonal was an agricultural dirt airstrip approximately 800 meters long, located in an underdeveloped area 23 miles northwest of Managua. By early 1981 the airstrip had been lengthened by 50 percent to approximately 1,200 meters, and a turnaround had been added to each end. A dispersal parking area with three hardstands—a feature typical of a military airfield—had been constructed at the western end of the runway. Three parking aprons had been cleared, and six hangar/storage buildings—each about 15 meters wide, and patterned after similar structures found at major Cuban

---

[66] Radio Reloj (San José) in Spanish, 1815 GMT, June 16, 1980; in FBIS, Latin America, June 17, 1980, p.P-3.

[67] AFP (Paris), June 17, 1980; in FBIS, Daily Report, Latin America, June 18, 1980, p.P-9. See also, "El Salvador Declares Air Alert," *Washington Post*, June 17, 1980, p.15.

[68] Radio Reloj (San José) in Spanish, 1815 GMT, June 16, 1980; in FBIS, Daily Report, Latin America, June 17, 1980, p.P-3. The Salvadoran press was less cautious. *La Prensa Grafica* reported on June 16, 1980, that the plane "with an enormous amount of ammunition and Sandinista weapons" had been seized. ACAN (Panama City), 1642 GMT, June 16, 1980; in FBIS, Daily Report, Latin America, June 17, 1980, p.P-4.

[69] Radio Cadena Sonora (San Salvador), 1750 GMT, June 16, 1980; in FBIS, Daily Report, Latin America, June 18, 1980, p.P-3.

airbases[70]—had been constructed on the aprons. Flights by C-47 cargo aircraft from Papalonal airfield corresponded with sightings in El Salvador.[71]

On January 25, 1981, El Salvador captured a Nicaraguan pilot and his twin-engined Cessna 310 airplane when he attempted to rescue the crew of another arms-smuggling Cessna that had crashed after experiencing mechanical difficulties. Various weapons and more than 9,000 rounds of ammunition were found at the scene. The pilot, Julio Romero Talevera—an international pilot for Nicaragua's Lanica Air Lines[72]—said he had previously made several flights from Nicaragua to El Salvador smuggling weapons to the insurgents, and said his country's government was behind the airlifting of weapons to rebels in El Salvador.[73]

The day after the Romero crash, another Nicaraguan light plane reportedly crashed in the same area of El Salvador. Before government forces could reach the site, local guerrillas had rescued the plane's occupants.[74]

On July 15, 1982, a Nicaraguan pilot named Francisco Torrealba sought asylum in San José, Costa Rica. During a press conference five days later, he stated that he had personal knowledge of Nicaraguan arms shipments to El Salvador originating at Managua's Sandino International Airport. The flights were made at night, and at least two of the pilots involved in the smuggling were Costa Rican. They were paid $8,000 for each flight, and flew unmarked C-47s (later incorporated into the Sandinista air force), Navajos, and Aztecs.[75]

Smuggling Arms By Sea. Another means of arms smuggling that has occurred since the early period is by small boat. Indeed, according to captured guerrilla documents, some of the first arms shipments went by boat. For example, a November 10, 1980, letter from "Comrade Marcial"

---

[70] Intelligence sources have confirmed Cuban involvement in their construction.

[71] See, e.g., Assistant Secretary of State Thomas O. Enders, testimony before Senate Foreign Relations Committee, April 12, 1983, published by Department of State as *Nicaragua: Threat to Peace in Central America*, Current Policy Series No. 476, p.4.

[72] There was some question as to Romero's employment status at the time of his capture. In Managua his brother told journalists that Romero was a Lanica pilot and had been "kidnapped" the day before the flight by a man who came to his home with a machine gun. (Radio Reloj [San José] in Spanish, 0100 GMT, January 27, 1981; in FBIS, Daily Report, Latin America, January 28, 1981, p. P-5.) However, the official Radio Sandino in Managua reported that, according to the airline, "Romero, who is Nicaraguan, left Lanica's service on 23 December, 1980, and has not reported for work ever since. . . ." (FBIS, Daily Report, Latin America, January 28, 1981, p.P-14.)

[73] Steve Bell, "Good Morning America," ABC Network Television, February 20, 1981, 7:00 a.m. See also, Jeffrey Antevil, "El Salvador rebels getting M-16s via Cuba, Nicaragua, U.S. says," *Philadelphia Inquirer*, January 29, 1981, p.D-1.

[74] ACAN (Panama City), 2137 GMT, January 26, 1981; in FBIS, Daily Report, Latin America, January 27, 1981, p.P-4. (Accounts of this incident are unclear, and this may well in reality be the same aircraft Romero was seeking to assist when he was apprehended.)

[75] "Statement and Background Papers released by Department of State to Press on Saturday, March 20, 1982."

(Cayetano Carpio, leader of the FPL)[76] to "Comrade Vladimir" (the DRU's logistics representative in Managua) forwarded complaints from the Salvadoran guerrilla Joint General Staff (EMGC) and the "logistical reception committee" that the Nicaraguan Front was overloading the capability of the logistics pipeline. As an example, he wrote: "The first military shipment was excessively overloaded and one of them foundered in Lagos territorial waters and the entire cargo was lost. They were successful in saving their shipmates. The other two were overloaded."[77]

A recently declassified summary of a debriefing in early 1985 of former FPL Central Committee member Napoleón Romero García reported:

Other routes include sea infiltration from the area of Chinandega, Nicaragua, to the Salvadoran coast around El Espino Beach, Usulutan Department. . . . Romero added that San Salvador was the principal logistics reception point. Material was stored in safehouses for pickup by couriers from the various fronts.[78]

According to Romero, such shipments are coordinated by coded radio contacts between the insurgents in El Salvador and their representatives in Managua.[79]

In September 1983, after Nicaraguan anti-government insurgents (Contras) of the Nicaraguan Democratic Force (FDN) attacked an alleged "center of logistical supply" on the island of La Concha in northwestern Nicaragua, the Nicaraguan government granted permission for several journalists to visit the site of the attack, which it described as "the state-financed Mario Carrillo fishing cooperative." When the journalists, armed with a letter of authorization from the government, first tried to visit the alleged "fishing cooperative" they were confronted by an armed guard who fired a shotgun to chase them away. Only after they presented their letter of authorization did the guard cooperate. As one of the journalists described the visit in the *Washington Post*:

[I]n two visits to La Concha, the swampy island base said by the government [of Nicaragua] to house the Mario Carrillo cooperative, reporters found no evidence the facility was ever used for fishing.

Instead, reporters found a Sandinista Army banner, a makeshift target with dozens of spent rifle shell casings, a radio antenna and three long, empty wooden boxes amid the ruins of the tin-roofed warehouse destroyed in the FDN attack.[80]

When asked about the antenna, the guard—who maintained that the facility was a fishing cooperative—said the facility's radio had been used to

---

[76] The letter is discussed in greater detail on pp.77-78, and Carpio is identified on p.48.

[77] Excerpt from report on work in Nicaragua, November 1-3, 1980, translated and reprinted in State, *Communist Interference in El Salvador*, op.cit., Document R, pp.2-3.

[78] Romero debriefing, op.cit.

[79] Ibid.

[80] Sam Dillon, "Base for Ferrying Arms to El Salvador Found in Nicaragua," *Washington Post*, September 21, 1983, p.A-29.

monitor Fisheries Ministry radio reports on fishing conditions. However, "[a] Fisheries Ministry official in Managua said the ministry does not broadcast fishing reports and knew of no fishing cooperatives equipped with two-way radios." Further, the *Post* account observed, "Officials in the Fisheries Ministry and the National Development Bank said . . . that the Mario Carrillo cooperative is not on the island and that no state-recognized cooperative operates in this region."[81]

After a second visit and interviews with fishermen and other residents in the area, the journalist wrote:

A radio-equipped warehouse and boat facility, disguised as a fishing cooperative on an island in northwestern Nicaragua, has served for three years as a transshipment point for smuggling arms to El Salvador, numerous residents here say.

Although the Nicaraguan government denies the operation, fishermen and others in several tiny coastal hamlets nearby say that soldiers in military vehicles regularly trucked wooden boxes to the water's edge and loaded them in motor-powered launches bound for El Salvador's coast 40 miles to the north.

Fishermen report occasionally finding similar wooden boxes containing foot-long "bazookas"—presumably mortar shells or similar munitions—on shore north of the mouth of this estuary where the boats battle the surf to enter the Pacific Ocean.

A 14-boat fleet, including half a dozen large dugout canoes that can carry thousands of pounds of cargo, has been involved in the operation, residents say, with regular departures at two-week intervals. . . .

Fishermen and other residents who live in huts lining this tangled estuary, and also small farmers and fishermen in Jipuilillo, Padre Ramos, Venecia, and other nearby hamlets, said La Concha island was not a fishing cooperative, but a "military base."

The island has been off limits to local residents for three years, they said. . . .

Some area residents were hesitant to discuss the La Concha activity, calling it a "delicate situation," but others openly talked with reporters.

"I don't get involved in politics, but everyone around here knows they are carrying arms to El Salvador," said the wife of a Padre Ramos fisherman. . . .

The fisherman said that weeks after the Sandinista-led ouster of president Anastasio Somoza in 1979 military men came to the village looking for experienced smugglers.

Beginning soon thereafter, Andres Lopez, identified by several residents as a smuggler who lives in Venecia on the northern shore of the estuary, emerged as the local leader of the operation, the fishermen said.

Then La Concha's guard . . . began to warn local residents away from the island and several unusually large launches appeared for the first time at the facility, residents said.[82]

La Concha had long been known by U.S. intelligence experts to be a base for shipping arms to Salvadoran insurgents.

---

[81] Ibid.
[82] Ibid.

On May 21, 1984, elements of the Salvadoran military in the Isla Montecristo area near the delta of the Rio Lempa exchanged fire with a small group of insurgents, killing two and capturing one. Four days later, acting on the basis of information provided by the prisoner, the Salvadoran Army located and destroyed a guerrilla base camp. Thirty-four large canoes were captured, along with maps and other documents depicting guerrilla supply routes.[83]

● Continuing Need for Ammunition

By 1983 the Nicaraguans had delivered thousands of modern military weapons to the Salvadoran insurgents. According to former Sandinista intelligence officer Miguel Bolaños Hunter in mid-1983: "They don't need any more arms, only ammunition. They already have five times more than what we had to overthrow Somoza."[84]

This account is supported by statements made by former Salvadoran guerrilla leader Napoleón Romero García, who said in 1985 that although shipments through 1983 were mostly weapons, the insurgents now have more weapons in storage than guerrillas to use them. The present priority, therefore, is for explosives and ammunition (especially cartridges for M-16 rifles, and for .50-caliber machine guns which are used as anti-aircraft weapons).[85] Shipments of ammunition and supplies have continued.[86]

Diplomats in Managua Confirm Arms Shipments

Nicaragua's efforts to destabilize the elected Government of El Salvador are common knowledge among the people and governments of the region. Consider, for example, this excerpt from an article which appeared in the *New York Times* in 1984:

MANAGUA, Nicaragua, April 10—Western European and Latin American diplomats here say the Nicaraguan Government is continuing to send military equipment to the Salvadoran insurgents and to operate training camps for them inside Nicaragua. . . .

The diplomats, including some from countries that have criticized United States policies in Central America, said military support to the Salvadoran rebels had dropped over the last year, but remained substantial. . . .

Western diplomats appear to be convinced of the general accuracy of American intelligence reports on the ties between Nicaragua and the Salvadoran rebels.

"I believe support for the revolutionaries in El Salvador is continuing and that is very important to the Sandinistas," said a European diplomat. . . .

---

[83] State/Defense, *Nicaragua's Military Buildup*, op.cit., pp.19-20.

[84] *Miguel Bolaños Transcripts*, op.cit., p.38.

[85] Romero debriefing, op.cit. Romero notes that one reason the insurgents no longer need rifles is that their ranks have dropped significantly since 1983. See Chapter 6.

[86] See, e.g., Richard Halloran, "U.S. Reports Sharp Rise in Arms Aid to Nicaragua," *New York Times*, August 2, 1983, p.8.

"Maybe not everything the Americans say is true, but logic and common sense support their case," said a Hispanic diplomat. "The Sandinistas' ideology dictates that they help other countries adopt political systems like their own."[87]

Providing Financial Support

The declassification in 1985 of several documents reporting information obtained during debriefings of former FPL Central Committee member Napoleón Romero García provided substantial insight into the financial activities of the FPL and the FMLN. As Secretary General of the FPL's Metropolitan Front in the San Salvador area, Romero was responsible for overseeing the receipt, control, conversion into local currency, and disbursement of FMLN funds received from abroad. The day-to-day handling of funds smuggled into San Salvador from Nicaragua was the responsibility of one of Romero's subordinates—a woman known as "Clara"—who handled all correspondence and was responsible for changing U.S. dollars into local currency on the San Salvador black market before distributing funds to other fronts.[88]

According to Romero, the FPL has a monthly operating budget of between U.S. $65,000 and $100,000. About $15,000 to $20,000 of this is raised inside El Salvador, and between $50,000 and $80,000 is received each month from the FPL National Finance Commission in Nicaragua.[89] Much of this external funding is provided by "solidarity committees" active in the United States and Europe and by friendly labor unions. Romero asserts that each of the FMLN factions also has representatives traveling through the United States and Europe raising funds for guerrilla activities—often in the guise of supporting legitimate development projects.[90]

Virtually all of the funds are forwarded to Managua, although a significant amount passes through Mexico City first—where, when necessary, it is converted into U.S. dollars. In Managua the money is turned over to the FPL Finance Committee representative, or to the representative of the FMLN

---

[87] Stephen Kinzer, "Salvador Rebels Still Said to Get Nicaraguan Aid," *New York Times*, April 11, 1984, p.A-1. See also, George de Lama, "U.S. fails to find arms bound for Salvador," *Chicago Tribune*, August 26, 1983, p.2: "[E]ven leftist sources in the region admit the Sandinista regime has been instrumental in providing Salvadoran rebels with material support and safe haven. More importantly, Managua, Nicaragua, has served as a military headquarters in exile, providing logistical, strategic and technical advice."

[88] Romero debriefing, op.cit.

[89] Ibid.

[90] Alejandro Montenegro, former Commander-in-Chief of the National Central Guerrilla Front (also based in the San Salvador area) addressed a gathering sponsored by the U.S. House of Representatives Republican Study Committee at which time he was asked to "describe the political support apparatus the FMLN has set up in the U.S. for solidarity with El Salvador's guerrillas." He responded: "The solidarity groups are instructed from Managua. What I want to make very clear is that Managua is where the command center is in every regard. The solidarity groups in other countries, not just in the United States, have two basic tasks: political propaganda favoring the FMLN and fund-raising to send funds to the guerrillas." Republican Study Committee, House, *Briefing with Montenegro*, op.cit., pp.4-5.

Finance Commission (COFIN). The money is then placed in concealment devices—hidden cavities of private automobiles, false bottoms of suitcases, ornamental dolls, picture frames, and so forth—so it can be smuggled into El Salvador.

Because of the increased security along the Honduran border, funds from Nicaragua destined for insurgents in El Salvador are often sent first by courier to Guatemala by air, and then smuggled into El Salvador from the north by private vehicle or public bus. Regardless of which route it takes, the external control point is Managua.[91]

Romero's account is consistent with several financial documents found in his possession at the time of his arrest. They indicated, for example, that during the month of February 1985 at least three deliveries of cash were received from Nicaragua. On February 1 Romero received U.S. $40,000; on February 18 he received $70,000; and on February 22 he received $60,000. According to Romero, this money was to be divided among the various insurgent fronts based on a percentage table established by the FPL high command.

Training Salvadoran Guerrillas

In addition to assisting in the smuggling of hundreds of tons of arms, ammunition, and equipment, to anti-government insurgents in El Salvador, the Sandinistas have played an instrumental role in training Salvadoran guerrillas in military tactics, weapons, communications, and explosives inside Nicaragua. Indeed, even before the victory over Somoza, Salvadoran insurgents were trained at FSLN base camps in Costa Rica.[92] Nicaragua has also facilitated the training of Salvadoran guerrillas in Cuba and other friendly countries.

At least four training camps inside Nicaragua, used extensively for training Salvadoran insurgents, have been identified: (1) the base of Ostional in the southern province of Rivas; (2) a converted National Guard camp in northwestern Nicaragua close to the Rio Tamarindo; (3) the camp of Tamagas, which specializes in teaching sabotage techniques, about 20 kilometers outside Managua; and (4) a new camp (which opened in 1984)

---

[91] One of the Romero debriefing summaries states that "Managua. . .is the collection point for all financial assistance obtained overseas by the Farabundo Marti National Liberation Front/Revolutionary Democratic Front (FMLN/FDR) solidarity groups."

[92] "[M]ore revealing were the statements of two members of the FARN arrested September 12, 1978, in connection with the kidnapping of a Swedish executive, Kjell Bjork [in El Salvador]. The two men, Miguel Angel Torres and Jesus Antonio Quintanilla, disclosed under interrogation that they had been trained at an FSLN guerrilla camp in Costa Rica by instructors from other Central American countries including FSLN Commander Zero." Arostegui, op.cit., p.96.

near Santa Julia on Nicaragua's Cosegüina Peninsula.[93] These camps are primarily staffed with Cuban instructors and administrators, but Nicaraguan government representatives are present and Nicaraguan soldiers provide security for the camps. At any given time, as many as a few hundred Salvadoran insurgents are reported to be receiving training in these camps.[94]

An even greater number of Salvadoran insurgents are flown to Cuba from Nicaragua for advanced training. One Salvadoran guerrilla who defected to Honduras in late 1981 reported that he had been one of a group of a dozen insurgents sent for extensive military training to Cuba, where over 900 Salvadorans were receiving training.[95]

Alejandro Montenegro, who led the guerrilla attack on Ilopango airfield outside San Salvador in January 1982—one of the most successful insurgent operations of the entire war[96]—has stated that the operation began when he received instructions from ERP chief Joaquin Villalobos to send seven of his best men to Nicaragua. They returned in October, after having received six months of advanced training for the operation in Cuba, and additional training in Nicaragua.[97]

Command and Control Assistance

Between May 5 and June 8, 1980, senior Salvadoran insurgent leaders visited Honduras, Guatemala, Costa Rica, Cuba, and Nicaragua. One member of this group—a member of the Political Commission of the Salvadoran Communist Party identified only as "Eduardo"—kept a record of the various meetings which was later captured by the Government of El Salvador. This excerpt appeared under the heading "MANAGUA":

Interview with the [Nicaraguan] Joint Directorate

—They offer the D.U. [Unified Directorate of Salvadoran insurgent groups] *headquarters with all measures of security* and they offered their (international) field of operations, which they control.

---

[93] State/Defense, *Nicaragua's Military Buildup*, op.cit., p.25; "U.S. Support for the Democratic Resistance Movement in Nicaragua," unclassified excerpts from the President's Report to the Congress, Pursuant to Section 8066 of the Continuing Resolution for FY1985, PL98-473, April 10, 1985, pp.5-6.

[94] In its Declaration of Intervention, *Nicaragua v. United States*, El Salvador charged that "since mid-1980 the Sandinista National Liberation Front has made available to the Salvadoran guerrillas training sites in Nicaraguan territory." Reprinted in *International Legal Materials* (published by the American Society for International Law), Vol. 24 (January 1985), p.39.

[95] State, *Nicaragua: Threat to Peace*, op.cit., p.4.

[96] For details on Ilopango raid—which destroyed 5 or 6 Huey UH-1H helicopters, 5 or 6 fighter aircraft, a training aircraft, and 3 C-47 cargo aircraft, and damaged two other C-47s—see Barbara Crossette, "U.S. Starts Replacing Salvadoran Copters Destroyed in Rebel Attack," *New York Times*, February 6, 1982, p.4.

[97] State, Interview with Montenegro, op.cit., p. 19; and Don Oberdorfer and Joanne Omang, "Nicaraguan Bares Plan to Discredit Foes," *Washington Post*, June 19, 1983, p.A-1.

—Offer "Ready to contribute in material terms". . . .

—The Joint Command assumes the cause of E.S. as their own.

—They are placing themselves at our disposal for the evaluation or exchange of information.[98]

The offer of a "headquarters" was accepted by the insurgent leaders. Pulitzer Prize-winning journalist Shirley Christian writes: "By May 1981, . . . Salvadoran guerrilla leaders were making public appearances in Managua, which was the headquarters of their high command."[99] A guerrilla leader told another American journalist in 1982 that the insurgents "have a permanent commission in Nicaragua overseeing the smuggling of weapons from that country to here."[100] In addition, the existence of a Salvadoran guerrilla headquarters inside Nicaragua has been confirmed by sensitive intelligence sources and by the testimony of numerous senior defectors and prisoners. For example, Alejandro Montenegro, former Commander-in-Chief of the National Central Guerrilla Front, told a U.S. Congressional group: "What I want to make very clear is that Managua is where the command center is in every regard."[101] After interviewing Montenegro, Bernard Weinraub wrote in the *New York Times*:

A former Salvadoran guerrilla . . . has told United States officials . . . that the guerrilla leadership is now operating from bases in Nicaragua. . . . By June 1980, Mr. Canadas [Montenegro] said, after guerrilla leaders, not including him, went to Havana, "arms began coming in and the commanders after that meeting did not return to Salvador." He said that was when the leaders moved . . . operations to Nicaragua.

"They never returned," he said, "with the exception of Villalobos, who was the last one to leave Salvador in February '81."[102]

Other former high-ranking Salvadoran insurgents have provided similar accounts. Moises López-Arriola, for example, reported that the Government of Nicaragua provided the Unified Revolutionary Directorate (DRU) and the FMLN with an extensive base of operations in and around Managua. He reported that representatives of the DRU from the five Salvadoran insurgent groups live in Managua and each of the forces has a command center there. U.S. intelligence sources have established that Nicaragua coordinates its support for the FMLN through a Comision Militar, which is jointly staffed by Nicaraguan and Cuban officers and operates under the supervision of the Nicaraguan Ministry of Defense. Joaquin Cuadra, the Cuban-trained Nicaraguan Army Chief of Staff, directs the day-to-day supervision of the Comision Militar.

---

[98] Report of trip of "Eduardo" from May 5 to June 8, 1980; translated and reprinted in State, *Communist Interference in El Salvador*, op.cit., Document D, pp.4-5. (Emphasis added.)

[99] Christian, op.cit., p.195.

[100] *San Diego Union*, March 1, 1982.

[101] Republican Study Committee, House, *Briefing with Montenegro*, op.cit., p.5.

[102] Bernard Weinraub, "Cuba Directs Salvador Insurgency, Former Guerrilla Lieutenant Says," *New York Times*, July 28, 1983, p.A-10.

One need not rely on captured documents and the testimony of senior defectors and prisoners to establish Nicaragua's role in the command and control of anti-government guerrilla forces in El Salvador. Consider this excerpt from El Salvador's declaration to the International Court of Justice:

The most positive proof of Nicaraguan intervention and participation in the subversive process against El Salvador was shown to the world the day of 10 January 1981, when the national radio of Nicaragua, Radio Sandino, was used for an entire day as an instrument of direct support, with harangues, instructions, and under the pretence of giving the news, events were described before they occurred. This clearly demonstrates Nicaragua's participation in the planning of the offensive.[103]

It is equally clear that key FMLN leaders have been operating out of Nicaragua. Indeed, Nicaragua's star witness before the International Court of Justice—former CIA contract employee David MacMichael—admitted as much in response to a question from one of the judges:

Q: . . . . To turn to another aspect of these facts, Mr. MacMichael, is it a fact that leaders of the El Salvadoran insurgency are based in Nicaragua and regularly operate without apparent interference from Nicaraguan authorities in Nicaragua?

A.: I think the response to that question would have to be a qualified yes, in that political leaders and, from time to time, military leaders, of the Salvadoran insurgency have [been] reported credibly to have operated from Nicaragua. . . ."[104]

In April 1983, two of the most senior Salvadoran insurgent leaders were killed inside Nicaragua—allegedly the result of a murder/suicide. In a eulogy delivered in Managua on April 9, 1983, Cayetano Carpio—leader of the Salvadoran guerrilla faction Popular Liberation Forces (FPL)—said:

Imperialism is accusing Nicaragua by saying that the leaders of the Salvadoran people are here, the leaders of the FMLN-FDR. In my opinion this charge was made as if one people's solidarity with another is something to be ashamed of. However, once this is evident, the members of the Directorate and all its working teams, some inside the country and others outside the country, are steadfastly at work fully aware of the need to unite the internal struggle with international solidarity and with the struggle of all peoples for the liberation of Central America and El Salvador. That is why we move from one country to another.[105]

Nicaraguan sources have also confirmed that key Salvadoran insurgent leaders have "lived" in Nicaragua. For example, former intelligence officer Miguel Bolaños Hunter—when asked by American journalists whether the Salvadorans "have a control center in Managua," responded: "They have two command centers in Managua. One for communications and the other to get together with the Nicaraguan high command." He added: "The high Salvadoran command stays in Managua all the time unless they go back to

---

[103] Declaration of Intervention of El Salvador in *Nicaragua v. United States*, *International Legal Materials*, Vol. 24 (January 1985), pp.38, 40.

[104] International Court of Justice, *Nicaragua v. United States*, Uncorrected Verbatim Record, September 16, 1985, CR 85/21, pp.34-35.

[105] Managua Domestic Service in Spanish, 1803 GMT, April 9, 1983; in FBIS, Daily Report, Latin America, April 11, 1983, p.P-8.

rally the troops. Then they are flown in for a day and flown back. The political people like Ungo have homes in Nicaragua."[106]

In talking with *Newsday* foreign affairs correspondent Roy Gutman about U.S.-Nicaraguan diplomatic exchanges, an unnamed senior Sandinista official complained that the Americans placed preconditions on talks: "They asked us to expel *the Salvadorans who sometimes* come through or *lived here*—what they called the center of command and control in Nicaragua—to cease all communications between Salvadorans that go through or live here [and those in] the exterior."[107]

Reportedly as a result of U.S. pressure, in late 1983 many if not all of the civilian leaders of the FMLN left Managua. However, the military command structure remained behind, and insurgent political leaders are still frequently seen in Managua—where, among other things, they often meet with visiting U.S. Congressional delegations.[108]

Providing a Clandestine Radio Station

In late 1980, the Salvadoran government captured an "official note" dated October 29, 1980 from the FMLN's Unified Revolutionary Directorate (DRU) in El Salvador to "DRU Comrades in Lago [Nicaragua]." In discussing certain decisions reached at a DRU meeting held two days earlier in San Salvador, the note stated:

THE LAGOS PROJECT-This would be the most strategic plan and would consist in the establishment of a clandestine radio in Lagos. To carry out this project the cooperation and assistance of the Island [Cuba] and the Laguenos [Nicaraguans] must be requested. It must be remembered that the Comrade Commander offered the equipment and assistance to this plan. It is up to you in Lagos to take all the necessary action to begin broadcasting operations as early as possible. The three organizations have already enlisted the personnel, or are about to, to form part of this operation, composed of at least six or more persons.

During this process arrangements should be made to authorize the operations on a short term and to be provided with the necessary technical and material support. The radio station will come under the responsibility of the Propaganda Commission, but at this time you are in charge of its installation. . . .

It should be a shortwave radio capable of reaching all of our territory and Central America.[109]

---

[106] *Miguel Bolaños Transcripts*, op.cit., p.38.

[107] Roy Gutman, "America's Diplomatic Charade," *Foreign Policy*, Fall 1984, pp.5-6. (Emphasis added.)

[108] U.S. Department of State, "U.S. Efforts to Achieve Peace in Central America," Report Submitted Pursuant to Section 109(f) of the Intelligence Authorization Act for Fiscal Year 1984, p.15. See also, Stephen Kinzer, "Salvadoran Rebels Still Said to Get Nicaraguan Aid," *New York Times*, April 11, 1984, p.A-1.

[109] Official Note, dated October 29, 1980, from DRU to DRU representatives in Nicaragua, translated and reprinted in State, *Communist Interference in El Salvador*, op.cit., Document P, pp.4-5. An earlier captured document—apparently notes taken during a DRU meeting of September 3, 1980—said: "The DRU is to ask the FSLN about a possibility of installing a radio and sharing expenses; or having the organizations provide whatever equipment they have."

Radio Liberación began broadcasting from within Nicaragua on December 15, 1980.[110] Its presence was ultimately admitted even by Nicaragua's star witness before the International Court of Justice, David MacMichael:

Q.: Mr. MacMichael, have you ever heard of Radio Liberación?

A.: I have heard of Radio Liberación, yes.

Q.: What is it? Can you tell the Court, please?

A.: It was a predecessor of the basic Radio Venceremos which is used by the FMLN in El Salvador. I believe that at one time a radio broadcast under the title of "Radio Liberación" was supposed to have originated from Nicaraguan soil.

Q.: Did they in fact originate from Nicaragua, to the best of your knowledge?

A.: To the best of my knowledge I think I would say yes, that is the information I have.[111]

According to Montenegro, in the early days one clandestine Salvadoran insurgent radio transmitter was located in a residential area at the end of Via Panama near the outskirts of Managua. However, its high frequency transmitters had long antennae that could be seen from the Pan American Highway, and when the authorities concluded that it was too visible it was moved to a more secluded location.[112]

Attempts to Influence Guerrilla Strategy

As already noted, for many years Cuba has tried to use the promise of arms and equipment to pressure feuding insurgent groups to work together in a united effort. This was done in Nicaragua, El Salvador, Honduras, and Guatemala. Working as partners in the effort to subvert the Government of El Salvador, both Cuba and Nicaragua have used their control over the supply of weapons and equipment to try to prevent infighting, and apparently also to influence the strategy and tactics of Salvadoran guerrillas.

---

[110] The close Cuban role in this program was emphasized when, after an off-the-air period, Radio Liberación was preparing to resume broadcasting in late January 1981. Cuban radio stations made the announcement two days before other stations received word from the FMLN. See FBIS, Daily Report, Latin America, January 26, 1981, p.P-13; and ibid., January 28, 1981, p.P-6 (translating an AFP—Agence France Presse—report).

[111] International Court of Justice, Nicaragua v. United States, Uncorrected Verbatim Record, September 16, 1985, CR 85/21, pp. 39-40. Shirley Christian writes: "Among other Salvadoran guerrilla undertakings in Nicaragua was the tower and operations center for their clandestine radio station, on the site of Cosigüina Volcano, just across the Gulf of Fonseca from El Salvador." Christian, op.cit., pp.195-196.

[112] Montenegro interview at Department of State, March 12, 1984, cited in State/Defense, Nicaragua's Military Buildup, op.cit., p.25, n.50. See also, Republican Study Committee, House, Briefing with Montenegro, p.6. ("Q. Where does Radio Venceremos broadcast from? A. [T]he principal station is in Managua. . . .because the press center is in Managua; called the information [or propaganda] command."); and David Wood, "Salvadoran Rebels Brag of Cuban Ties," Los Angeles Times, March 13, 1983 ("The broadcast [was] transmitted from a secret location in neighboring Nicaragua—whose Marxist-led Sandinista regime has allowed the Salvadoran guerrillas to establish their headquarters in Managua. . . .").

This was true from the very beginning. Shortly before the first anniversary of the Sandinista victory in Nicaragua, a delegation of senior Salvadoran guerrilla leaders visited Managua on July 13, 1980, in search of aid. According to a captured report of that trip, the Salvadorans were at first unable to meet with Bayardo Arce or other senior Nicaraguan officials because "they were very busy with the celebration." However, the guerrillas were able to meet with one of Arce's assistants—identified in the report only as "G." The trip report states that during this meeting, the Salvadorans were told that the Nicaraguans "had stopped all the shipments until they knew the plan." In response, according to the report, the guerrillas complained "that they [the Nicaraguans] had made the aid which they gave conditional upon their approval of the plan. . . . [W]hat they were asserting was a political condition." Arce's assistant subsequently withdrew this condition.[113]

One of the three Salvadoran guerrilla groups to take part in the Havana unification talks in December 1979 was the Armed Forces of National Resistance (FARN)—a splinter group that had left the People's Revolutionary Army (ERP) in the mid-1970s. Although FARN had joined the DRU in 1980, later that year it withdrew—a step which caused deep concern that other Salvadoran insurgent groups would lose their Cuban support. A captured letter to the DRU dated August 31, 1980, from "the members of the DRU who are fulfilling missions in foreign places" (one of which was "Lagos") spoke of returning home "after we fulfill the remaining tasks which are: . . . b) the visit to the Esmeraldian Management (a quick visit) in order to inform them about the background and real scope of the anti-unity decision made by Rene and to provide them with sufficient elements of guidance. . . ." Expanding on this subject, the letter said:

7) In light of the fact that we think comrade Mart. is extremely worried about this situation and that any price should be paid to solve the "division," we decided to ask permission to go to Esmeralda in order to report directly to the "Esmeraldan" management about the background of the problem, the ways taken by Rene in his divisive position, and the scope of this action so that the management could have enough elements to consider when judging the situation and making a final decision. We fear very much the effects that this anti-unity decision made by Rene will have on the joint logistics matters that had already been resolved and were moving very fast. The host managers [Nicaraguans] have informed us that the shipment will still be sent to us at least for the time being. However, there might be negative possibilities in this field in the near future. For this reason, we have decided to go to Esmeralda in order to provide them with the information needed to deal with the real situation. We asked for permission in writing Saturday morning before we left for Arenas.[114]

The letter was signed by Jonás Montalvo, Eduardo, and Marcial. It included a postscript stating that on September 1 the writers had met with "the public relations representative of the host management." The postscript continued:

---

[113] Trip Report, captured from Salvadoran insurgents, translated and reprinted in State, *Communist Interference in El Salvador*, op.cit., Document G, pp.1-2.

[114] "Letter to DRU, dated August 31, 1980, from three members of DRU in Nicaragua."

After getting to the bottom of the problem, he officially stated that the shipment of materials will not be stopped and that more will be sent depending on the transportation capacity of the DRU. This means that we will have much more responsibility on the reception side of the deal. We have to make sure that our capacity to receive materials is not slowed down.[115]

The Nicaraguans did not cease trying to influence Salvadoran guerrilla strategy. The decision to rush massive amounts of arms and equipment into El Salvador in late 1980 in order to launch a major nationwide "final offensive" in January 1981, for example, was reportedly made by the Sandinistas and imposed upon the Salvadorans. For example, Alejandro Montenegro has stated:

In Managua we were pressured no end to carry out the offensive as soon as possible, because according to a political analysis that had been prepared in Managua, it was feared that Ronald Reagan would come to power. The Managua leadership feared that Reagan would spoil all their plans. With his policy of non-intervention in Central America, President Carter indirectly aided the Cubans and caused the conflict to intensify.[116]

Captured documents established that the early delivery schedules for shipping arms and equipment from Nicaragua to El Salvador were drawn up by the Sandinistas without considering the ability of the Salvadoran insurgents to absorb the massive influx of new supplies. Indeed, this was a source of some dismay to the Salvadoran insurgents. A November 1, 1980, report from "Vladimir"—the FMLN's chief logistics representative in Managua—to three senior FMLN leaders in El Salvador, complained that "these people from Lago" were "pushing us" to move shipments more quickly, and commented: "[T]his cannot be endured much longer."[117] The letter also made clear that Nicaragua maintained a great deal of control over arms smuggling decisions. Consider this excerpt:

On 19 October we forwarded an enclosed plan subject to the confirmation of the points dealing with the reception submitted by the comrades from domestic logistics; this plan was approved by the [Sandinista] Front, but dates were changed on the 25th thereby scheduling the first shipments to begin on the fourth. They also said we would be getting the shipping schedule this week. Yesterday, 30 October, they handed me a schedule that practically doubles the previous projected amount, with a plan to smuggle into the country 109 tons this month alone, which represents 90% of the total stored here. They appear to be in a hurry and determined. . . . I believe it is almost impossible to smuggle 109 tons this month, but we must make every effort to bring in as much as we can.[118]

At almost the same time, the DRU dispatched an individual identified only as "Rodrigo" to Nicaragua "to put together a schedule of shipments related

---

[115] Ibid.

[116] State, *Interview with Montenegro*, op.cit., p.11. Salvadoran guerrillas openly proclaimed that it was their intention to create an "irreversible" military situation by launching a "final offensive" in El Salvador before President Reagan assumed office. See, e.g., David Wood, "Carter Orders Military Supplies to Embattled Junta in Salvador," *Washington Star*, January 15, 1981, p.1; Karen DeYoung, "State's Latin Bureau Urges Resumption of Arms Aid to Salvador," *Washington Post*, January 10, 1981, p.1.

[117] State, *Communist Interference in El Salvador*, op.cit., Document K, p.1.

[118] Ibid., pp.2-3.

76

to all available alternatives." Rodrigo's report to the DRU was eventually captured by the Salvadoran government. It notes that he met twice with Comrade Vladimir for a total of four hours, and (ironically in view of Vladimir's almost simultaneous protest) Rodrigo seems to have blamed Vladimir for the pressure to move shipments more quickly:

These meetings were restricted to a report presented by comrade Vladimir dealing with the prospect of sending materials to our country and to the presentation of a shipment schedule put together by our comrades of the Front. I personally made sure that comrade Vladimir understood the impossibility of receiving these materials if we followed the schedule presented by him. I insisted that the schedule had been prepared without previous consultation of the Reception Commission. This consultation was necessary so that the schedule would fit all the alternatives available to us.

My arguments were not taken into account. Comrade Vladimir restricted himself to saying that we should take the schedule with us, that we should do all we could, and that if something could not be done, we should let it be known through the instituted means in order to carry out the necessary suspensions.

I believe that the participation by a member of the Reception Commission in the program planning and preparation of the schedule must be a full one since this person has complete knowledge of the internal situation. . . .

On the day [a particular] shipment left, the comrade in charge of the operation indicated to the comrades of the Front that they were overloaded and that these could have problems.

This recommendation was not taken into account.

I write this letter so that my arguments will be studied by our directorate.[119]

On November 10, on behalf of the DRU, Comrade Marcial (Cayetano Carpio, leader of the FPL guerrilla group) responded to Comrade Vladimir's note of November 1.[120] He passed along to the DRU's logistics representative in Managua some of the complaints he had received from other guerrilla leaders in El Salvador about the arms shipment schedule:

7. In my position as general coordinator [of the DRU] I received reports from the bodies of the DRU and I try to have contacts and meetings with the comrade coordinators of each body. Both in the EMGC [Guerrilla Joint General Staff] and the logistical reception [committee] they have shared with me some of their concerns about logistical shipments and deliveries.

8. That in Lagos (the reference is primarily the [Sandinista] Front comrades, but in part also you) it would be necessary that they take more into consideration the opinions and plans prepared here by the committee of logistical reception; and that they feel the plans are not so much taken into consideration specifically concerning the location, capacities, etc., but that they do it "at random."

They gave examples: a) The first military shipment was excessively overloaded and one of them foundered in Lagos territorial waters and the entire cargo was lost. They were successful in saving their shipmates. The other two were overloaded. b) In view of the fact that they were

---

[119] Excerpt from report on work in Nicaragua, November 1-3, 1980; translated and reprinted in ibid., Document R, pp.1-3.

[120] This was clearly identified as a specific response to the November 1 report from Vladimir. See note 119 above.

overloaded more than had been expected, the comrades decided to send 100 more men and because of this they had a collision on the coastal highway. (An accident which neither eliminates nor invalidates the route or the location; but it is an example of the measures which they suddenly have to take, when over there, measures are not coordinated with the plans and capacities given by the domestic reception.) This has been pointed out to the comrades—not that measures should be taken to reduce the shipments but that there be more coordination with those within.[121]

Statements by former senior guerrilla leaders suggest that the Nicaraguans may use their control of the warehouses in which the arms are stored as a lever to influence guerrilla policy in El Salvador. It is at least clear that, for whatever reason, the Nicaraguans maintain formal control over the weapons. For example, a summary of a debriefing of former insurgent leader Moises López-Arriola said that "The Nicaraguans control the distribution of all weapons stockpiled in their country and López-Arriola had been told by a fellow FMLN leader that when the FMLN was in need of weapons, the United Revolutionary Directorate (DRU) asked the Nicaraguans for permission to draw from available supplies."

This practice still continues, according to Napoleón Romero García, a member of the Central Committee of the Popular Liberation Forces (FPL), who was arrested in April 1985. He stated that during the February 1985 FPL Central Committee meeting, Secretary General Leonel Gonzales asserted that the FMLN had obtained "authorization" from the "Sandinistas and Cubans" to receive shoulder-fired anti-aircraft missiles.[122] Romero indicated that at the time of his capture he was unaware of any tactical plan to introduce such weapons into El Salvador, but he thought some Salvadoran insurgents had already been trained in the use of such weapons in the course of anti-aircraft instruction in Nicaragua.[123]

Statements by Nicaragua's Neighbors

Both El Salvador and Honduras have frequently and formally gone on record in protest against Nicaragua's unlawful intervention in the internal affairs of El Salvador.

● El Salvador

Since at least 1980, Salvadoran government officials have protested against Nicaraguan intervention in the internal affairs of El Salvador by smuggling arms and taking other actions to assist Salvadoran insurgents.[124]

---

[121] Ibid., pp.2-3.

[122] Although Romero referred to the missiles as "Ojos Rojos" ("Red Eyes"—the designation of a U.S. version of this weapon), it is likely that the guerrillas had in mind the Soviet-made SAM-7.

[123] Declassified cable summarizing Romero debriefing.

[124] For example, in May 1980 a Nicaraguan official noted his country's "deteriorating relations" with El Salvador, and placed the blame on "the various statements made by a number of

To mention just a few examples, during the "final offensive" in January 1981 President José Napoleón Duarte frequently denounced both Nicaraguan and Cuban intervention, and called for U.S. assistance in meeting the aggression. As the *Washington Post* reported at the time: "Duarte has denounced alleged Cuban and Nicaraguan intervention in El Salvador several times during the last few days. . . . He has also called on U.S. President-elect Ronald Reagan to 'export democracy' to El Salvador and the world and to increase aid to the government here, particularly economic aid."[125]

On March 28, 1983, Salvadoran Foreign Minister Fidel Chávez-Meña warned the United Nations Security Council that El Salvador was the victim of "belligerent and hostile acts," and charged that Nicaragua "does not practice, and respects even less, the principle of non-interference in the internal affairs of Central American states." He stated:

Everyone is aware that the armed groups operating in El Salvador have their central headquarters in Nicaragua. It is there that decisions are made and logistic support is channelled—logistic support without which it would be impossible for them to continue in their struggle and without which they would have joined in the democratic process.[126]

During a visit to Washington in August 1983 seeking further assistance in meeting external aggression, Salvadoran President Alvaro Magaña Borja stated:

Foreign military intervention in domestic affairs constitutes the main obstacle to our efforts to attain peace. The interference of extracontinental communist countries by way of Cuba and Nicaragua in support of armed groups against a legitimate constitutionally elected government, is a form of aggression which violates the essence of international law, specifically the principle of non-intervention in the internal affairs of other states.[127]

On November 9, 1983, El Salvador's representative to the United Nations, Ambassador Rosales Rivera, told the General Assembly that Nicaragua was following "an interventionist policy," and that the Government of Nicaragua was "the primary factor in the instability of Central America."

Salvadoran Government officials seeking to connect the Nicaraguan Government junta with Salvadoran guerrilla forces." The diplomat added that it was evident that those accusing the Nicaraguan government had no proof of its alliance with the Salvadoran guerrillas. . . ." Radio Cadena, YSKL (San Salvador), 1815 GMT, May 30, 1980; in FBIS, Daily Report, Latin America, June 3, 1980, p.P-2. See also, ACAN (Panama City), 1642 GMT, June 16, 1980; in FBIS, Daily Report, Latin America, June 17, 1980, p.P-5 (noting that Salvadoran junta member Col. Jaime Abdul Gutierrez had in the past stated "that the Nicaraguan Government is supporting the armed struggle in El Salvador.").

[125] Christopher Dickey, "Fighting Subsides in El Salvador; 3 Journalists Hurt," *Washington Post*, January 13, 1981, p.1. See also, January 11, 1981, news conference by Vice President Jaime Abdul Gutierrez; reprinted in FBIS, Daily Report, Latin America, January 12, 1981, p.P-2.

[126] S/PV.2425, 7, March 28, 1983. See also, Chávez-Meña's speech before the thirty-eighth session of the UN General Assembly, A/38/PV/21 (October 7, 1983).

[127] "Remarks of President Alvaro Magaña Borja of El Salvador," *Department of State Bulletin*, August 1983, p.84.

[M]y country has been the victim, among other warlike and hostile acts, of a continuing traffic in weapons, with Nicaragua as the last link in the chain. From there orders are sent to armed groups of the extreme left operating in El Salvador. These groups have their headquarters in Nicaragua and logistic support is channelled through them.[128]

The following month, President Magaña was interviewed by the Spanish newspaper, *ABC*, during which this exchange occurred:

QUESTION: Mr. President, how do the guerrillas supply themselves and where from?

ANSWER: Be sure of this: from Nicaragua, and only from Nicaragua. In the past 2 weeks we have detected 68 incursions by aircraft which parachuted equipment, weapons and ammunition into the Morazán area, which is where the guerrillas are most concentrated. . . .

QUESTION: I would remind you, Mr. President, that one of Lenin's maxims was: "Against bodies, violence; against souls, lies."

ANSWER: Well, they have learned the lesson very well. While Nicaragua draws the world's attention by claiming for the past 2 years that it is about to be invaded, *they have not ceased for one moment to invade our country*. There is only one point of departure for the armed subversion, Nicaragua.[129]

In May 1984 José Napoleón Duarte was chosen President of El Salvador in a runoff election that was witnessed by scores of international observers and widely praised for its honesty and fairness.[130] In his inaugural address on June 1, President Duarte warned:

Salvadorans, we must bravely, frankly, and realistically acknowledge the fact that our homeland is immersed in an armed conflict that affects each and every one of us; that this armed conflict has gone beyond our borders and has become a focal point in the struggle between the big world power blocs. With the aid of Marxist governments like Nicaragua, Cuba, and the Soviet Union, an army has been trained and armed and has invaded our homeland. Its actions are directed from abroad.[131]

A month later, President Duarte said in a San Salvador press conference:

What I have said, from the Salvadoran standpoint, is that we have a problem of aggression by a nation called Nicaragua against El Salvador, that these gentlemen are sending in weapons, training people, transporting bullets and what not, and bringing all of that to El Salvador. I said that at this very minute they are using fishing boats as a disguise and are introducing weapons into El Salvador in boats at night. . . . [W]e are trying to get Nicaragua to behave like a sister nation, to *stop exporting revolution* and to respect our country.[132]

---

[128] UN General Assembly, A/38/PV.49, 17 (November 9, 1983).

[129] Interview with Salvadoran President Alvaro Magaña, *ABC* (Madrid), December 22, 1983, translated and reprinted in U.S. Counter-Memorial, annex 51. (Emphasis added.) See also, State/Defense, *Nicaragua's Military Buildup*, op.cit., p.23.

[130] See, e.g., John Vinocur, "West Europeans Hail Salvadoran Vote Result," *New York Times*, May 10, 1984, p. 19. Vinocur quotes, inter alia, observers from the West German Christian Democratic Party calling the election "an unequivocal confirmation of the view that people in El Salvador favor democracy and oppose the guerrillas."

[131] Duarte Inaugural Address; translated in FBIS, Daily Report, Latin America, June 4, 1984, pp.P-5-7.

[132] Duarte Press Conference, Radio Cadena YSKL (San Salvador), in Spanish, 1735 GMT, July 27, 1984; translated in FBIS, Daily Report, Latin America, July 30, 1984, p.P-2, included in U.S. Counter-Memorial annex 53. (Emphasis added.)

When asked about his view on anti-government forces (Contras) fighting in Nicaragua, Duarte responded:

In view of this situation, El Salvador must stop this somehow. The contras . . . are creating a sort of barrier that prevents the Nicaraguans from continuing to send arms to El Salvador by land. What they have done instead is to send them by sea, and they are now getting them in through Monte Cristo, El Coco, and El Espino. This is because they cannot do so overland, because the contras are in those areas, in one way or another. . . . I am not opposed to the prevention of weapons entering El Salvador. If by some action in the world these weapons are prevented from entering El Salvador, it is welcome, because this will rid us of the constant problem of so many deaths, murders, and problems in our homeland. This is what must be prevented.[133]

In addition to calling the attention of the people of El Salvador and the world to Nicaraguan aggression, the Government of El Salvador has frequently submitted formal protests to the Government of Nicaragua. For example, on August 24, 1984, the Salvadoran Foreign Ministry delivered a document to the Nicaraguan Chargé d'Affaires which, inter alia, stated that Nicaraguan intervention in the internal affairs of El Salvador and the material and logistical support given to the rebel groups "represent a flagrant violation of the most elemental norms of international law."[134]

● Honduras

Nicaraguan aggression against El Salvador has in the process flagrantly violated the territorial integrity of Honduras as well. Although Honduras has for many years quarreled with El Salvador about many issues—not the least of which is a major boundary dispute—the Government of Honduras has on several occasions expressed its deep concern about these Nicaraguan violations of international law.

Such criticism has not been limited to comments on Nicaraguan intervention against Honduras itself. For example, in April 1983 the Honduran Army issued a report which accused the FSLN of using Honduran territory to support the Salvadoran guerrillas—charging specifically that the Sandinistas had established "a corridor in Honduran territory to send men, weapons and equipment to the Salvadoran guerrillas."[135] Similarly, when Honduran Foreign Minister Eduardo Paz Barnica visited Panama in January 1984 he charged that "the Nicaraguan Revolutionary regime traffics in arms for the Salvadoran guerrillas, and . . . this aggravates the Central American crisis."[136] A more detailed discussion of Honduran complaints about Nicaraguan efforts to subvert its neighbors appears in Chapter 4.

---

[133] Ibid., pp.P-4-5.

[134] Reported by ACAN (Panama City), in Spanish, 0221 GMT, August 24, 1984.

[135] Cadena Audio Video (Tegucigalpa), in Spanish, 1145 GMT, April 5, 1983.

[136] DPA (Hamburg), in Spanish, 0050 GMT, January 7, 1984.

Statements by Individuals Who Have Had Access
to Sensitive Intelligence Information

By using sophisticated intelligence gathering procedures—overhead imagery, interception of electronic signals, secret agents, and other techniques—the United States and its allies have been able to obtain vast amounts of information far more persuasive than the unclassified material mentioned in this study. A limited amount of relatively less sensitive intelligence data has been made public from time to time,[137] but the most revealing material properly remains highly classified. It is unfortunate that the United States government is not able to share this information with its citizens and foreign friends, without in the process making it available to potential adversaries, but that is a reality of the modern world. Virtually every disclosure of sensitive intelligence information carries with it a risk that America's adversaries will discover their own weaknesses and take countermeasures making it more difficult—and perhaps impossible—for the United States to gather similar information during a future crisis.

That this has been more than a theoretical problem with respect to El Salvador and Nicaragua was brought home with the arrest of FPL Central Committee member Napoleón Romero Garcïa. Among the many documents found in the guerrilla safehouse in which Romero was apprehended were several "one-time pads" for encrypting sensitive data. Many code systems used to encrypt secrets for radio transmission can, with great effort or modern technology, be deciphered or "broken." "One-time pads" are inconvenient to use, but because they have no connecting logic they are essentially unbreakable. Romero said that the pads were used for all sensitive guerrilla communications, and that "introduction of the pads was prompted by the disclosure of information related to encrypted insurgent communications in a publication issued by the U.S. Congress."[138] In this instance, a decision to make public information derived from sensitive sources and methods resulted in increased communications security by anti-government forces in El Salvador and their supporters in Nicaragua—

---

[137] See, for example, the infrared photographs taken from AC-130 aircraft showing arms-smuggling trawlers off the coast of El Salvador in June 1984, which were made public by General Paul F. Gorman, Commander-in-Chief, U.S. Southern Command, in State/Defense, *External Support of Guerrillas in El Salvador*, op.cit., pp.8-12. Other recently declassified intelligence material is also included in this briefing. It is worth noting that General Gorman's account is supported by information provided by Napoleón Romero Garcïa, former member of the FPL Central Committee arrested in April 1985. A recently declassified cable summarizing a debriefing interview with Romero stated: "[A]rms shipments—which Romero believes may originate in the area of Chinandega, Nicaragua—are received on the beaches of Usulutan Department, either to the south of Jucuaran . . . or in the vicinity of Montecristo Island . . . at the mouth of the Rio Lempa. The deliveries are made at night, using no more than three launches or large canoes. . . . Shipments are coordinated by coded radio contacts between the insurgents in El Salvador and their representatives in Managua, Nicaragua."

[138] Declassified cable summarizing debriefing of Romero.

almost certainly in the process denying the Government of El Salvador important tactical information about guerrilla plans and operations that might have saved the lives of Salvadoran citizens and soldiers. Similarly, when information derived from clandestine human intelligence sources (e.g., intelligence agents) is made public, not only the continued effectiveness but even the lives of the agents may be placed in jeopardy.

Senior officials of the Carter Administration who had access to sensitive intelligence information were convinced, as former Secretary of State Edmund Muskie put it, that there was "no question" that leftist guerrillas in El Salvador were receiving arms through Nicaragua under circumstances that could force an end to U.S. assistance to the Sandinista regime.[139] Indeed, it was in large part because of this external assistance to the insurgents that the Carter Administration decided to resume military aid to the Government of El Salvador,[140] and to halt further aid to Nicaragua.

Even strong critics of the Reagan Administration who had access to intelligence data during the Carter Administration have conceded the Nicaraguan role in arming Salvadoran insurgents. For example, former Ambassador to El Salvador Robert White told Congress that the evidence of Nicaraguan intervention contained in a lengthy State Department white paper "was genuine,"[141] and acknowledged that the guerrillas had "imported massive quantities of arms" by way of Nicaragua.[142]

Sensitive intelligence information concerning Nicaragua's intervention in El Salvador has also been made available in great detail to the House and Senate intelligence committees; and, while endeavoring to avoid unauthorized disclosures of sensitive material, the committees have both issued public statements of their findings. The reports of the House Permanent Select Committee on Intelligence are particularly useful, because for several years a majority of that committee has been critical of U.S. policy toward Nicaragua, and thus has had little incentive to overstate facts which would almost certainly be used in debate to undermine the Committee's position.

---

[139] John M. Goshko, "Nicaragua Helping Aid El Salvador Leftists, Muskie Says," *Washington Post*, January 30, 1981, p.20. See also, Karen DeYoung, "Carter Decides to Resume Military Aid to El Salvador," *Washington Post*, January 14, 1981, p.18: "Both Muskie and the U.S. Embassy in El Salvador, which had similar reservations [about resuming military aid], now believe that leftist guerrillas . . . have received substantial new arms shipments and pose a strong threat to the U.S.-backed regime."

[140] See, e.g., Karen DeYoung, "Carter Decides to Resume Military Aid to El Salvador," *Washington Post*, January 14, 1981, p.18; and Janet Battaile, "U.S. Set to Resume Military Assistance to Salvador," *New York Times*, January 14, 1981, p.3.

[141] Richard Whittle, "Reagan Weighs Military Aid to Counter Soviet, Cuban 'Interference' in El Salvador," *Congressional Quarterly*, February 28, 1981, p.389. The State Department white paper, entitled *Communist Interference in El Salvador*, op.cit., February 23, 1981, includes documents which have been cited extensively in this study.

[142] Margot Hornblower, "Ousted Envoy Hits Arms Aid to Salvador," *Washington Post*, February 26, 1981, p.1.

On March 4, 1982, following a lengthy briefing of the House Intelligence Committee, Chairman Edward Boland issued a public statement which said:

The Committee has received a briefing concerning the situation in El Salvador, with particular emphasis on the question of foreign support for the insurgency. The insurgents are well-trained, well-equipped with modern weapons and supplies, and rely on the use of sites in Nicaragua for command and control and for logistical support. The intelligence supporting these judgments provided to the committee is convincing.

There is further persuasive evidence that the Sandinista Government of Nicaragua is helping train insurgents and is transferring arms and financial support from and through Nicaragua to the insurgents. They are further providing the insurgents bases of operations in Nicaragua. Cuban involvement—especially in providing arms—is also evident.

What this says is that, contrary to the repeated denials of Nicaraguan officials, that country is thoroughly involved in supporting the Salvadoran insurgency. That support is such as to greatly aid the insurgents in their struggle with government forces in El Salvador.[143]

In its May 13, 1983 report accompanying the Intelligence Authorization bill, the House Intelligence Committee provided a detailed discussion of Nicaraguan involvement in El Salvador. After noting in its introduction that "this insurgency depends for its lifeblood—arms, ammunition, financing, logistics and command-and-control facilities—upon outside assistance from Nicaragua and Cuba,"[144] the Committee included a section entitled "Activities of Cuba and Nicaragua" which stated:

The Committee has regularly reviewed voluminous intelligence materials on Nicaraguan and Cuban support for leftist insurgencies since the 1979 Sandinista victory in Nicaragua. . . .

Full discussion of intelligence materials in public reports would pose serious security risks to intelligence sources and methods. Necessarily, therefore, the Committee must limit its treatment of Cuban and Nicaraguan aid for insurgencies to the judgments it has reached. Such judgments nonetheless constitute a clear picture of active promotion for "revolution without frontiers" throughout Central America by Cuba and Nicaragua. . . .

At the time of the filing of this report, the Committee believes that the intelligence available to it continues to support the following judgments with certainty:

A major portion of the arms and other material sent by Cuba and other communist countries to the Salvadoran insurgents transits Nicaragua with the permission and assistance of the Sandinistas.

The Salvadoran insurgents rely on the use of sites in Nicaragua, some of which are located in Managua itself, for communications, command-and-control, and for the logistics to conduct their financial, material, and propaganda activities.

The Sandinista leadership sanctions and directly facilitates all of the above functions.

Nicaragua provides a range of other support activities, including secure transit of insurgents to and from Cuba, and assistance to the insurgents in planning their activities in El Salvador.

---

[143] Statement released by House Permanent Select Committee on Intelligence Chairman Edward Boland, March 4, 1982.

[144] U.S. Congress, House, Permanent Select Committee on Intelligence, Amendment to the Intelligence Authorization Act for Fiscal Year 1983, House Report 98-122, pt. 1, 98th Congress, 1st Session, May 13, 1983, p.2.

84

In addition, Nicaragua and Cuba have provided—and appear to continue providing—training to the Salvadoran insurgents.[145]

A clear majority of the House Permanent Select Committee on Intelligence publicly opposed U.S. policy toward Nicaragua, evidenced by votes between 1983 and 1987 to deny funding for the Nicaraguan Contras. When the Committee submitted its report in connection with the fiscal year 1985 intelligence authorization bill, it did not include a discussion of Nicaraguan intervention in El Salvador. However, when the bill reached the House floor for debate, Congressman Thomas Coleman of Missouri called the attention of Chairman Boland—who was leading the opposition to aid to the Contras—to the lack of similar report language in the 1984 report, and asked whether in the Committee's view the situation had changed. This exchange then occurred:

MR. BOLAND: Pointing to and indicating that there is clear and convincing evidence that military equipment is going to El Salvador and transiting through Nicaragua, is that the question?

MR. COLEMAN of Missouri: Right. Is that true today? Because I see nothing in the report.

MR. BOLAND: That is true today, as it was at the time of that [May 1983] report. The evidence is less concrete, more circumstantial,[146] but it still supports that conclusion. We have never backed away from that statement.

MR. COLEMAN of Missouri: . . . Let me ask another question. . . . Another statement which was made with great certainty by the committee in May 1983 was that the Salvadoran insurgents rely on the use of its sites in Nicaragua, some of which are located in Managua itself, for communications, command and control, and for the logistics to conduct their financial, material, and propaganda activities. Is that true today?

MR. BOLAND: That was true in 1983 and it is true today. My answer would be yes.

MR. COLEMAN of Missouri: Along the same lines, Mr. Chairman, with certainty the committee stated that the Sandinista leadership sanctions and directly facilitates all of these functions. And, further, Nicaragua provides a range of other support activities, including secure transit of insurgents to and from Cuba, and assistance to the insurgents in planning their activities in El Salvador. Is that true today also?

MR. BOLAND: It was true then. It is true today. And the committee has never backed away from that statement.[147]

Like its House counterpart, the Senate Select Committee on Intelligence has on occasion issued public statements summarizing its conclusions following sensitive intelligence briefings. For example, on March 2, 1982, Committee Chairman Barry Goldwater issued a press release which said in part:

The [several-hour-long intelligence briefing] left no doubt that there is active involvement by Sandinista Government officials in support of the Salvadoran guerrilla movement. This support

---

[145] Ibid., p.6. This report also found it especially "ominous" that "the Sandinistas have stepped up their support for insurgents in Honduras." Ibid., p.3.

[146] This may be explained in part as a consequence of the use of "one-time pads" and other security measures by the insurgents aimed precisely at preventing the United States from gathering the kind of hard, clear evidence it had been able to obtain during the earlier stages of the conflict.

[147] *Congressional Record*, Vol. 130, pp.H 8268-8269 (daily edition, August 2, 1984).

includes arrangements for the use of Nicaraguan territory for the movement of arms and ammunition to guerrillas in El Salvador, the continuing passage of guerrillas in and out of Nicaragua for advanced training in sabotage and other terrorist tactics, and the presence of high-level guerrilla headquarters elements in Nicaragua. There is strong evidence of a great surge in the delivery of arms, ammunitions, and related materials from Nicaragua to El Salvador.

Speaking as chairman of the committee, I must stress the sensitive nature of the intelligence provided us. The details must remain secret, but the American people deserve to know that the officials charged with developing and implementing U.S. policy in this area are doing so on the basis of solid information.[148]

Similarly, in March 1984 the Vice Chairman of the Senate Select Committee on Intelligence, Senator Daniel Patrick Moynihan, said on the Senate floor:

It is the judgment of the Intelligence Committee that Nicaragua's involvement in the affairs of El Salvador and, to a lesser degree, its other neighbors, continues. As such, our duty, or at very least our right, now as it was [in November 1983,] is to respond to these violations of international law and uphold the charter of the OAS. . . .

In sum, the Sandinista support for the insurgency in El Salvador has not appreciably lessened; nor, therefore, has their violation of the OAS charter abated.[149]

Not only have both Congressional intelligence committees consistently concluded that Nicaragua has been intervening in the internal affairs of El Salvador by supporting the insurgents, but the entire Congress has gone on record with a similar conclusion. For example, section 109(a) of the Intelligence Authorization Act for Fiscal Year 1984 provided in part:

Sec. 109(a) the Congress finds that—

(1) The Government of National Reconstruction of Nicaragua has failed to keep solemn promises, made to the Organization of American States in July 1979, to . . . pursue a foreign policy of nonaggression and nonintervention;

(2) By providing military support (including arms, training, and logistical, command and control, and communications facilities) to groups seeking to overthrow the Government of El Salvador and other Central American governments, the Government of National Reconstruction of Nicaragua has violated article 18 of the Charter of the Organization of American States which declares that no state has the right to intervene, directly or indirectly, for any reason whatsoever, in the internal affairs of any other state. . . .[150]

Similarly, in the International Security and Development Cooperation Act of 1985, Congress found that "the . . . Government of Nicaragua . . . has flagrantly violated . . . the security of the nations in the region, in that it . . . has committed and refused to cease aggression in the form of armed subversion against its neighbors. . . ."[151]

---

[148] Press release issued by Senate Select Committee on Intelligence Chairman Barry Goldwater, March 2, 1982.

[149] Reprinted in "For the Record," *Washington Post*, April 10, 1984.

[150] Intelligence Authorization Act for Fiscal Year 1984, Public Law 98-215 [H.R. 2968], 97 Stat. 1475, December 9, 1983.

[151] International Security and Development Cooperation Act of 1985, Section 722(c)(2)(C).

The National Bipartisan Commission on Central America (the so-called Kissinger Commission) was also provided a certain amount of sensitive intelligence information as a part of its responsibilities to make recommendations to the President on future U.S. policy in the region. In its final report, the Commission concluded:

External Intervention. Whatever the social and economic conditions that invited insurgency in the region, outside intervention is what gives the conflict its present character. . . .

Propaganda support, money, sanctuary, arms, supplies, training, communications, intelligence, logistics, all are important in both morale and operational terms. Without such support from Cuba, Nicaragua, and the Soviet Union, neither in El Salvador nor elsewhere in Central America would such an insurgency pose so severe a threat to the government. . . . As a mainland platform, therefore, Nicaragua is a crucial steppingstone for Cuban and Soviet efforts to promote armed insurgency in Central America. Its location explains why the Nicaraguan revolution of 1979, like the Cuban revolution 20 years earlier, was a decisive turning point in the affairs of the region. With the victory of the Sandinistas in Nicaragua, the levels of violence and counter-violence in Central America rapidly increased, engulfing the entire region.[152]

Public Statements by Sandinista Comandantes

Although Nicaraguan officials have usually denied giving any assistance to insurgents in El Salvador, there have been a number of relatively candid moments which shed light on their objectives and activities. Sergio Ramírez, who became Nicaragua's Vice President in 1984, said in an interview with a Mexican journalist in January 1980 that "deeper social change cannot take place in one country without a similar transformation in those that surround it." He added: "To be specific, a process of change in one Central American country requires that a similar process be in progress in the others. . . . [W]e cannot neglect giving special attention to our immediate neighbors."[153] Comandante Tomás Borge Martinez, Nicaragua's Interior Minister and the only surviving founder of the FSLN, told a North Korean audience in June 1980 that "the Nicaraguan revolutionaries will not be content until the imperialists have been overthrown in all parts of the world. . . . We stand with the forces of peace and progress, which are the socialist countries."[154] In early 1982 he told the closing session of the Fifth Permanent Conference of Latin American Political Parties:

How can a patriot be indifferent to the fate of his Latin American brothers? . . . How can we keep our arms folded in the face of the crimes that are being committed in El Salvador and

---

[152] *Report of the President's National Bipartisan Commission on Central America,* January 10, 1984, pp.87-88, excerpted in U.S. Counter-Memorial, annex 45. Under the heading "The Situation in El Salvador," the Commission concluded: "The guerrilla front (. . .FMLN) has established a unified military command with headquarters near Managua." Ibid., p.97.

[153] Interview with Sergio Ramírez, *Cuadernos de Marcha* (Mexico), reprinted in Leiken and Rubin, op.cit., p.214.

[154] Pyongyang KCNA in English, 0400 GMT June 10, 1980; reprinted in FBIS, Daily Report, East Asia, June 12, 1980, p.D-16.

Guatemala? . . . We have shown our solidarity with all Latin American peoples in the past, we are doing so at present and will continue to do so in the future.[155]

In a lengthy interview in *Playboy* magazine in September 1983, Borge was asked how he would respond to a lengthy quotation from the United States Ambassador to the United Nations, Dr. Jeane Kirkpatrick. This exchange occurred:

PLAYBOY: Then will you respond to the general thrust of her remarks—that Nicaragua is the first domino in Latin America? That since the revolution triumphed here, *it will be exported to El Salvador*, then Guatemala, then Honduras, then Mexico?

BORGE: That is one historical prophecy of Ronald Reagan's that is *absolutely true!*[156]

Consider also the statements of Comandante Humberto Ortega Saavedra, Nicaragua's Defense Minister, who has been quoted in the American press as having stated: "Of course we are not ashamed to be helping El Salvador. We would like to help all revolutionaries."[157] Humberto Ortega has also been quoted by Panamanian news sources as having said:

Nicaragua must express its solidarity with the other Latin American peoples struggling against or defeating imperialism or trying to shake off the yoke of foreign masters. . . . That is what we must learn from our Cuban brothers, who, despite their limitations and their poverty, have been generous with our people.[158]

Lest there be any misunderstanding about what Comandante Ortega had in mind in suggesting that Nicaragua "learn" from the "generosity" of its "Cuban brothers," consider this statement he made the following year about the Cuban role in aiding Nicaragua:

The socialist camp has to sacrifice a major part of its economy to defend itself and to help other peoples to defend themselves. This is, for example, the case with Cuba, which without aid from the Soviet Union would not have the weapons to defend its revolution. This is also the case with Nicaragua, because we have had the unconditional, unqualified support, above all, of Cuba, led by Fidel Castro.[159]

Another key Sandinista Comandante who implicitly confirmed Nicaragua's support for Salvadoran insurgents is Bayardo Arce, one of the nine members of the FSLN's National Directorate, Coordinator of the Front's Political Committee, and the Nicaraguan official most closely associated

---

[155] Managua domestic service, February 21, 1982. On January 21, 1982, Borge said in a message to the Continental Conference for Peace, Human Rights, and Self-Determination of El Salvador: "The struggle of the Salvadoran people is the struggle of all honest men and women of the continent. . . . This is the struggle of all those who feel dutybound to support a brave David facing a criminal and arrogant Goliath, it is the continuation of the struggle of Sandino, Farabundo Martí, Ché Guevara, and Salvador Allende." Radio Sandino, January 21, 1982.

[156] Dreifus, op.cit., p.192. (Emphasis added.)

[157] Kramer, op.cit., p.39.

[158] Remarks at ceremony in Havana marking 21st anniversary of Cuban Revolution, reported by Panamanian news agency ACAN, January 4, 1980.

[159] Speech by Humberto Ortega Saavedra, Nicaraguan Minister of Defense, at closing session of the Meeting of Specialists; date and place not given. Reprinted in *La Prensa* (Managua), October 27, 1981, pp.16-19.

with foreign insurgent groups.[160] According to the *Washington Post*, "Speaking March 3 [1983] at a funeral for 17 adolescent Sandinistas killed by counterrevolutionaries, Nicaraguan commander Bayardo Arce warned that his party's 'internationalism will not bend' and that 'while Salvadorans are fighting to win their liberty Nicaragua will maintain its solidarity.'"[161] A few months later, he was quoted in another American journal as saying: "We will never give up supporting our brothers in El Salvador."[162]

In May 1984 Comandante Arce delivered a revealing speech about the upcoming Nicaraguan presidential election to the political committee of the Nicaraguan Socialist Party (PSN) in Managua. Although not intended to be made public, the meeting was secretly taped and after the speech was published its authenticity was confirmed to journalists by no less an authority than Comandante Daniel Ortega—the current President of Nicaragua.[163] While stressing that the election was "a nuisance" that would have been "totally out of place in terms of its usefulness" were it not for United States pressure, Comandante Arce explained:

[I]t is well to be able to call elections and take away from American policy one of its justifications for aggression against Nicaragua, because *the other two factors cannot be conceded*.

Imperialism asks three things of us: *to abandon interventionism*, to abandon our strategic ties with the Soviet Union and the socialist community, and to be democratic. *We cannot cease being internationalists unless we cease being revolutionaries.* We cannot discontinue strategic relationships unless we cease being revolutionaries. It is impossible even to consider this.[164]

Although no longer a member of the Sandinista government, Edén Pastora was once the most famous comandante of all. In a rare contribution to an American scholarly journal, Comandante Cero wrote:

When the Managua government, personified by the nine top Communists, was planning the insurrection in El Salvador, I was a participant in the meetings of the National Leadership; I was in effect the tenth member of the National Leadership without having formally been so

---

[160] Arce has been so identified by former Salvadoran insurgent leader Napoleón Romero García. See also, State, *Communist Interference in El Salvador*, op.cit., Document G, pp. 1, 8; and State/Defense, *Nicaragua's Military Buildup*, op.cit., pp. 17-18: "The Nicaraguan support structure for the Salvadoran DRU (Unified Revolutionary Directorate) has been incorporated into the FSLN's party structure and state apparatus. The 'Comisión Política,' headed by FSLN national coordinator Bayardo Arce, is in charge of facilitating propaganda and diplomatic support for the Salvadoran guerrillas."

[161] Christopher Dickey, "Leftist Guerrillas in El Salvador Defend Cuban Ties," *Washington Post*, March 11, 1983.

[162] Kramer, op.cit., p.39.

[163] ". . . Ortega made several comments suggesting that differences do exist within the directorate regarding the planned elections for a president, vice president and an assembly. In particular, he said that recently disclosed comments by Sandinista Political Commission head Bayardo Arce 'do not represent the official position of the Sandinista front.' . . . Ortega did not deny that Arce . . . had made the comments. . . ." Robert J. McCartney, "Nicaraguan Hails 'Fluid' Talks with U.S. on Security," *Washington Post*, August 12, 1984, p.A-1.

[164] State, *Bayardo Arce's Secret Speech*, op.cit., p.4. (Emphasis added.) For a discussion of the effectiveness of U.S. pressure on the Government of Nicaragua, see Chapter 6.

designated. With care and much diplomacy, I told the rest of the leaders that I did not agree with the idea of launching the Salvadorans into an insurrection. . . .[165]

There have been other direct and indirect implications by Sandinista leaders that they continue to supply arms to Salvadoran guerrillas. For example, in researching an article on U.S.-Nicaraguan negotiations for *Foreign Policy* quarterly, *Newsday* foreign affairs correspondent Roy Gutman spoke at length with Nicaraguan officials. He later wrote:

[U.S. Assistant Secretary of State Thomas] Enders also told them that only if the flow of arms to El Salvador were stopped would the United States be willing to enter agreements [with Nicaragua]. . . .

But whether or not originally intended as a precondition, it was formally presented as one by Enders later that month in a letter to Nicaraguan Foreign Minister Reverend Miguel D'Escoto Brockman shown to this writer by Arana and confirmed as authentic by the State Department. "The continued use of Nicaraguan territory to support and funnel arms to insurgent movements in the area will create an insuperable barrier to the development of normal relations," Enders wrote. "Unless this support is terminated right now, I don't think that there can be the proposed dialogue, so I will say this has to be a sine qua non for *any* dialogue." As incentives, Enders offered security guarantees and economic aid.

The Nicaraguan leaders told Enders they were willing to negotiate but without any preconditions. "And that if they were waiting for us to accept their conditions and demands, then we were not willing to proceed," the party official continued. "They considered that we did not take the steps. So the dialogue did not progress."[166]

Given Nicaragua's alleged desire to negotiate with the United States, were the Enders "precondition" in reality already satisfied (i.e., had Nicaragua already ceased aiding Salvadoran insurgents), one would have expected Foreign Minister D'Escoto simply to announce that fact and urge that negotiations begin.

Nicaraguan officials have also on occasion in private meetings admitted their intervention in El Salvador. For example, the Government of El Salvador has noted that in a July 1983 meeting of the Contadora Group, Nicaraguan Foreign Minister D'Escoto admitted that his country had been giving material aid to Salvadoran guerrillas.[167] In January 1985, Nicara-

---

[165] Edén Pastora Gómez, "Nicaragua 1983-1985: Two Years' Struggle Against Soviet Intervention," *Journal of Contemporary Studies*, Spring/Summer 1985, pp.9-10.

[166] Gutman, op.cit., p.6.

[167] Declaration of Intervention of the Republic of El Salvador, *Nicaragua v. United States*, submitted to the International Court of Justice, August 15, 1984, pp.10-11. On several occasions surrounding the January 1981 "final offensive" in El Salvador, D'Escoto virtually admitted that Nicaraguans were fighting alongside the Salvadoran insurgents. For example, on January 14, 1981, he said: "[I]t is not unusual for Nicaraguan guerrillas to be in El Salvador participating in the struggle the Salvadoran people are waging for their liberation." He said that "a difference must be made between a mercenary, who struggles in another country for a salary or for pay, and a guerrilla, who struggles out of solidarity with a people pursuing their liberation or ideals." AFP (Paris), 2130 GMT, January 14, 1981; reprinted in FBIS, Daily Report, Latin America, January 15, 1981, p.P-17. See also, Panama City National Television, 1130 GMT, January 7, 1981; in FBIS, Daily Report, Latin America, January 8, 1981, p.P-13.

guan President Daniel Ortega Saavedra was interviewed by Mario Vargas Llosa, the distinguished Peruvian novelist, who later recounted the conversation in an article in the *New York Times* Magazine. According to Mr. Vargas, in discussing possible negotiations with the United States, President Ortega said: "We've said that we're . . . willing to stop the movement of military aid, or any other kind of aid, through Nicaragua to El Salvador. . . ."[168] A similar statement was made in April 1986 to a *Wall Street Journal* writer, who quoted Ortega as saying, "Nicaragua is ready to agree to . . . a halt to aid for 'irregular forces' in the region," if the United States would "end its military pressure on Nicaragua and cease military maneuvers in the region."[169] Since this was described by Ortega as "a reciprocal arrangement,"[170] it constitutes an admission of some importance. Similar admissions have been made during conversations with members of the United States Congress. Consider this account by Representative F. James Sensenbrenner:

I asked [Daniel] Ortega specifically to swear off the doctrine of "revolution without borders," and he refused to do so. He said that Nicaraguans would talk about stopping their exportation of revolution if the United States would cut off aid to the "Contras," stop military maneuvers in Honduras and the naval maneuvers off the coast of Nicaragua.[171]

Evidence of Nicaragua's efforts to destabilize the Government of El Salvador can also be found in numerous documents that have surfaced in recent years. Particularly important in this regard was a 36-page document summarizing the results of the "First National Assembly of Cadres of the Sandinist National Liberation Front (FSLN)" which took place in Managua between September 21 and 23, 1979—just two months following the seizure of power from the Somoza regime. Formally entitled *Analysis of the Situation and Tasks of the Sandinist People's Revolution*, but commonly referred to as the "Seventy-Two-Hour Document," it set forth "general-guidelines . . . on the basis of which we will have to begin issuing specific instructions for the various work spheres and for the various sectors involved in our revolutionary process."[172] In addressing foreign policy matters, the document says:

The foreign policy of the Sandinist People's Revolution is based on the full exercise of national sovereignty and independence and on the principle of revolutionary internationalism. The goal of the FSLN's foreign policy is to consolidate the Nicaraguan revolution, because this will help to strengthen the Central American, Latin American and worldwide revolution. . . . This will be our general approach to foreign policy, the guidelines of which are as follows: . . . .

---

[168] Mario Vargas Llosa, "In Nicaragua," *New York Times* Magazine, April 28, 1985, p.37.

[169] Clifford Krauss, "Nicaragua Again Offers to Talk Peace with US, but Washington is Skeptical," *Wall Street Journal*, April 18, 1986, p.24.

[170] Ibid.

[171] Rep. F. James Sensenbrenner, "Q & A: Nicaragua's Words and its Deeds," *Washington Times*, November 8, 1983, p.2.

[172] FSLN, *Analysis. . .of the Sandinist People's Revolution*, op. cit., p.1.

c) Help further the struggles of Latin American nations against fascist dictatorships and for democracy and national liberation.

d) The same principles apply to Central America, which has great strategic importance at present; we should underscore the need to counteract the aggressive policy of the military dictatorships in Guatemala and El Salvador by taking proper advantage of the frictions there, while stressing our differences with Honduras and the friendly conduct of Costa Rica and Panama.[173]

As will be shown in Chapter 5, not even peaceful Costa Rica would be spared in the end from Nicaraguan intervention.

Admissions by Salvadoran Insurgent Leaders

Finally, Salvadoran insurgents have on occasion acknowledged publicly the assistance they have received from Nicaragua and other countries. Thus, in an article on the FMLN, Alan Riding wrote in the *New York Times* in 1982:

[T]he guerrillas acknowledge that, in the past, they received arms from Cuba through Nicaragua, as the Reagan Administration maintains. . . . And finally, the guerrillas now concede, Cuba agreed to supply them with the necessary armaments—many of them transshipped through Nicaragua—to enable them to open their "final offensive" on January 10, 1981, just days before President Reagan took office.[174]

Consider also this account from the *Los Angeles Times*:

El Salvador's leftist guerrilla movement boasted Sunday of its close ties to Cuba and Nicaragua and declared that it sees its struggle against the U.S.-backed government in San Salvador as part of a wider regional conflict. . . .

The broadcast, transmitted from a secret location in neighboring Nicaragua—whose Marxist-led Sandinista regime has allowed the Salvadoran guerrillas to establish their headquarters in Managua—also boasted that the rebels have imported arms "through all routes that we could" and that "we have used all of Central America and other countries" for that purpose.

The broadcast appeared to support charges made by the Reagan Administration that the insurgency is at least encouraged and armed, if not directed, by the Soviet Union, Cuba and Nicaragua and is aimed at toppling one moderate government after another throughout the region.[175]

Consequences of Nicaraguan Intervention

According to a Sandinista organizer, guerrillas must solve three essential problems. They must have an "adequate arsenal," they must overcome "internal fighting," and they must have "public support." "Unless rebels solve these problems, they will have no chance for progress or victory."[176]

---

[173] Ibid., pp.30-31.

[174] Alan Riding, "Salvador Rebels: Five-Sided Alliance Searching for New, Moderate Image," *New York Times*, March 18, 1982, p.A-1.

[175] David Wood, "Salvadoran Rebels Brag of Cuban Ties," *Los Angeles Times*, March 13, 1983. See also, Christopher Dickey, "Leftist Guerrillas in El Salvador Defend Cuba Ties," *Washington Post*, March 11, 1983.

[176] Gertrudis de Ramírez, wife of junta member Sergio Ramírez Mercado, quoted in Beth Nissen, "Nicaraguan Echo: Overthrow of Somoza Spurs Other Guerrillas in Central America," *Wall Street Journal*, July 27, 1979.

The Government of Nicaragua and the Sandinista National Liberation Front—working in close cooperation with Cuba and other radical states—played an instrumental role in resolving two of these problems for the insurgency movement in El Salvador.

First of all, Sandinista officials joined with Fidel Castro in using the promise of massive amounts of arms and equipment to persuade the five feuding and ineffective Marxist guerrilla organizations to set aside their differences and work together under the banner of the FMLN. The importance of this step was emphasized by a spokesman for one leftist splinter group prior to the formation of the FMLN. He told an American journalist, less than two months following the Sandinista victory in Nicaragua, that "the military part of the [Salvadoran] revolution has to wait until the rebel factions are unified. A full-blown revolt . . . is inevitable but not imminent."[177]

More recently, looking back on the formation of the Front, Comandante Fermán Cienfuegos of the FMLN told a foreign debt conference in Havana in August 1985:

In 1980, the patriots, democrats, socialists, Christians, Marxists, and the various political movements of the Salvadoran people united to create the FMLN and the FDR, an unbreakable alliance that established the pace of the great leap that began with the [final offensive] campaign of 10 January 1981. *Nothing would have been possible without that unification.*[178]

At the time of the Sandinista victory in Nicaragua, anti-government guerrillas in El Salvador numbered by most estimates only a few hundred.[179] Their tactics were limited largely to kidnappings, bank robberies, and occasional bombings and assassinations.[180] As Sandinista support increased,[181] guerrilla groups began targeting El Salvador's economy. Consider this account from the *Wall Street Journal*, written six months after the Sandinista victory:

---

[177] Joe Frazier, "El Salvador battle grows," *Philadelphia Inquirer*, September 16, 1979, p.A-16.

[178] Speech by Comandante Fermán Cienfuegos, member of FMLN general command, at foreign debt conference in Havana; FBIS, Daily Report, Latin America, August 5, 1985, p.Q-11. (Emphasis added.) According to Radio Venceremos, the January 1981 "final offensive" was "possible thanks to the union of our four main revolutionary forces. . . ." Radio Venceremos, in Spanish, 1210 GMT, January 29, 1981; in FBIS, Daily Report, Latin America, January 30, 1981, p.P-8.

[179] See, e.g., Bob Adams, "El Salvador: ready to explode," *Chicago Sun-Times*, September 24, 1979, p.17 ("The guerrillas number only a few hundred by most estimates."); and Christopher Dickey, "El Salvador's Shadowy War," *Washington Post*, June 30, 1980, p.1, who reports that there were "believed to be in the neighborhood of . . . a few hundred [guerrillas] a year ago" in El Salvador.

[180] See, e.g., Arostegui, op.cit., p.96.

[181] As has already been noted (p.46, fn.2), even prior to the overthrow of Somoza the FSLN was providing some assistance to the Salvadoran rebels.

He calls himself a "front-line soldier in the quietest war," this thin rebel guarding the entrance of a guerrilla-occupied coffee factory. "We are not strong enough to win our revolution by destroying the army," he says, hefting his rusted rifle. "But we can cause chaos by destroying the businesses."[182]

Six months later, a spokesman for the FPL told a *Washington Post* reporter that the military balance was "still unfavorable to us,"[183] but already the picture was beginning to change. Guerrilla strength increased dramatically as Havana and Managua helped bring unity to the rival insurgent groups, and by September 1980 a campaign of economic sabotage had destroyed more than 200 urban and intercity buses, and seriously damaged numerous electrical transmission lines.[184] A month later, diplomatic and intelligence sources—as well as representatives of Salvadoran guerrilla groups—were quoted as saying the revolutionary forces were "better trained, better equipped and better able to mount major assaults on the Salvadoran government's troops than ever before."[185]

Following the continued influx of massive amounts of arms and equipment from and through Nicaragua, by the time of the January 1981 "final offensive" the Government of El Salvador was confronted by a dramatically changed situation. U.S. Ambassador Robert White, who ten months earlier had characterized El Salvador as being in "a prerevolutionary situation,"[186] noted that there had been a "change [in] the nature" of the conflict by January 1981.[187] *Le Monde* observed that the "quality and firepower of [Salvadoran guerrilla] arms seem to have improved";[188] and the *Washington Post* reported that "the guerrillas have proven they can mount coordinated actions virtually anywhere in this overcrowded Central American country and operate almost freely in the rural areas."[189]

---

[182] Beth Nissen, "The Quiet War: Salvadorean Guerrillas Take Aim at Economy in Bid to Unseat Junta," *Wall Street Journal,* December 13, 1979.

[183] Christopher Dickey, "El Salvador's Shadowy War," *Washington Post,* June 30, 1980, p.1. As early as April, "political and diplomatic analysts" were reported to have warned that "general armed rebellion could erupt in this poor, overcrowded central American nation within two to three months." "El Salvador Tilts Further Toward Full Civil War," *New York Times,* April 6, 1980, p.E-2.

[184] Juan de Onis, "U.S. Plans More Aid for Salvador to Offset Sabotage," *New York Times,* September 9, 1980, p.13.

[185] Christopher Dickey, "U.S. Training Salvadorans in Panama," *Washington Post,* October 9, 1980, p.1.

[186] "El Salvador Tilts Further Toward Full Civil War," *New York Times,* April 6, 1980, p.E-2.

[187] David Wood, "Carter Orders Military Supplies to Embattled Junta in Salvador," *Washington Star,* January 15, 1981, p.1; and "Flow of Arms to Rebels Given as Reason for Aid," *New York Times,* January 19, 1981, p.A-11.

[188] *Le Monde* (Paris), January 9, 1981, p.7.

[189] Christopher Dickey, "U.S. Adds 'Lethal' Aid to El Salvador," *Washington Post,* January 18, 1981, p.1. See also, Jack Anderson, "Salvadoran Rebels Given Military Edge," *Washington Post,* January 20, 1981, p.C-22. Anderson quotes "intelligence sources" as saying, "A year ago, the guerrillas and the government were about even militarily. But now the guerrillas have the edge."

The "final offensive"—which included guerrilla attacks on nearly 50 different targets across El Salvador—demonstrated that the guerrillas lacked popular support,[190] but it also showed the impact of their unity and of the massive assistance they had received from Nicaragua. It marked the start of a major civil war that has threatened the very survival of democratic El Salvador, and has cost the people of El Salvador horrendously. In economic damage alone, the war by early 1985 had cost in excess of one billion dollars.[191] This figure continues to increase,[192] but as huge as it is it represents only a small measure of the true damage done to El Salvador—in large part due to the efforts of Nicaragua.

According to the Red Cross, during one week in January 1981, 600 Salvadorans were killed during the "final offensive."[193] It is often difficult to determine whether casualties in El Salvador have been produced by the notorious right-wing "death squads" or are a product of the Marxist-Leninist insurgency. In its declaration to the International Court of Justice, the Government of El Salvador stated that "half a million persons have been internally displaced and over 30,000 persons have been killed in the conflict since it was unleashed in 1979."[194] FMLN high command Comandante Fermán Cienfuegos announced in Havana in August 1985 that since the "final offensive," FMLN forces "have inflicted over 18,000 casualties on the enemy's Army, and have destroyed at least 43 aircraft."[195] He stated that

---

[190] The offensive was in military terms an utter failure, since contrary to apparent guerrilla expectations the people of El Salvador ignored their calls for a mass uprising to overthrow the government. Montenegro notes that the guerrillas who entered San Salvador for the final offensive were shocked when they went into the streets and called upon the people to join in the revolution, and found no support—only locked doors. (See pp.143-144.)

[191] State/Defense, *Soviet-Cuban Connection,* op.cit., p.1. See also, Warren Hoge, "War Saps Salvador Economy," *New York Times,* March 18, 1982, p.A-1. José Napoleón Romero and other defectors have reported that a major objective of guerrilla strategy is "the destruction of El Salvador's economic infrastructure."

[192] For example, on January 8, 1986, a single guerrilla attack burned 1,000 sacks of coffee beans. The following day, another attack destroyed 5,000 sacks of coffee beans—with an estimated value of about $1 million. "Rebels Disrupt Salvadoran Coffee Harvest," *Washington Times,* January 10, 1986, p.B-10.

[193] Christopher Dickey, "U.S. Adds 'Lethal' Aid to El Salvador," *Washington Post,* January 18, 1981, p.1. The Government of El Salvador reported that during the nine-day period following the start of the offensive on January 10, 1981, a total of 1,122 people died as a result of the fighting. Statement of Defense Minister José Guillermo García, January 19, 1981; translated and reprinted in FBIS, Daily Report, Latin America, January 21, 1981, p.P-4.

[194] Declaration of Intervention of the Republic of El Salvador, *Nicaragua v. United States, International Legal Materials,* Vol. 24 (January 1985), pp.38, 40.

[195] Speech by Comandante Fermán Cienfuegos at foreign debt conference in Havana; FBIS, Daily Report, Latin America, August 5, 1985, p. Q-11. In just one attack on San Salvador's Ilopango airfield on January 27, 1982—for which carefully selected guerrillas were sent first to Nicaragua and then to Cuba for special training (discussed on p.70)—insurgents destroyed 5 or 6 helicopters, 5 or 6 fighter aircraft, one training plane, and 3 C-47 cargo planes. Two additional C-47s were damaged. Barbara Crossette, "U.S. Starts Replacing Salvadoran Copters Destroyed in Rebel Attack," *New York Times,* February 6, 1982, p.4.

"In the first six months of 1985 alone, . . . we have inflicted an average of 400 casualties per month."

In addition to the damage to the Salvadoran economy and the military casualties of the conflict, the guerrillas of the FMLN have engaged in an active campaign of political assassination that has left hundreds if not thousands of Salvadoran civilians dead.[196] And it is worth noting that these tactics predated even U.S. military aid to El Salvador, much less to Nicaraguan opposition forces. Consider this account from the *Washington Post* in June 1980:

As for the numerous incidents in which villages are briefly taken over and suspected informers are shot or, in some cases, killed with machetes, the guerrilla spokesman said: "In taking the villages we establish people's courts before we try to execute anyone. But we don't do this without gathering every bit of evidence proving that they have participated in massacres and murders."

There are many members of the newly formed Revolutionary Democratic Front, a coalition of guerrilla, political, union and popular groups, who do not condone such actions. . . .

But the leftist front is so structured that these people have little voice in the way the war is conducted. When asked, they will say frankly that they do not speak for the guerrillas.[197]

On one day alone during the 1981 "final offensive," no fewer than seven "civilian patrolmen" were murdered in San Salvador by "leftist guerrillas."[198]

The murder of civilian noncombatants in El Salvador by Nicaraguan- and Cuban-trained insurgents has continued, and the victims are not even limited to individuals who have in any way personally harmed the guerrillas. It is sufficient to be related to someone who has incurred the wrath of the revolutionary forces. For example, at about 1:00 a.m. on July 20, 1985, guerrillas entered a village near Chinameca, San Miguel, and kidnapped four men. All four were taken to a nearby ditch and executed. One victim, Adan Ramos Campos—who suffered from multiple sclerosis—was the father of a maid working for an American Embassy family. The others, Antonio Granados, Adrian Solorziano, and Atilio Quintanilla, each had relatives working for the Salvadoran government.[199]

---

[196] Precise figures on political assassinations are unavailable because political violence from both the right and left in El Salvador is sufficiently pervasive to make it difficult in many instances to determine the source of such acts of terrorism.

[197] Christopher Dickey, "El Salvador's Shadowy War," *Washington Post*, June 30, 1980, p.1. See also, "El Salvador Tilts Further Toward Full Civil War," *New York Times*, April 6, 1980, p.E-2: "In the small town of Armenia, 30 miles northwest of [San Salvador], the mayor, a member of the ruling party, was murdered in April. Last week, his replacement also was assassinated."

[198] Karen DeYoung, "State's Latin Bureau Urges Resumption of Arms Aid to Salvador," *Washington Post*, January 10, 1981, p.1.

[199] Account based on unclassified State Department cable (R251616Z, July 1985) from American Embassy, San Salvador, Subject: "Four Civilians Murdered by Guerrillas Near Chinameca."

Consider also this account from the *Washington Post*:

Daniel was one of 20 villagers, including four small children, killed during a four-hour attack by leftist guerrillas Monday night on this hamlet, 35 miles southeast of the capital, San Salvador.

While some of the dead were local militiamen who apparently were the direct targets of the attack, residents say that at least 12 were unarmed civilians.

The attack, and the summary execution of some of the dead, marked a conspicuous return by the guerrillas to the tactic of executing government supporters in villages, and appeared to be part of a new rebel push to expand their military domain south of El Salvador's capital.

The incident brought sharp condemnation of the rebels today by human rights groups in El Salvador and the United States. . . .

Summary executions of local government officials and Civil Defense commanders were a regular rebel tactic in 1979 and 1980, the early years of El Salvador's civil war.[200]

In a broadcast on December 31, 1985, Radio Venceremos announced the FMLN was launching a "national campaign to exterminate . . . enemy groups who commit crimes against the people. . . ."[201]

While opposition to the Government of El Salvador would no doubt continue to exist in the absence of Nicaraguan intervention, the conflict would not nearly approach its current magnitude were it not for Nicaraguan support and other external assistance funneled largely through Nicaragua with the cooperation of the Sandinista regime. It is this external intervention that has given the conflict its international character, and has dissuaded the Salvadoran insurgents from accepting the invitations of El Salvador's elected government to participate in the political process.

---

[200] Julia Preston, "Salvadoran Rebels Kill 20 Villagers," *Washington Post*, April 11, 1985.
[201] "Salvador Rebels Vow to 'Exterminate' Foes," *Washington Times*, January 1, 1986, p.D-4.

4. Nicaraguan Aggression Against Honduras

. . . Nicaragua's subversive activities in Central America, and more specifically, in Honduras, began about six months after the Marxist Government assumed power in Nicaragua. I am talking about the year 1979. Therefore, Nicaragua's attack cannot be a reaction to Honduras' alleged help for the contras.

General Gustavo Alvarez Martinez,
Chief of the Honduran Armed Forces[1]

Nicaragua's unlawful intervention in the internal affairs of Honduras has not thus far approached the level of its aggression against El Salvador, but it has nevertheless been substantial. And while some of these activities may have been motivated by something other than a desire to destabilize or assist in the overthrow of the Honduran government,[2] it is equally clear that other activities initiated or supported by Nicaragua are directed at precisely those objectives—and are a consequence of an ideological commitment to assist unlawfully the efforts of revolutionary movements in other Central American states to overthrow legitimate governments by armed force.[3]

Support for Terrorism

On November 27, 1981, Honduran police raided a safehouse of the Morazanist Front for the Liberation of Honduras in Tegucigalpa, and following a gunfight apprehended a Honduran, a Uruguayan, and several Nicaraguan terrorists. The terrorists stated that the Government of Nicaragua had provided them with funds and explosives. Documents captured during the raid, and statements made by captured guerrillas, indicated that the group was formed in Nicaragua at the instigation of senior Sandinista leaders. Members of the group were trained both in Nicaragua and Cuba, and their chief of operations was located in Managua.[4]

On July 4, 1982, the main power station in Tegucigalpa was sabotaged, and a month later several U.S. businesses (including Air Florida and IBM) were

---

[1] Tegucigalpa Cadena Audio Video in Spanish, 1145 GMT, February 3, 1984.

[2] For example, in September 1979 Major Pablo Emilio Salazar—who as "Comandante Bravo" had been widely regarded as one of Somoza's most competent field commanders in the Nicaraguan National Guard—was assassinated in Honduras.

[3] Shortly after the 1979 Sandinista victory, leaflets reportedly appeared in Honduras featuring a photograph of Tomás Borge with Fidel Castro in Havana, promising to join forces "with the revolutionary organizations of Latin America," and hailing "development of the Central American revolution." Rowland Evans and Robert Novak, "Latin Dominoes," *Washington /Post*, August 1, 1979, p.21.

[4] For additional details, see State, *Central America*, op.cit., pp.11,12.

bombed. A Salvadoran guerrilla captured by Honduran authorities admitted to helping in the sabotage of the power station and the attack on the IBM office. He said he had obtained explosives from Nicaragua, and had transported them to Honduras concealed in a truck modified for arms smuggling in a Nicaraguan workshop.[5]

On September 11, 1982, Rodolfo Gutierrez Gonzales, a Nicaraguan Embassy official in Tegucigalpa, was escorted to the border and turned over to Nicaraguan authorities for actions "contrary to the national interest, sovereignty, and security of the country." Unofficial sources indicated that Gutierrez had been linked to terrorist groups in documents captured from insurgent groups by Honduran authorities.

Building a Communist Infrastructure

Between February and April 1981, Nicaragua and Cuba began the first phase of a program designed to build a strong communist infrastructure inside Honduras. Once established, the infrastructure was to engage in guerrilla warfare against the Honduran government—and eventually to overthrow that government.

Phase one involved the recruitment inside Honduras of potential guerrillas for training in Nicaragua and Cuba. According to the testimony of recruits who later defected to the Honduran government, they were enticed to leave Honduras with promises of technical education abroad in fields such as automobile mechanics and with assurances that their families would receive $50 a month during their absence. Most of the initial group of "recruits" apparently had no idea they would be taken to Cuba in the first part of 1981 for political indoctrination and military training at Pinar del Rio.[6]

● The Olancho Infiltration (July 1983)

The first group of 96 guerrillas—under the leadership of Central American Workers Revolutionary Party (PRTC) leader Dr. Antonio Reyes Mata, long regarded as Honduras' leading Marxist[7]—returned from Cuba to Nicaragua beginning in September 1982. They continued their military training in Nicaragua, and obtained combat experience in operations against the Contras. Once they had acquired sufficient combat training, they were provided with equipment, weapons, and ammunition by the Nicaraguan government. According to guerrillas who subsequently defected, each

---

[5] State/Defense, *Nicaragua's Military Buildup*, op.cit., p.28.

[6] A detailed unclassified account of this operation—based largely on debriefings of defectors and captured guerrillas—was released in November 1984 by the U.S. Army Southern Command (SOUTHCOM), *Cuban-Nicaraguan Support for Subversion in Honduras: El Paraiso, July 1984*. (Hereinafter cited as U.S. Army, *Subversion in Honduras*.)

[7] Loren Jenkins, "Honduran Army Defeats Cuban-trained Rebel Unit," *Washington Post*, November 22, 1983, p.A-1.

guerrilla was expected to carry an average of 60 pounds of equipment—including an extra M-16 rifle to give to his first new recruit in Honduras.[8] The PRTC group of 96 insurgents was divided into three elements of 30 members each (plus a command group), and infiltrated from Nicaragua into Honduras' Olancho department on July 16, 17, and 18, 1983. The guerrillas were inadequately motivated (many had been recruited with false promises of foreign education), and the operation was not well planned. Nicaragua had promised to airdrop additional supplies, but a joint U.S.-Honduran military exercise in the area apparently deterred the promised resupply effort.[9] On August 1, two guerrillas defected from their unit, and five days later turned themselves in to Honduran authorities. On the basis of information provided by these two, elements of the Honduran armed forces were able to promptly neutralize the remaining guerrillas. Reyes Mata was reportedly killed during the ensuing struggle.[10]

Lest there be any doubt about the extent of Nicaraguan government involvement in this operation, it is worth noting that defectors reported that after learning of the real purpose behind their recruitment some of their colleagues had attempted to desert in Nicaragua. These individuals were promptly imprisoned by Sandinista security forces.[11] According to the defectors, once the first group had established an adequate logistical base a larger force of 166 guerrillas was to follow from Nicaragua.[12]

Discussing the Olancho operation in early 1984, an American journalist observed: "If the Sandinistas had just wanted to free their own people from dictatorship, such events as these would not have been the outcome. One can see today unmistakably their expansionist ideology at work."[13]

● The Paraiso Infiltration (July 1984)

Another group of 19 recruits returned to Nicaragua early in 1983 after completing their training in Cuba. They, too, received a brief period of combat training as a part of regular Nicaraguan Army units that were fighting the Contras, and then they were reconstituted under Honduras' Revolutionary Popular Front Lorenzo Zelaya (FPP-LZ)—a clandestine communist organization responsible for several terrorist acts in Honduras beginning in 1980. After receiving arms, ammunition, equipment, and money from the Nicaraguan government, this so-called Camilo Torres

---

[8] U.S. Army, *Subversion in Honduras*, op.cit., p.22.

[9] Loren Jenkins, "Honduran Army Defeats Cuban-trained Rebel Unit," *Washington Post*, November 22, 1983, p.A-1.

[10] U.S. Army, *Subversion in Honduras*, op.cit., p.22.

[11] State/Defense, *Nicaragua's Military Buildup*, op.cit., p.27.

[12] Loren Jenkins, "Honduran Army Defeats Cuban-trained Rebel Unit," *Washington Post*, November 22, 1983, p.A-1.

[13] Georgie Anne Geyer, "Central America faces up to Sandinista expansionism," *Washington Times*, January 10, 1984, p.C-2.

group was supposed to be infiltrated into Honduras at the end of July 1983. However, the failure of the Reyes Mata group persuaded the Nicaraguans to delay the second infiltration for one year. In July 1984 the second group began infiltration in three-to-five-man teams from El Escambray, Nicaragua, into the Honduran department of Paraiso, with the mission of organizing a support network for insurgency and preparing the way for future military operations against the Government of Honduras. Statements by FPR-LZ guerrillas, and a master plan found by Honduran intelligence, indicate that the Nicaraguans and Cubans expected the FPR-LZ to establish regional commands during the second half of 1984 which would be responsible for the conduct of hostilities in their areas of responsibility and would recruit new guerrillas. This group, too, was quickly compromised by defections, and suffered a fate similar to that of the Reyes Mata contingent.[14]

Despite these earlier failures, it is clear that Nicaragua has not abandoned its efforts to undermine the Government of Honduras. Between April 11 and 14, 1985, seven Nicaraguans were arrested in Paraiso department trying to infiltrate arms to Cinchoneros guerrillas based in Olancho department. One of the arrested individuals admitted to being a member of the Nicaraguan Directorate for State Security (DGSE), and said he had coordinated similar arms infiltrations during the previous five-month period.

Border Incidents

Since the Sandinistas seized power in Nicaragua in July 1979 there have been numerous incidents in which Sandinista soldiers unlawfully entered Honduran territory along the common 570-mile border and murdered, kidnapped, or harassed Honduran citizens. On many other occasions, Sandinista soldiers located near the border have intentionally fired their weapons into Honduras—killing and wounding citizens and destroying their property.

During the first eight months of 1982, for example, the Honduran government compiled a list of nearly three dozen incidents of this type. These included:

March 4—Elements of the Sandinista Armed Forces penetrated the sector of GUAPINOL, kidnapping the Honduran citizens CORNELIO RUBIO and DANIEL GONZALEZ, taking also their boat.

March 18—Sandinista elements penetrated to the community of RAYA, 30 miles inside Honduran waters capturing 48 lobster fishermen and the boat DERVEEQEE, taking them kidnapped towards Nicaraguan waters; their whereabouts unknown.

May 16—A Sandinista Army patrol entered Honduran territory up to the community of CAGUASCA, kidnapping FRANCISCO LOPEZ VASQUEZ, who was later murdered.

[14] U.S. Army, *Subversion in Honduras*, op.cit., pp.5, 19, 24.

August 6—The Corporal in charge of the post at EL OYOTO informs that on this date at 7:14 P.M. 10 Sandinista elements arrived at his home, broke down the door with rifle butts, aiming their guns at his family and hitting him with their rifles. They returned to Nicaragua after they stole his regulation weapon, home utilities, clothing, food and 260.00 Lempiras cash.[15]

Nicaragua has contended that such border violations are a consequence of alleged operations by Contras located inside Honduras against Nicaragua. However, according to former Nicaraguan intelligence officer Miguel Bo-laños Hunter, such rhetoric is largely aimed at setting the international stage for an eventual Nicaraguan armed offensive against Honduras. He stated in June 1983:

They [the Sandinistas] have the army to fight if the contras come down as a group. The ultimate target is Honduras, not the contras. If the contras attacked[,] a portion [of] the army would help the militia but the rest would wage conventional war with Honduras.

If the Sandinistas fight Honduras there will be a big push in El Salvador to distract attention. They have carried out operations in Honduras one and a half years ago [i.e., since late 1981]. . . . So far, Nicaragua has been taking more of a diplomatic role accusing Honduras of soldiers coming into Nicaraguan territory to help the counter-revolutionaries. All of that is propaganda to prepare for the conventional attack to come so world opinion will be on the side of Nicaragua.[16]

Honduran Government Statements

The Government of Honduras has on numerous occasions protested against these and other acts of unlawful intervention by Nicaragua. For example, on August 23, 1982, Honduran Foreign Minister Edgardo Paz Barnica sent copies of the aforementioned 1982 compilation of incidents of Nicaraguan intervention to the United Nations Security Council and the Organization of American States, with a cover letter denouncing these acts.

In a July 14, 1983 speech, Honduran Ambassador Roberto Martinez Ordonez reported to the Organization of American States on the extent of Nicaraguan aggression:

It is important to bring to the attention of the distinguished representatives the fact that the totalitarian Nicaraguan regime is the main factor in the emergence of the regional crisis, because it has unleashed actions aimed at destabilizing governments in other Central American countries. These actions include, among others, direct support for terrorist and subversive groups. . . . The incidents. . .show the aggravation of the Central American situation as the direct and immediate result of the warmongering and threatening attitude of the Sandinist regime.

Nicaragua has continued its spiraling arms buildup. It has continued the trafficking of weapons from several places through its territory, particularly to El Salvador, violating our sovereignty.

---

[15] The full report appears in annex 62 to the United States Counter-Memorial, submitted to the International Court of Justice in the case of Nicaragua v. United States of America (Jurisdiction), August 17, 1984.

[16] *Miguel Bolaños Transcripts*, op.cit., p. 17.

The actions for the political destabilization of the area have not been interrupted; on the contrary, they have been increased. The acts of provocation and aggression against Honduras have not ceased; rather they have flared up. . . .

All this clearly shows that Central America is experiencing a widespread conflict provoked by Nicaragua, which has consequences for all countries in the region. . . .[I]t is of the highest priority for the rest of the Central American countries to discuss the regional problems created by Nicaragua because of its worrisome arms buildup, its direct participation in the destabilization of the other Central American governments, and its clandestine arms trafficking. . . .

In our analysis of the incidents occurring in Central America, with which most countries are familiar, we warn that our continent is facing a war without borders that is encouraged, promoted, supported, and, at times, even led by foreign Marxist forces that are trying to impose, through the armed struggle, their totalitarian political-social system on us.[17]

There is a special irony in the timing of this speech, since it occurred less than one week before the final two infiltrations of guerrillas from Nicaragua into Olancho department of Honduras—but more than two weeks before these operations came to the attention of Honduran authorities through the defections of guerrillas.

On April 4, 1984, Ambassador Flores Bermudez, the Honduran Representative to the United Nations Security Council, informed that organ:

Despite this democratic path which is now being strengthened in Honduras, my country is the object of aggression made manifest through a number of incidents by Nicaragua against our territorial integrity and civilian population. Those elements, which have obligated [Honduras] to strengthen its defences, are mainly the disproportionate amount of arms in Nicaragua, the constant harassment along our borders, the promotion of guerrilla groups which seek to undermine our democratic institutions, and the warmongering attitude of the Sandinist commanders. . . .

Among other Nicaraguan activities that pose a threat to peace are the continuation of the illegal traffic in arms by guerrilla groups in other countries; it is also continuing to provide logistic support to insurgents in neighboring States, while its agents visit Libya, Iran and North Korea, among other countries, for the purpose of acquiring more weapons.[18]

Just two weeks later, in a note addressed to the Secretary General of the United Nations, the Government of Honduras warned: "The Government of Nicaragua is engaged in the destabilization of neighboring governments by providing encouragement, financing, training, and logistical and communications assistance to groups of insurgents from other Central American countries with a view to establishing sympathetic governments within those countries."[19]

---

[17] Tegucigalpa Domestic Service in Spanish, 1957 GMT, July 14, 1983; in FBIS, Daily Report, Latin America, July 20 1983, p.A-1. Included as annex 59 to the United States Counter-Memorial, *Nicaragua v. United States.*

[18] Remarks of Mr. Flores Bermudez, Representative of Honduras, Before the United Nations Security Council, April 4, 1984, S/PV.2529, pp.37-38, 44; reprinted in part in annex 60 to the United States Counter-Memorial, *Nicaragua v. United States.*

[19] Reprinted in annex 104 to the United States Counter-Memorial, *Nicaragua v. United States.*

5. Nicaraguan Intervention in Costa Rica

Costa Rican President Luis Alberto Monge Alvarez charged that "In our country terrorism and subversion can only exist with outside help because among the Costa Ricans objective conditions do not exist for these two phenomena to occur." The President commented on this matter when he confirmed that he had asked former President José Figueres to speak to Fidel Castro and to the Sandinist leaders of the concern regarding the participation of Nicaraguan diplomats in acts of terrorism and subversion. . . .

The President asked Figueres to tell Fidel Castro and the Sandinist leaders that the participation of Nicaraguan Embassy and consulate leaders in terrorist actions had been proven.

He also sent them the message that he had information, which was very difficult to prove, that there was a plan to destabilize our country and thereby destroy our democratic system.

> "Monge dice que terrorismo se da con el apoyo externo"
> *La Nación* (San José, Costa Rica)
> August 1, 1982, p.A-4

Costa Rica is a particularly unlikely target for revolution. It has a long tradition of democratic government and the highest standard of living and social services in Central America.[1] Despite growing troubles in other parts of Central America, prior to 1981 terrorism was virtually unknown in Costa Rica.[2] However, at least as early as 1970 the FSLN considered that part of its "fundamental mission" was "to aid the revolutionary movements in all of Central America, including bourgeois democratic Costa Rica."[3]

Support for Terrorism

Since 1981 Costa Rica has been the victim of sporadic acts of terrorism, including bombings and kidnappings, and several of these acts have been traced directly to Nicaragua. For example, on March 17, 1981, leftist terrorists attacked a group of U.S. Marine guards assigned to the American Embassy in San José. While this was taking place, another group of terrorists exploded a bomb at the Honduran Embassy in San José. A little over a month later, on April 20, 1981, four leftist terrorists were arrested during a shootout near the President's House in Zapote. Another shootout occurred in the San José suburb of Calle Blancos on June 12, in which three policemen, a taxi driver, and one leftist terrorist were killed.

---

[1] Furthermore, the Sandinistas should have been particularly indebted to their southern neighbors, since Costa Rican government officials rather openly supported the Sandinista effort to overthrow the Somoza regime. See pp. 4,12, 37.

[2] State, *Cuban Support for Terrorism*, op.cit., p.3.

[3] Nolan, op.cit., pp.38-39.

In January 1982 an effort by Salvadoran and Guatemalan terrorists to kidnap Salvadoran businessman Roberto Palomo was thwarted by Costa Rican authorities. Three terrorists were killed, and two were arrested. The two arrested terrorists, Luis Jonathan Rodriguez and José Roberto Marroquin, were tried and convicted on September 2, 1983. During their trial, they testified that they had received logistical support and military and ideological training in Nicaragua. The same court also sentenced 13 other members of the terrorist group "La Familia," which was found responsible for both the Palomo kidnapping attempt and the attack on the U.S. Marines.

On March 15, 1982, Costa Rican security forces raided a San José safehouse and captured nine terrorists—including two Nicaraguans—and a large supply of weapons, equipment, documents (including fake passports and immigration stamps from more than thirty countries), and vehicles. Of the approximately 175 weapons recovered, 70 were U.S.-made M-16s, and 50 of these were subsequently traced by their serial numbers to weapons abandoned to the communists in Vietnam.[4] Several of the vehicles were found to have been modified with hidden compartments—apparently for use in arms smuggling.

On July 3, 1982, the San José office of the Honduran National Airline (SAHSA) was bombed by terrorists. Eleven days later Costa Rican authorities arrested German Pinzon Zora, a member of the Colombian terrorist group M-19, for the attack. He confessed to setting the bomb, and identified three Sandinista diplomats assigned to the Nicaraguan Embassy in San José as having directed the attack and assisted in its planning and execution. He indicated further that the July 3 attack was part of a broader Nicaraguan plan that included sabotage, kidnapping, bank robberies, and other terrorist acts designed to discredit Costa Rica internationally.[5]

On July 27 the Government of Costa Rica declared Nicaraguan diplomat German Altamirano Palacios and two other officials of the Nicaraguan Embassy *persona non grata* because of their participation in the attack on the Honduran airline office. In explaining this decision to other governments represented in San José, the Costa Rican Foreign Ministry wrote:

The Office of National Security was able to arrest German Pinzon Zora, a Colombian national, who confessed. . . that he was responsible for that serious act of terrorism together with German Altamirano Palacios. According to that statement, the bomb planted in the SAHSA offices in San José was part of a plan to destabilize Costa Rica and discredit it internationally. The plan included operations to sabotage important facilities in Costa Rica, other terrorist acts, kidnappings, attacks on banks and acts against public institutions, agencies, and companies of other Central American countries. According to the

---

[4] These may have been part of the shipment of M-16s from Vietnam to Nicaragua for eventual use in El Salvador, mentioned on pp. 54-58.
[5] State, *Central America*, op.cit., p.13.

informant, the plan was devised and directed from Managua, Nicaragua, by Rafael Lacayo of the Nicaraguan Ministry of Interior. . . .

Yesterday morning [27 July 1982] Oscar Ramon Tellez, the Nicaraguan Chargé d'Affaires, called the Costa Rican Foreign Ministry to request that Altamirano Palacios be released. . . . [H]e pointed out that Altamirano Palacios was accredited as an attache at the Embassy of Nicaragua in Costa Rica. Altamirano Palacios was released during the afternoon. . . .

In view of the seriousness of the acts of which Altamirano Palacios together with Alvara Ruiz Tapia, First Secretary of the Nicaraguan Embassy in Costa Rica, and Cairo Arevalo Baltodano, Assistant in the Nicaraguan Consular Office, are accused, the Government of Costa Rica decided to declare them persona non grata and request that they leave Costa Rica as soon as possible. . . .

The serious acts for which the three aforementioned diplomats were expelled from the country are yet another manifestation of the attitude of the Nicaraguan Government, which is contrary not only to the principles and rules of present international law, but also to those that govern two neighboring countries with long-standing cultural ties.[6]

On August 2, 1982, Costa Rican President Luis Alberto Monge Alvarez—who had been elected in May—sharply criticized Nicaragua for failing to punish the three diplomats involved in terrorist activities and for provocations on the country's northern border.[7]

It is worth noting that the SAHSA bombing—and all of the other terrorist acts mentioned above—occurred long before Nicaragua first charged that Contras were operating on Costa Rican soil.[8] Nicaraguan involvement in terrorist acts in Costa Rica continued after the reported establishment by former Sandinista war hero Edén Pastora and disillusioned Nicaraguan junta member Alfonso Robelo of the ARDE Contra group near the Nicaraguan-Costa Rican border. For example, on June 29, 1983, one Nicaraguan was killed and another seriously wounded when a bomb they were carrying exploded in their automobile. Both men had recently come into Costa Rica from Nicaragua.

On July 11, 1983, the San José newspaper *La Republica* reported: "Confidential government sources have revealed that Cuba and Nicaragua are training Costa Ricans to stage subversive actions in the country's Atlantic Zone. . . . Nicaraguan advisers would be in charge of directing the initial phase of the operation."[9] At about the same time, former Sandinista intelligence officer Miguel Bolaños Hunter told reporters from the *Washington Post*:

---

[6] Costa Rican Ministry of Foreign Relations and Worship, *Las Relaciones Entre Costa Rica Y Nicaragua*, July 28, 1982, translated in annex 57 of the United States Counter-Memorial, *Nicaragua v. United States*.

[7] ACAN (Panama City), in Spanish, 0054 GMT, August 2, 1982.

[8] The first Nicaraguan complaint to Costa Rica alleging the presence of Contras on Costa Rican soil occurred on December 2, 1982.

[9] *La República* (San José), in Spanish, July 11, 1983, p.3.

Since 1979 there has been a plan to neutralize democracy in Costa Rica. They are doing it covertly in Costa Rica. They are training guerrilla groups and infiltrating unions to cause agitation. The idea is to cause clashes with the police and Costa Rican soldiers and to cause a break between the unions and the president. When the economy gets worse they will be able to have an organized popular force aided by guerrilla forces already there.[10]

According to Alvaro José Baldizon Aviles—a full member of the Sandinista party and the former Chief Investigator of the Special Investigations Commission of the Nicaraguan Ministry of the Interior—in March 1983 a group of approximately 45 members of the Costa Rican Popular Vanguard Party (PVP) was being trained in guerrilla warfare in Nicaragua. Baldizon testified that the training took place on the property of the African Oil Palm Cultivation Project near El Castillo in southern Nicaragua. He was informed that when the group he observed had completed its six-month course of instruction, it would return to Costa Rica and be replaced by a new group for training.[11]

On September 8, 1983, Costa Rican authorities apprehended Gregorio Jimenez, a member of the Basque terrorist group ETA, while he was drawing plans of the residence of former Sandinista leader Edén Pastora. Jimenez and other ETA members were using a safehouse belonging to "Costa Ricans closely connected with the Managua regime," according to the Costa Rican Ministry of Public Security. On September 16, *El Pais* (Madrid) reported that the Spanish Ministry of Interior had complained in the past about Sandinista training of ETA terrorists, and the following day the same daily reported that Costa Rican police had learned that the terrorist plot against Pastora also included plans to attack electrical installations and airports in Costa Rica, using airplanes presumably to be provided by Nicaragua.

Costa Rican Government Statements

On October 18, 1982—in the aftermath of incidents like the SAHSA bombing in San José—the Government of Costa Rica announced that in an effort to reduce the chances of further subversive activity it would double its guards on the border with Nicaragua. Costa Rican officials have frequently called international attention to Nicaraguan intervention in its internal affairs,[12] and have also protested directly to the Government of Nicaragua.[13]

---

[10] *Miguel Bolaños Transcripts*, op.cit., p.32.

[11] U.S. Department of State, Office of Public Diplomacy for Latin America and the Caribbean, *Inside the Sandinista Regime: A Special Investigator's Perspective*, p.25 (1985). Mr. Baldizon defected on July 1, 1985.

[12] "Relations between the two countries appear to be cooling, as Costa Rica seeks international support for its claims of Nicaraguan aggression. This morning the Costa Rican Foreign Minister, Dr. Carlos Jose Gutierrez, called a meeting of ambassadors to the Organization of American States here [in San José] to present what he said was concrete evidence of Nicaraguan moves into Costa Rica over the last year." "Costa Rican Civil Guard Trades Fire With Sandinista Soldiers," *New York Times*, May 4, 1984.

[13] See, for example, the note of protest from Costa Rican Foreign Minister Fernando Volio Jimenez to the Acting Foreign Minister of Nicaragua (Nora Astorga) dated September 30,

As already observed,[14] in July 1982 Costa Rican President Luis Alberto Monge Alvarez denounced the participation of Nicaraguan diplomats in acts of terrorism and subversion in Costa Rica. In a conversation with an American journalist eighteen months later, President Monge was quoted as saying with respect to Nicaraguan intervention: "I never thought I would say, as I do now, that we have it worse in four years [of Sandinismo] than in 40 years of Somoza. . . . [W]hen we had differences with Somoza, still he never had a political party inside Costa Rica that was in solidarity with him."[15] He concluded: "[W]e see ourselves as a country under attack . . . ."[16]

On Sunday, February 2, 1986, Costa Ricans turned out in record numbers to elect Oscar Arias Sanchez their new president. Like President Monge, Arias is a member of the National Liberation Party (PLN) and is an advocate of Costa Rican neutrality. However, he told the press that he supported U.S. assistance to the rebels fighting in Nicaragua "only if it is used as an instrument of pressure to make the Sandinistas sit down and negotiate."[17] Nicaraguan intervention in Costa Rica has continued, and, after nearly 100 incidents leading to diplomatic protests, the Government of Costa Rica on February 19, 1985, ordered Nicaragua to reduce its embassy staff from 47 to 10.

1983 (reprinted as annex 63 to the U.S. Counter-Memorial *Nicaragua v. United States*), which said in part: "The Government of Costa Rica condemns and repudiates with profound indignation the attack on Costa Rican territory, on members of the Armed Forces of Costa Rica and on the country's installations at the Penas Blancas border post carried out by the Sandinista Popular Army with the evident purpose of attacking us."

[14] See the quotation at the beginning of this chapter.

[15] Georgie Anne Geyer, "Central America faces up to Sandinista expansionism," *Washington Times*, January 10, 1984, p.C-2.

[16] Georgie Anne Geyer, "Costa Rica's Leader Must Contend with Chaos After Nicaraguan Revolt," *Columbia Missourian*, January 5, 1984.

[17] "Peace Theme Wins Election in Costa Rica," *Washington Times*, February 4, 1986, p.A-5.

6. United States Aid to the Contras: A Necessary and Proportional Response to Aggression

Consistent with positions taken by the United Nations and the Organization of American States, in 1979 the United States facilitated the transfer of power in Nicaragua from the Somoza dictatorship to the Sandinista regime. Despite some misgivings about the Marxist-Leninist nature of its leadership, the United States went to extraordinary efforts to establish a friendly and cooperative relationship with the new regime in Managua. Among other things, the United States gave the Sandinista government, during its first eighteen months in office, more economic assistance than did any other country, and more aid than it gave to the rest of Central America combined.[1]

Although Congress required by law that aid be terminated unless the President could certify that Nicaragua was not supporting terrorism in neighboring states, even after there was significant evidence of Nicaraguan subversive activities against El Salvador the U.S. response was to send a senior State Department official to Managua—to inform the Nicaraguan leaders of the evidence against them, and to plead that these activities cease lest the United States be forced by law to terminate assistance.

After a brief pause in the shipment of arms and military equipment from Nicaragua to El Salvador, a massive logistical effort was undertaken in late 1980 in support of the unsuccessful "final offensive" of January 1981. Under the circumstances, despite its desire to cultivate good relations with the Managua regime, the United States had no choice but to comply with the law and suspend further deliveries of assistance. Given Nicaragua's contention that the difficulties in U.S.-Nicaraguan relations somehow are a product of the election of President Reagan, it should be emphasized that both the decision to suspend foreign assistance to Nicaragua and the decision to resume military aid to El Salvador were made during the final days of the Carter Administration.

It is important to keep in mind that U.S. support for the use of military force against the Sandinista regime did not begin until well over a year after Nicaragua launched a major campaign to overthrow the governments of neighboring states. The facts on this point are clear and are beyond serious question, despite Nicaragua's sworn affidavit to the International Court of

---

[1] See p.8, fn.37.

Justice denying having provided arms or other supplies to Salvadoran guerrillas.

Indeed, according to the *New York Times*, prior to oral argument Nicaragua's American lawyers believed that the Managua government would admit having provided assistance to the insurgents in El Salvador in 1980 and 1981.[2] Perhaps recognizing that such an admission would both establish the perjury of their Foreign Minister[3] and strengthen the U.S. contention that it was entitled to use necessary and proportional armed force in defense of victims of Nicaraguan aggression, when the case was argued no such admission was forthcoming from Nicaragua or its American lawyers. The blanket D'Escoto denial was never withdrawn, and in his prepared statement Professor Abram Chayes tried to hedge the issue by asserting that Nicaragua "was not supplying arms to El Salvador either now or in the *relevant* past. . . ."[4] Nicaragua's agent before the Court, Ambassador Carlos Arguello Gómez, could do little better. When asked by one of the judges about the clear evidence of Nicaraguan arms smuggling in 1980 and 1981, Ambassador Arguello replied: "The position of Nicaragua and of any objective reasoning in this case is that it is *of no relevance* to discuss happenings five years ago. . . ."[5]

To understand the shift in Nicaragua's position from denying in April 1984 that it had ever given any assistance to Salvadoran guerrillas, to asserting on September 19, 1985 that such assistance was somehow "irrelevant," it is helpful to review the testimony of Nicaragua's "star witness" on September 16, 1985—just three days before the implicit admission. David MacMichael worked for two years in Washington, D.C., as a mid-level contract employee of the Central Intelligence Agency, during which time he reportedly had access to certain classified information regarding Central America. An opponent of United States policy in the region, when his contract was not renewed he became an outspoken public critic of U.S. policy toward Nicaragua. He was presented to the International Court of Justice as an

---

[2] See, e.g., *New York Times*, September 8, 1985. This account quoted Professor Abram Chayes and Attorney Paul Reichler as having said "that they would acknowledge that the Managua Government supplied weapons to the Salvador guerrillas for the big January 1981 offensive against the United States-backed government in El Salvador." On September 14, 1985, the *New York Times* reported that "American lawyers for the Nicaraguan government . . . have acknowledged that weapons were shipped to El Salvador before the January 1981 guerrilla offensive there. . . ."

[3] In a sworn affidavit dated April 21, 1984, Foreign Minister Miguel D'Escoto Brockmann had already told the Court: "In truth, my government is not engaged, and has not been engaged, in the provision of arms or other supplies to either of the factions engaged in the civil war in El Salvador."

[4] International Court of Justice, *Nicaragua v. United States*, Uncorrected Verbatim Record, September 19, 1985, CR 85/26, p.30. (Emphasis added.)

[5] Ibid., CR 85/25, p.15.

expert witness for Nicaragua, during which time the following exchange occurred in response to questions from one of the judges:

Q.: In an interview with the *Washington Post* published on 30 January 1981, the outgoing Secretary of State, Edmund Muskie, stated that arms and supplies being used in El Salvador's bloody civil war were flown from Nicaragua "certainly with the knowledge, and to some extent the help of Nicaraguan authorities." . . . Do you think that Mr. Muskie was speaking the truth?

A.: Oh yes, in that case. . . .

Q.: I understand you to be saying, Mr. MacMichael, that you believe that it could be taken as a fact that at least in late 1980/early 1981 the Nicaraguan Government was involved in the supply of arms to the Salvadoran insurgency. Is that the conclusion I can draw from your remarks?

A.: I hate to have it appear that you are drawing this from me like a nail out of a block of wood but, yes, that is my opinion.[6]

The United States has argued that its support for the Contras is a defensive response to Nicaraguan aggression against its neighbors—particularly El Salvador.[7] Obviously, a critical factual question is which side first resorted to the use of armed force. Like a schoolyard bully, Nicaragua—in arguing that its support for guerrillas seeking to overthrow the Government of El Salvador in 1980 and 1981 is "irrelevant"—seems to be crying: "He hit me back first!"

During the oral argument before the World Court in September 1985, Nicaraguan representatives made two other admissions that are of relevance in considering the legality of U.S. support for the Contras. On September 12, Nicaragua's Vice Minister of Interior Luis Carrión—who told the Court he was "in charge of all State security matters"[8]—had this exchange with one of his own lawyers:

Q.: In what condition were the anti-government forces prior to December 1981?

A.: They were just a few small bands very poorly armed, scattered along the northern border of Nicaragua and they were composed mainly of ex-members of the Somoza's National Guard. They did not have any military effectiveness and what they mainly did was rustling cattle and killing some civilians near the border lines.[9]

---

[6] Ibid., September 16, 1985, CR 85/21, pp.40-41.

[7] See, e.g., Presidential Message to Congress on Assistance to Democratic Resistance Forces in Nicaragua, February 25, 1986, p.4: "My request affirms that our actions are consistent with our right to defend ourselves and assist our allies. . . ." For an earlier assertion that the U.S. action is premised upon the right of self-defense, see the speech by UN Ambassador Jeane Kirkpatrick to the American Society of International Law, excerpted in the *Washington Post* on April 15, 1984, in which she asserted: "There can be no question by reasonable persons that Nicaragua is engaged in a continuing, determined, armed attack against its neighbors, and that under the Charter of the United Nations, if not according to the laws of the class struggle, those neighbors have the right of individual or collective self-defense."

[8] International Court of Justice, *Nicaragua v. United States*, Uncorrected Verbatim Record, September 12, 1985, CR 85/19, p.21.

[9] Ibid., p.23.

On September 18, Mr. Paul Reichler—whose law firm represented Nicaragua in the case—told the Court that the armed opposition to Nicaragua prior to 1982 was "militarily and politically insignificant."[10] This admission is important not only because it establishes that—more than a year after the Sandinista regime began its campaign to overthrow the governments of neighboring states—Nicaragua faced no armed opposition that would justify its use of force against its neighbors; but also because it reinforces the view presented earlier that Nicaragua's massive arms buildup was not in response to any military threat.[11]

On a related matter, Nicaraguan officials and spokesmen admitted to the Court that the U.S. decision to provide support for the Contras was not made until December 1981—and that it was nearly a year later before the first major military operation by the Contras was launched.[12] Thus, the record before the World Court established beyond reasonable doubt that Nicaragua was engaged in unlawful aggression against its neighbors long before the United States provided any support to any group seeking to use force against Nicaragua. From a legal perspective, this is significant.

Legal Rights and Duties

A detailed legal analysis of United States support for the Nicaraguan opposition is beyond the scope of this study, and would at best duplicate an excellent analysis recently published in the *American Journal of International Law*.[13] However, it may be useful to look briefly at the core legal principles which govern this case: the complementary doctrines that (a) force may not be used as a means of effecting international change; but that (b) states which are victims of armed aggression may use necessary and proportional force in self-defense, and may also ask other states to use such force on their behalf to prevent the aggression from prevailing.

The general prohibition against using armed force is set forth in article 2(4) of the United Nations Charter, which provides:

All Members shall refrain in their international relations from the threat or use of force against the territorial integrity or political independence of any state, or in any other manner *inconsistent with the Purposes of the United Nations.*[14]

---

[10] Ibid., September 18, 1985, CR 85/24, p.16.
[11] See p.16.
[12] See, e.g., International Court of Justice, *Nicaragua v. United States*, Uncorrected Verbatim Record, September 12, 1985, CR 85/19, p.26.
[13] John Norton Moore, "The Secret War in Central America and the Future of World Order," *American Journal of International Law*, Vol. 80 (1986), p.43. An expanded and updated version of this article has recently been published. See John Norton Moore, *The Secret War in Central America* (Frederick, Md.: University Publications of America, 1987).
[14] Emphasis added.

The very first "purpose" set forth in article 1(1) of the UN Charter is "[t]o maintain international peace and security, and to that end: to take effective collective measures for the prevention and removal of threats to the peace, and for the suppression of acts of aggression or other breaches of peace. . . ." In furtherance of this fundamental principle, an exception to the prohibition against using force is contained in article 51 of the UN Charter:

Nothing in the present Charter shall impair the inherent right of individual or collective self-defense if an armed attack occurs against a Member of the United Nations, until the Security Council has taken measures necessary to maintain international peace and security.

These complementary rules are also embodied in the Revised Charter of the Organization of American States. Thus, article 18 provides:

No State or group of States has the right to intervene, directly or indirectly, for any reason whatever, in the internal or external affairs of any other State. The foregoing principle prohibits not only armed force but also any other form of interference or attempted threat against the personality of the State or against its political, economic and cultural elements.

However, this is qualified by article 22, which expressly provides:

Measures adopted for the maintenance of peace and security in accordance with existing treaties do not constitute a violation of the principles set forth in Articles 18 and 20.

Numerous other provisions of the OAS Charter also make clear that member states may use force "in the case of self-defense in accordance with existing treaties"; that "[e]very act of aggression by a State against the territorial integrity or the inviolability of the territory or against the sovereignty or political independence of an American State shall be considered an act of aggression against the other American States"; and that "None of the provisions of this Charter shall be construed as impairing the rights and obligations of the Member States under the Charter of the United Nations."[15]

One might argue that Nicaragua's intervention in El Salvador—although clearly a flagrant violation of international law as codified in article 2(4) of the UN Charter and article 18 of the OAS Charter—does not permit the United States to give aid to anti-government forces in Nicaragua, because Nicaragua's action does not meet the standard of an "armed attack" set forth in article 51 of the UN Charter. In this connection it is worth noting that the French version of article 51—which is equally authentic with the English—does not say "armed attack" but "armed aggression" (aggression armée).

The United States government has consistently recognized that armed force may be used in collective self-defense in response to "indirect" armed aggression. In May 1947, when the UN Commission of Investigation Concerning Greek Frontier Incidents reported to the United Nations that Yugoslavia, Albania, and Bulgaria were supporting guerrillas fighting in Greece, the United States representative noted that a failure of the Security

---

[15] Articles 21, 27, and 137.

Council to act would not preclude individual or collective action by states willing to act, so long as the action taken was consistent with the general purposes and principles of the United Nations.[16]

In 1949 the issue arose again, during Senate consideration of the North Atlantic Treaty. Appearing before the Senate Foreign Relations Committee, Secretary of State Dean Acheson was asked by Senator Fulbright: "Would an internal revolution, perhaps aided and abetted by an outside state, in which armed force was being used in an attempt to drive the recognized government from power be deemed an "armed attack" within the meaning of article 5 [of the NATO Treaty]? Secretary Acheson responded: "I think it would be an armed attack."[17]

In a lengthy statement to the Senate on this treaty, Committee Chairman Senator Arthur Vandenburg—who four years earlier had chaired the committee at the San Francisco Conference which drafted article 51 of the UN Charter—explained:

Are we bound to support a member state against internal attack which seeks to overthrow the government? We are not bound, directly or indirectly, to take sides in civil wars. We are pledged only against armed aggression by one state against another. If civil war should include external armed aggression, identified by us as such, we would be obligated to take such steps against the external armed aggressor as we would deem necessary to restore and maintain the security of the North American area.[18]

The Organization of American States has also taken the position that armed force could be used in collective self-defense in response to precisely the sort of intervention that Nicaragua has committed against its neighbors. For example, in November 1963 Venezuela complained to the OAS that Cuba was smuggling guns to guerrillas in Venezuela. The OAS appointed a committee to investigate, which concluded that the shipment of arms by Cuba to Venezuelan guerrillas "constituted a policy of aggression on the part of the present Government of Cuba against the territorial integrity, the political sovereignty, and the stability of the democratic institutions of Venezuela."[19]

This led to the convening of the Ninth Meeting of Consultation of Ministers of Foreign Affairs of the OAS, on July 21, 1964. After extensive debate and

---

[16] See Robert F. Turner, "Peace and the World Court: A Comment on the Paramilitary Activities Case," *Vanderbilt Journal of Transnational Law*, Vol. 20, No. 1 (1987), p. 62.

[17] Quoted in Marjorie M. Whiteman, *Digest of International Law* (Washington, D.C.: U.S. Government Printing Office, 1971), Vol. 12, p.232.

[18] *Congressional Record*, Vol. 95, p.8897 (1949). The Foreign Relations Committee report to the Senate on the Treaty said that "if a revolution were aided and abetted by an outside power such assistance might possibly be considered an armed attack. Each party would have to decide, in the light of the circumstances surrounding the case and the nature and extent of the assistance, whether, in fact, an armed attack had occurred and article 5 thus brought into play." U.S. Congress, Senate, *North Atlantic Treaty*, Report of the Committee on Foreign Relations, on Ex. L., 81st Congress, 1st Session, Senate Executive Report 8, p.13; quoted in Whiteman, Vol. 12, op. cit., p. 856.

[19] Ibid., p.815.

review of the facts, the OAS Foreign Ministers passed Resolution I, which resolved in part:

2. To condemn emphatically the present Government of Cuba for its acts of aggression and of intervention against the territorial integrity, the sovereignty, and the political independence of Venezuela. . . .

5. To warn the Government of Cuba that if it should persist in carrying out acts that possess characteristics of aggression and intervention against one or more of the member states of the Organization, the member states shall preserve their essential rights as sovereign states by the use of self-defense in either individual or collective form, *which could go so far as resort to armed force*, until such time as the Organ of Consultation takes measures to guarantee the peace and security of the hemisphere.[20]

Professors Ann V. Thomas and A.J. Thomas, Jr., experts on the OAS system, have observed that "the OAS has labelled assistance by a state to a revolutionary group in another state for purposes of subversion as being aggression or intervention. If this subversive intervention culminates in an armed attack by the rebel group, it can be said that an armed attack . . . has occurred."[21] Similarly, Professor Hans Kelsen has interpreted article 51 of the UN Charter to permit defensive measures in the event of "a revolutionary movement which takes place in one state but which is initiated or supported by another state."[22]

Indeed, even the Soviet Draft Definition of Aggression states: ". . . that State shall be declared the attacker which first commits . . . [s]upport of armed bands . . . which invade the territory of another State, or refusal, on being requested by the invaded State, to take in its own territory any action within its power to deny such bands any aid or protection."[23] Further, it is not insignificant that El Salvador has formally informed the International Court of Justice that "we are the victims of aggression and armed attack from Nicaragua and have been since at least 1980."[24]

It might also be argued that the United States may not use force in defense of an attacked State without that State's request. But in this case, it is clear that El Salvador has sought the assistance of the United States in responding to Nicaraguan aggression. In its Declaration of Intervention to the International Court of Justice in the case of *Nicaragua v. United States*, El Salvador stated:

[O]ur nation cannot, and must not, remain indifferent in the face of this manifest aggression and violent destabilization of . . . Salvadoran society which oblige the State and the

---

[20] Quoted in Francisco V. García-Amador, "The Rio de Janeiro Treaty," *University of Miami Inter-American Law Review*, Vol. 17 (1985), pp.18-19. (Emphasis added.)

[21] Quoted in Moore, *AJIL*, op.cit., p.84.

[22] Ibid.

[23] Ibid., p.86.

[24] Declaration of Intervention of the Republic of El Salvador, *Nicaragua v. United States*, *International Legal Materials*, Vol. 24 (January 1985), p.39.

Government to legitimately defend themselves. For that reason we have sought and continue to seek assistance from the United States of America. . . to defend ourselves from this foreign aggression that supports subversive terrorism in El Salvador. . . .

In the opinion of El Salvador . . . it is not possible for the Court to adjudicate Nicaragua's claims against the United States without determining the legitimacy or the legality of any armed action in which Nicaragua claims the United States has engaged and, hence, without determining the rights of El Salvador and the United States to engage in collective actions of legitimate defense. . . .

Any case against the United States based on the aid provided by that nation at El Salvador's express request, in order to exercise the legitimate act of self-defence, cannot be carried out without involving some adjudication, acknowledgment, or attribution of the rights which any nation has under Article 51 of the United Nations Charter to act collectively in legitimate defence.[25]

In addition to its strong moral commitment to the right of all peoples to self-determination—which by itself would lead the American people to favor assistance to democratically-elected governments which are threatened by externally-supported insurgencies aimed at substituting the power of armed force for the democratic process—the United States in Central America has not only a right, but a legally-binding treaty obligation, to assist States which are victims of international aggression. Article 3 of the Inter-American Treaty of Reciprocal Assistance (Rio Pact) of 1947 provides in part:

1. The High Contracting Parties agree that an armed attack by any State against an American State shall be considered as an attack against all the American States and, consequently, each one of the said Contracting Parties undertakes to assist in meeting the attack in the exercise of the inherent right of individual or collective self-defense by Article 51 of the Charter of the United Nations.

2. On the request of the State or States directly attacked and until the decision of the Organ of Consultation of the Inter-American System, each one of the Contracting Parties may determine the immediate measures which it may individually take in fulfillment of the obligation contained in the preceding paragraph and in accordance with the principle of continental solidarity. . . .

3. Measures of self-defense provided for under this Article may be taken until the Security Council of the United Nations has taken the measures necessary to maintain international peace and security.

Therefore, for both moral and legal reasons—despite its strong desire to establish a positive and cooperative relationship with the Sandinista government in Nicaragua—the United States could not sit idly by in the face of flagrant international aggression by Nicaragua against its neighbors.[26]

---

[25] Ibid., pp.39, 41.

[26] Given the strength of the U.S. legal position, it might be asked why it refused to participate in the case brought by Nicaragua in the International Court of Justice. Candidly, I believe the United States made a bad decision—if for no other reason than it gave the appearance of being in the wrong. A detailed discussion of the jurisdictional arguments against the case is beyond the scope of this study; however, in my view the case falls clearly within one of the reservations announced by the United States in 1946 when jurisdiction under article 36(2)

116

Attempts at Peaceful Resolution Failed

It is important to note that the United States did not respond to evidence of Sandinista aggression against its neighbors by immediately supporting the use of military force against Nicaragua. The initial U.S. response to Nicaraguan efforts to destabilize the Government of El Salvador was diplomatic.[27] Former Sandinista junta member Arturo Cruz has written:

> In August of 1981, the Assistant Secretary of State for Inter-American Affairs, Thomas Enders, met with my superiors in Managua, at the highest level. His message was clear: in exchange for non-exportation of insurrection and a reduction in Nicaragua's armed forces, the United States pledged to support Nicaragua through mutual regional security arrangements as well as continuing economic aid. His government did not intend to interfere in our internal affairs. . . . My perception was that, despite its peremptory nature, the U.S. position vis-a-vis Nicaragua was defined by Mr. Enders with frankness, but also with respect for Nicaragua's right to choose its own destiny.[28]

A somewhat similar account is provided by former Sandinista Comandante Cero, Edén Pastora, who wrote in the *Journal of Contemporary Studies*:

> When Daniel Ortega told Fidel Castro of the FSLN talks with Thomas Enders, . . . he said that Enders had confided privately that as a U.S. representative, he had come to Managua not to defend the rights of the democratic opposition, but rather to insist that the FSLN meddling in El Salvador must stop. . . . Enders had told Daniel that the Nicaraguans could do whatever they wished—that they could impose communism, they could take over *La Prensa*, they could expropriate private property, they could suit themselves—but they must not continue meddling in El Salvador, dragging Nicaragua into an East-West confrontation, and if they continued along these lines, they would be smashed.[29]

---

of the ICJ Statute was accepted. The so-called "Vandenberg" or "Multilateral Treaty" reservation excluded from the Court's jurisdiction "Disputes arising under a multilateral treaty, unless (1) all Parties to the treaty affected by the decision are also Parties to the case before the Court, or (2) the United States of America specially agrees to jurisdiction." In discussing this reservation before the ICJ, Nicaraguan counsel Professor Abram Chayes said: "The problem envisaged is that in a case arising under a multilateral treaty, the United States, as defendant, might be bound by a judgment to a certain course of action when other parties to the same treaty who were not parties to the case would be able to pursue that very course of action to the detriment of the United States." (International Court of Justice, *Nicaragua v. United States*, Uncorrected Verbatim Record, September 19, 1985, CR 85/26, p. 28.) Since the case was brought in part under article 2(4) of the UN Charter, since both Cuba and the Soviet Union have been actively involved in Nicaragua's effort to overthrow the governments of neighboring states, and since neither Cuba nor the Soviet Union accepts any article 36(2) jurisdiction of the World Court, the ICJ is clearly incapable of resolving the underlying problem.

[27] Such as the September 1980 visit to Managua by Deputy Assistant Secretary of State James Cheek, discussed on pp. 8, 139.

[28] Arturo J. Cruz, "Nicaragua's Imperiled Revolution," *Foreign Affairs*, Summer 1983, pp.1041-1042. See also, Don Oberdorfer and Patrick E. Tyler, "U.S.-Backed Nicaraguan Rebel Army Swells to 7,000 Men," *Washington Post*, May 8, 1983, p.1. Oberdorfer and Tyler reported: "For the new administration, 1981 was a year of deepening concern about Central America and high-level conflict over what to do. The insurgency in El Salvador continued apace and, by the end of October, the State Department had failed in efforts to negotiate a cutoff of Nicaraguan support for the Salvadoran rebels."

[29] Edén Pastora, op.cit., pp.10-11.

It was not until two years after the first Nicaraguan support for Salvadoran guerrillas—and after reasonable peaceful efforts, using both positive and negative incentives to resolve the situation, had been exhausted—that the United States began giving assistance to anti-government insurgents in Nicaragua similar to that being given by the Sandinistas to Salvadoran insurgents.

Obviously, every opportunity must be explored for serious negotiations which might lead to a peaceful resolution of the dispute. Critics of current policy who urge greater emphasis on negotiations have their basic priorities right—resort to armed force, be it direct or indirect, must always be viewed as a last resort after alternative approaches have failed.

But critics who believe that negotiations alone are sufficient—that all that is necessary is to persuade the Sandinistas to sign a new agreement—are naive at best. After all, the Nicaraguan government is already a party to several fundamental international agreements which, if adhered to, would resolve the current conflict. As already noted,[30] the provision of arms to insurgent groups to promote the overthrow of a sovereign government is a flagrant violation of article 2(4) of the United Nations Charter and article 18 of the Charter of the Organization of American States. Anyone who argues that the Sandinistas can now be relied upon to adhere to a new agreement to cease their ongoing armed aggression against their neighbors—in the absence of significant pressure from the United States—have the burden of explaining why such an agreement would be given greater respect than the Sandinistas have shown toward their obligations under the most fundamental charters of international law. A recent editorial in the *New Republic* argued:

With a free hand, does anyone imagine that they will adhere to their agreements any more than, say, the Vietnamese adhered to theirs? We have experience with Sandinista parchment. In 1979 they pledged to the Organization of American States to establish an open, democratic, and pluralistic society.[31]

That is not to say that opportunities for negotiations should be ignored. Indeed, if sufficient pressure is maintained and the Sandinistas eventually perceive that the costs of international aggression will outweigh any perceived benefits, a verifiable negotiated solution may be possible. But as we remain willing to negotiate, we must never lose sight of the traditional Marxist-Leninist tactic of "diplomatic struggle." We must recognize that the Sandinistas are using the desire of the United States and its allies for a peaceful solution as a weapon to promote false hopes, to brand the United States government as the impediment to peace, to promote dissension between the U.S. government, its people, and its allies, and thus to

---

[30] See pp. 113–117.
[31] Editorial, "The Case for the Contras," *New Republic*, March 24, 1986, p.8.

undermine efforts to deter Sandinista armed aggression.[32] If the Sandinistas really wanted "peace" in the region, all they would need to do is to halt their efforts to undermine their neighbors by armed force. If Comandante Ortega and his comrades would simply abide by their *existing* international commitments—such as the United Nations and OAS Charters—no further "negotiations" would be necessary to restore peace to the region.

United States Support for the Contras

Confronted by the massive Nicaraguan intervention in the internal affairs of El Salvador, and unable to bring this aggression to a halt through diplomatic or economic pressure, the United States government found itself in a dilemma. To allow the aggression to continue unchallenged would both encourage further aggression and contribute to the destruction of the right of self-determination of the Salvadoran people. On the other hand, the United States had no desire to intervene in Central America with its own armed forces. According to the *Washington Post*, after diplomatic initiatives proved unsuccessful,

Some officials. . . favored a naval quarantine of Cuba and Nicaragua, but the Pentagon was leery. As the result of a National Security Council meeting on Nov. 16, 1981, Reagan approved a 10-point program including economic and military aid to friendly nations, U.S. contingency planning and military preparedness—but no U.S. military action.

One of the 10 points, according to NSC records, was to "work with foreign governments as appropriate" to conduct political and paramilitary operations "against [the] Cuban presence and Cuban-Sandinista support infrastructure in Nicaragua and elsewhere in Central America."

An accompanying document explained that this initially would involve a $19 million program to build a 500-man force, but that "more funds and manpower will be needed. ". . . A few days later, on Dec. 1, Reagan signed the required "finding" that this new undercover effort in Central America was in the national interest.[33]

According to the same press account, when the Congressional intelligence committees were briefed in December 1981, CIA Director William Casey "portrayed the program as resulting from inquiries from neighboring countries, such as Honduras and Costa Rica, about help against the spread of revolution." The mission of the operation was characterized to Congress as "the interdiction of arms traffic through Nicaragua to leftist rebels in El Salvador and the exertion of pressure to force the leftist Sandinista leadership of Nicaragua to 'look inward' rather than exporting revolution, according to participants in the congressional briefings."[34] The first reports of significant Contra activities inside Nicaragua emanated from Managua on March 14, 1982, when a state of emergency was declared following the

---

[32] See pp. 40–42, 144.

[33] Don Oberdorfer and Patrick E. Tyler, "U.S.-Backed Nicaraguan Rebel Army Swells to 7,000 Men," *Washington Post*, May 8, 1983, p.1.

[34] Ibid.

destruction of two bridges near the Honduran border by anti-government Nicaraguan guerrillas.[35]

The following month, a classified National Security Council study—which was obtained and published without authorization by the *New York Times*[36]—gave as a key element of strategy: "Increasing the pressure on Nicaragua and Cuba to increase for them the costs of interventionism." In May of the following year, *Time* magazine wrote that "The full-scale CIA association with the Nicaraguan *contras* began last October [1982]." It quoted a State Department official as arguing that

the growing strength of the *contras* provides an effective way for the U.S. to apply pressure on the Sandinista government to end its backing of rebels in El Salvador. Agrees a senior State Department official in Washington, "Now we have got an element of reciprocity that gives Nicaragua an incentive to sit down and talk. We've got some bargaining chips: you call off your dogs and we'll call off ours."[37]

According to the *Washington Post*, in July 1983 the President signed a new "finding" on the Nicaraguan program, directed more toward "stopping [Nicaragua's] efforts to export revolution" than simply interdicting the flow of arms.[38] Thus, from its inception, the purpose behind the U.S. program of support for anti-government guerrillas in Nicaragua has been to pressure Nicaragua to cease its unlawful aggression against its neighbors.

Who Are the Contras?

Much of the criticism of U.S. support for the Nicaraguan resistance has been directed against the nature of the Contras themselves. The Sandinistas have sought to portray them as gangs of "mercenaries" composed almost exclusively of former members of Somoza's National Guard,[39] and

---

[35] Ibid. Both bridges were thought to have been used to smuggle arms from Nicaragua into El Salvador via Honduras.

[36] "U.S. Policy in Central America and Cuba Through F.Y.'84, Summary Paper," published in "National Security Council Document on Policy in Central America and Cuba," *New York Times*, April 7, 1983, p.16.

[37] "Uneasy over a Secret War," *Time*, May 16, 1983, p.12.

[38] Fred Hiatt, "Administration 'Finding' Justifies Covert Operation in Nicaragua," *Washington Post*, July 27, 1983, p. 1. See also, Joanne Omang, "New Justification for U.S. Activity in Nicaragua Offered," ibid., September 21, 1983, p.29.

[39] See, e.g., Vargas Llosa, op.cit., p.41. The charge that the majority of the Contras are former guardsmen is not even theoretically possible unless one includes the thousands of low-ranking recruits and draftees inducted into the Guard during Somoza's final year—mostly young men who can hardly be held accountable for the excesses of their government. In 1978 the National Guard totaled about 7,000 men. Interior Minister Tomás Borge acknowledges that a third of Nicaragua's admitted 6,000 prisoners are former guardsmen (presumably not predominately individuals drafted or recruited in the final days of the old regime). Even if every remaining veteran guardsman joined the Contras, it is doubtful they would total more than a third of the estimated force of 14,000. In reality, as will be discussed later, the figure seems to be approximately two percent. It is worth noting that—despite Sandinista claims that the Contras are predominantly former guardsmen—Nicaraguan Vice Minister of Interior Luis Carrión told the ICJ that the CIA had set up "a full

120

this characterization has been accepted by many Americans. The reality, however, is more complex.

Most of the criticism has been directed against the largest Contra organization, the Nicaraguan Democratic Force (Fuerza Democratico Nicaraguense—FDN), since it would be extremely difficult to portray ARDE and its founders—former Sandinista junta member Alfonso Robelo, and the greatest hero of the Sandinista army that overthrew Somoza, Edén Pastora (Comandante Cero)—as Somoscistas. Further, there was enough involvement by former guardsmen in the early days of the FDN to give a kernel of credibility to the Sandinista charge.

The Contras are not "mercenaries."[40] According to the *Washington Post*, the United States government provided each Contra soldier with a "subsistence fee" of $23 per month.[41] The average monthly salary for a "worker" in Nicaragua in January 1985 "ranged between $110 and $150."[42] Thus, in addition to enduring the hardship and danger of guerrilla life, Contra soldiers were paid on the average about one-fifth as much money as they would have made had they chosen jobs as "workers." This hardly suggests that their motivation in taking up arms was money.

Nor do the facts support the charge that most of the Contras are former members of Somoza's National Guard. Although Enrique Bermudez Varela, the Chief of the FDN Strategic Military Command, did serve in the National Guard under Somoza, he was hardly a Somoza confidant. Indeed, during the three years preceding the 1979 Sandinista victory, Colonel Bermudez was assigned as a military attache in Washington. In 1979, when the Carter Administration suggested that Bermudez be placed in command of the National Guard after Somoza's departure, Somoza rejected the recommen-

---

training structure. . . to teach the contras how to use these weapons. Many of them never had anything to do with weapons. . . ." (International Court of Justice, *Nicaragua v. United States*, Uncorrected Verbatim Record, September 12, 1985, CR 85/19, pp.40-41.) It is difficult to reconcile the theory that the Contras are essentially the old Somoza National Guard with the suggestion that the CIA had to train them to use weapons because they "never had anything to do with weapons. . . ."

[40] Nicaraguan Foreign Minister Miguel D'Escoto said in 1981 (justifying participation by Nicaraguans in the "final offensive" in El Salvador) that "a difference must be made between a mercenary, who struggles in another country for a salary or for pay, and a guerrilla, who struggles out of solidarity with a people pursuing their liberation or ideas." AFP (Paris), 2130 GMT, January 14, 1981; reprinted in FBIS, Daily Report, Latin America, January 15, 1981, p.P-17.

[41] Don Oberdorfer and Patrick E. Tyler, "U.S.-Backed Nicaraguan Rebel Army Swells to 7,000 Men," *Washington Post*, May 8, 1983, p.1. One scholar who has researched the question reports that "the overwhelming majority of recruits to both ARDE and FDN receive no payment, and only a few leaders receive support for their families." Michael S. Radu, *The Origins and Evolution of the Nicaraguan Insurgencies, 1979-1985* (Philadelphia, Pa.: Foreign Policy Research Institute, 1986), p. 21.

[42] Vargas Llosa, op.cit., p.45. Nicaragua's per capita income in 1983 was estimated to be $846. Central Intelligence Agency, *The World Factbook—1984* (Washington, D.C.: U.S. Government Printing Office, 1984), p.179.

dation. Even Sandinista Army spokesman Robert Sanchez conceded in December 1982 that Bermudez had never been identified with "war crimes" committed under the Somoza regime.[43]

The President of the FDN National Directorate and Commander-in-Chief of FDN armed forces since 1983 is Adolfo Calero Portocarrero, who not only did not support the Somoza regime, but actually was a leader of the business opposition to the dictatorship. A 1978 *New York Times* article about five Nicaraguan opposition leaders who might eventually succeed Somoza stated:

ADOLFO CALERO PORTOCARRERO—Probably the most forceful of them all, Calero, 52 . . . has been a life-long opponent of the Somozas and speaks passionately about "the corrupt political system" he charges they created. . . .Calero demands an honest government in Nicaragua based on a real democracy and a capitalist economy. . . . He heads the moderate faction in the Broad Opposition Front.[44]

According to information gathered in early 1985 by members of the U.S. Congress and its intelligence committees, of the top 56 FDN leaders only 13 were at any time members of Somoza's National Guard. By contrast, more than twice that number are former Sandinistas.[45] At the lower levels of Contra leadership, the numbers are even more striking. Roughly 80 percent of the group leaders, and "nearly all" of the detachment leaders, have no prior Guard service.[46] When the lower ranks are included, of the reported 14,000 Contras in early 1985, about 40 officers and 200 soldiers had served in Somoza's National Guard—roughly two percent of the total FDN membership.[47] About 15 percent were former Sandinistas.

If any one category properly describes the large majority of the men and women who have taken up arms against the Sandinista regime in Nicaragua, it is that they are peasants. As Peruvian writer Mario Vargas Llosa wrote in the *New York Times* Magazine following a month-long visit to Nicaragua in early 1985: "[O]ne point is clear: The 'bourgeoisie' is not at the front. This is a war between poor men. Most of the *contras* . . . are peasants."[48]

---

[43] U.S. Department of State, *Documents on the Nicaraguan Resistance*, Special Report No. 142, 1986, p.6.

[44] Gordon D. Mott, *New York Times*, October 23, 1978, p.27.

[45] *Congressional Record*, p.H 2323 (daily edition, April 23, 1985, Representative Cheney).

[46] Arms Control and Foreign Policy Caucus, "Who Are the Contras?," *Congressional Record*, p.H 2335-2336 (daily edition, April 23, 1985, inserted by Representative Richardson). Each group consists of about 70 guerrillas; there are four detachments in a group, consisting of nearly 20 guerrillas each.

[47] *Washington Post*, February 28, 1985, quoted in *Congressional Record*, p.H 2324 (daily edition, April 23, 1985, Representative Livingston). A more recent U.S. government study—which may reflect more recent information—asserted that "Of the approximately 17,000 in the FDN, fewer than 200 were once in the guard." State/Defense, *Challenge to Democracy in Central America*, op. cit., p.41.

[48] Vargas Llosa, op.cit., p.41. A study on the Contras prepared by the Congressional Arms Control and Foreign Policy Caucus and inserted into the *Congressional Record*, p.H-2335

Not only are the Contras peasants, but they have substantial support from the Nicaraguan people. Following a 1984 visit to Nicaragua, Robert Leiken—a vocal supporter of the Sandinistas in the early days—wrote in the *New Republic*:

Sympathy with the *contras* is becoming more open and more pervasive. I was stunned to hear peasants refer to the *contras* as "Los Muchachos," the boys—the admiring term used to describe the Sandinistas when they were battling the National Guard. It was apparent that many Nicaraguans are listening to the "Fifteenth of September," the *contra* radio station.[49]

It is obviously difficult to assess how the Nicaraguan people would vote if permitted a free election in which all parties could present their policies under fair conditions. However, it is perhaps worth noting that—unlike the situation in El Salvador, where the insurgents have been invited to participate in elections but have refused (acknowledging to the press in the process that they realized they would lose[50])—it is the Government of Nicaragua that has prevented free and fair elections from taking place. The various armed opposition groups have on several occasions expressed a willingness to lay down their arms and participate in free elections under effective supervision, and have even agreed that Daniel Ortega could remain as president until after elections were held.[51]

Human Rights and the CIA "Murder Manual"

Perhaps a few words should be said at this point about the allegations that the Contras are as a matter of policy regularly engaging in the commission of war crimes—and even that "terror tactics" have been encouraged and taught by the United States. While it is almost certainly true that atrocities and other "war crimes" have been committed by Contra soldiers from time to time[52]—a statement which would also appear to apply to Sandinista soldiers[53]—

(daily edition, April 23, 1985) by Representative Richardson (in opposition to U.S. assistance to the Contras) concluded: "FDN and U.S. Government claims that the FDN is largely a 'peasant army' of Nicaraguans disaffected with their government are accurate." See also, *Washington Post*, February 28, 1985, quoted in *Congressional Record*, p.H 2324 (daily edition, April 23, 1985).

[49] Robert S. Leiken, "Nicaragua's Untold Stories," *New Republic*, October 8, 1984, p.20.

[50] See p. 51, fn.25.

[51] See, e.g., Vicki Rivera, "Statement of Principles by Nicaraguan Rebels Wins Shultz Endorsement," *Washington Times*, January 29, 1986, p.C-7; and the Document on National Dialogue of the Nicaraguan Resistance done in San José, Costa Rica, on March 2, 1985, excerpted in Moore, *AJIL*, op.cit., pp.74-75.

[52] Even were there no reliable accounts of such activities (and in this instance there are), the fact that the Contra force is composed largely of uneducated campesinos makes abuses of the laws of war more likely. This is further exacerbated by Nicaragua's "macho" culture, and by the intensity of the hatred felt by both sides in the conflict. None of these factors in any way *justifies* a single human rights abuse; but they help explain *why* they occur and should serve as a warning for the need of special precautions and training to prevent their occurrence in the future.

[53] Former Sandinista intelligence officer Miguel Bolaños Hunter has stated: "[I]n the north they are using all sorts of brutality against the contras. They are killed in masses. If they capture 15, they will take two for briefing in Managua and are put on TV, the rest will be killed. They are killed by stabbing to death and also the 'vest cut.' They cut off both arms and legs alive and let them bleed to death." *Miguel Bolaños Transcripts*, op.cit., p.40.

Nicaragua's political warfare offensive has grossly misrepresented U.S. policy on this issue.

For example, Professor Abram Chayes told the International Court of Justice that "the most shameful episode in this whole sorry affair"[54] was the preparation by the Central Intelligence Agency of a manual on *Psychological Operations in Guerrilla Warfare.* An early version of the document was given to American journalists during the 1984 U.S. presidential campaign. By focusing attention on a few out-of-context sentences, the entire manual was presented to the American people as an "assassination manual" or "murder manual."[55] Attorney Paul Reichler told the World Court that the Contras adopted the "widespread use of terror tactics. . .with the advice, encouragement and approval of the United States."[56] He continued:

Such madness was not without its method. It had a very clear purpose. Commander Carrión testified that

"all of these terrorist instructions have the main purpose of alienating the population from the Government through creating a climate of terror and fear so that nobody would dare to support the Government." (CR 85/19, p.34).

In order to instruct the *contra* forces in these tactics the CIA prepared a manual called "Psychological Operations in Guerrilla Warfare. ". . .The Court will undoubtedly recall the testimony that Commander Carrión gave on 12 September when he read aloud excerpts from this manual. . . . *I do not believe it is necessary to quote further from this appalling pamphlet.* It is in evidence and it speaks for itself.[57]

Without seeking to justify or defend every passage in the manual, a few additional facts are useful to put the matter in perspective. In the first place, the manual was not in any real sense "prepared" by the CIA—it was largely a translation of a training document prepared by the U.S. Army in 1968. Rather than teaching "terror tactics," the clear focus of the manual was on discouraging human rights abuses. It was part of a training program aimed at educating the *campesinos* who had joined the Contras about the need to maintain the support of the population. After referring to two or three well-publicized paragraphs, it is not surprising that Mr. Reichler told the Court that it was not "necessary" to quote further from the manual. Had he done so, here are some of the passages he might have encountered:

Armed propaganda includes every act carried out, and the good impression that this armed force causes will result in positive attitudes in the population toward that force; and it does not

[54] International Court of Justice, *Nicaragua v. United States*, Uncorrected Verbatim Record, September 19, 1985, CR 85/26, p.20.

[55] See, e.g., "The CIA's Murder Manual," editorial in the *Washington Post*, October 21, 1984. Two days later, a *Post* article alleged that the manual "instructed rebels in Nicaragua in the art of assassination and subversion."

[56] International Court of Justice, *Nicaragua v. United States*, Uncorrected Verbatim Record, September 18, 1985, CR 85/24, pp.32-33.

[57] Ibid., p.33. (Emphasis added.)

include forced indoctrination. Armed propaganda improves the behavior of the population toward them, and it is not achieved by force.

This means that a guerrilla armed unit in a rural town will not give the impression that arms are their strength over the peasants, but rather that they are the strength of the peasants against the Sandinista government of repression. This is achieved through a close identification with the people as follows: hanging up weapons and working together with them on their crops, in construction, in the harvesting of grains, in fishing, etc. . . . [A]s long as explicit coercion is avoided, positive attitudes can be achieved with respect to the presence of armed guerrillas within the population.[58]

Or consider this passage:

The combatant-propagandist guerrilla is the result of a continuous program of indoctrination and motivation. They will have the mission of showing the people how great and fair our movement is in the eyes of all Nicaraguans and the world. Identifying themselves with our people, they will increase the sympathy towards our movement, which will result in greater support of the population for the freedom commandos, taking away support for the regime in power.

Armed propaganda will extend this identification process of the people with the Christian guerrillas.[59]

Under the title "Political Awareness," the manual states:

The individual political awareness of the guerrilla, the reason for his struggle, will be as important as his ability in combat. This political awareness and motivation will be achieved:. . .

By the guerrilla recognizing himself as a vital tie between the democratic guerrillas and the people, whose support is essential for the subsistence of both.

By fostering the support of the population for the national insurgency through the support for the guerrillas of the locale. . . .

By developing trust in the guerrillas and in the population, for the reconstruction of a local and national government.

By developing in each guerrilla the ability of persuasion face-to-face, at the local level, to win the support of the population, which is essential for success in guerrilla warfare.[60]

This is followed by a section entitled "Group Dynamics," which calls for regular "group discussions" among guerrillas. It provides in part:

These group discussions will give special emphasis to:

Creating a favorable opinion of our movement. . . .

Showing each guerrilla the need for good behavior to win the support of the population. Discussion guides should convince the guerrillas that the attitude and opinion of the population play a decisive role, because victory is impossible without popular support.[61]

Another section is entitled "Interaction with the People," and it explains in part:

---

[58] The text of the manual has been published by Random House under the title *Psychological Operations in Guerrilla Warfare*, with essays by Joanne Omang and Aryeh Neier (New York: Vintage Books, 1985), and this passage appears on pages 35-36.

[59] Ibid., p.39.

[60] Ibid., pp.40-41.

[61] Ibid., pp.41-42.

In order to ensure popular support, essential for the good development of guerrilla warfare, the leaders should induce a positive interaction between the civilians and the guerrillas, through the principle of "live, eat, and work with the people," and maintain control of their activities. In group discussions, the leaders and political cadres should give emphasis to positively identifying themselves with the people. . . .

Whenever there is a chance, groups of members should be chosen who have high political awareness. . . to be sent to the populous areas in order to direct the armed propaganda, where they should persuade the people through dialogue in face-to-face confrontations, where these principles should be followed:

Respect for human rights and others' property.

Helping the people in community work.

Protecting the people from Communist aggressions.

Teaching the people environmental hygiene, to read, etc., in order to win their trust, which will lead to a better democratic ideological preparation.

This attitude will foster the sympathy of the peasants for our movement, and they will immediately become one of us, through logistical support, coverage and intelligence information on the enemy or participation in combat. The guerrillas should be persuasive through the word and not dictatorial with weapons. If they behave in this way, the people will feel respected, will be more inclined to accept our message and will consolidate into popular support.[62]

Sandinista efforts to depict this manual as a "terror" handbook were helped by its frequent use of the term "armed propaganda"—which admittedly sounds like a euphemism for coercive combat. In reality, however, the manual explains that "armed propaganda" means something much different:

Frequently a misunderstanding exists on "armed propaganda" that this tactic is a compulsion of the people with arms. In reality, it does not include compulsion. . . .

Close Identification with the People

Armed propaganda includes all acts carried out by an armed force, whose results improve the attitude of the people toward this force, and it does not include forced indoctrination. This is carried out by a close identification with the people on any occasion. For example:

- Putting aside weapons and working side by side with the peasants in the countryside: building, fishing, repairing roofs, transporting water, etc.

- When working with the people, the guerrillas can use slogans such as "many hands doing small things, but doing them together."

- Participating in the tasks of the people, they can establish a strong tie between them and the guerrillas, and at the same time a popular support for our movement is generated.

During the patrols and other operations around or in the midst of villages, each guerrilla should be respectful and courteous with the people. . . . Even in war, it is possible to smile, laugh or greet people. Truly, the cause of our revolutionary base, the reason why we are struggling, is our people. We must be respectful to them on all occasions that present themselves.[63]

---

[62] Ibid., pp.47-48.
[63] Ibid., pp.49-50.

126

Not only does the manual not advocate using indiscriminate "terror" against the population; but, on the contrary, it urges the guerrillas to avoid combat near villages:

[T]he Armed Propaganda Team cadres should not turn the town into a battlefield. Generally, our guerrillas will be better armed, so that they will obtain greater respect from the population if they carry out appropriate maneuvers instead of endangering their lives, or even destroying their houses in an encounter with the enemy within the town.[64]

Clearly, the overall theme of the manual was not the teaching of terrorism, but rather teaching the guerrillas the importance of *not* mistreating civilians. The purpose of the manual was the promotion of human rights.

Some readers may wonder, if the details set forth above are accurate,[65] how this manual came to be so misunderstood in the United States and around the world. Part of the answer may be found in unusually careless journalism and the normal partisan misrepresentation of a presidential campaign. But a more nefarious explanation may also exist. It is offered here only as a theory, but it does seem to fit the odd-shaped gap in the puzzle nicely.

Put simply, the explanation may be that what began as a praiseworthy CIA effort to promote greater respect for human rights by the Contras was turned into a tragic "dirty trick" by a Sandinista "mole" or sympathizer in the Contra high command. The probable suspect is Edgar Chamorro, a member of one of Nicaragua's most prominent families—whose members are divided between supporters of the Sandinistas and the Contras[66]—and until 1984 essentially the public affairs spokesman for the FDN. After numerous apparent "admissions" to the press which seriously damaged the public image of the Contras,[67] and in other ways harmed their cause,[68] Chamorro was removed from the FDN in 1984.

Chamorro's indiscretions, considered by themselves, could as easily be attributed to incompetence or to a personal commitment to truth and honor as to more devious causes. But other parts of the overall picture are far more conducive to a conspiracy theory than to more simple explanations.

From the author's own research, several facts seem clear. First of all, the entire *Psychological Operations* manual project was carried out under Chamorro's general direction. The American and the two Nicaraguans who actually participated in the translation of the manual have independently confirmed this fact in separate conversations with the author, and Edgar

---

[64] Ibid., p.71.

[65] Readers are encouraged to examine the manual and judge for themselves. As noted above in fn. 58, a commercial edition of an English translation is widely available.

[66] For background on the Chamorro family, see Christian, op. cit.

[67] Such as "admitting" that Contra soldiers killed prisoners and committed other war crimes.

[68] Such as implicating the Government of Honduras as a supporter of the Contras, which resulted in further constraints being placed on the FDN by Honduras.

Chamorro had told American journalists that "only he, the American author and two anti-Sandinista guerrillas who translated the work into Spanish had seen the book before its publication."[69] All three of the other participants told the author that Chamorro took the draft manuscript from them to do the final editing, and a fourth person—Chamorro's special assistant—stated that Chamorro had sole possession of the manuscript for approximately one week before it was delivered to the printer.

The author has compared the version of the manual which Chamorro had delivered to the printer—what might best be called the "Chamorro edition"—with the original U.S. Army lesson plans on which it was based, and most of the offensive paragraphs did not appear in the original. When shown the language in the Chamorro edition, the American and both Nicaraguans directly involved in the translation of the original draft all expressed shock. They unanimously agreed that several passages in the Chamorro edition had not been in their draft when it was taken from them by Chamorro. These passages stand out in stark contrast to the rest of the manual, which clearly promotes human rights and deemphasizes violence.

Chamorro and the others involved agree that, after the manual was returned from the printer, most of the offensive passages were promptly identified by Contra leaders, who insisted that two pages (actually four pages, counting front and back) be removed from all copies and replaced with less offensive language. There is disagreement about who first discovered the problem and demanded the change. Two senior FDN leaders told the author in separate interviews that, almost simultaneously, both of them found the passages and were outraged. They say they complained to Chamorro, who agreed to have the pages replaced. Chamorro, on the other hand, has testified under oath that he discovered the problem and insisted that the pages be removed:

Before the manual was distributed, I attempted to excise two passages that I thought were immoral and dangerous . . . . I locked up all the copies of the manual and hired two youths to cut out the offending pages and glue in expurgated pages. About 2,000 copies of the manual, with only those two passages changed, were then distributed to FDN troops. Upon reflection, I found many of the tactics advocated in the manual to be offensive, and I complained to the CIA station chief in Tegucigalpa.[70]

Nearly a year before the above statement, Chamorro told a *New York Times* writer that two pages of "some copies" of the manual had been "ripped out" because "we didn't like some of what it said."[71] Since Chamorro has

---

[69] *Philadelphia Inquirer*, October 21, 1984. Nearly a year later, Chamorro told the International Court of Justice that "I assisted 'Kirkpatrick' [the American] in translating certain parts of the manual, and the manuscript was typed by my secretary." Affidavit of Edgar Chamorro to the International Court of Justice in the case of *Nicaragua v. United States*, September 5, 1985, reprinted in Leiken and Rubin, op. cit., p.270 (hereinafter cited as "Chamorro ICJ Affidavit").

[70] Chamorro ICJ Affidavit, op. cit., p.270.

[71] *New York Times*, October 21, 1984, p.E-5. (Emphasis added.)

128

admitted having seen the manuscript before the manual was published,[72] and everyone else involved in the project asserted that he had sole possession of the manuscript before it was sent to the printer, his contention that he was the individual who objected to the offending passages after the manual was printed is not very credible. Had he really found the language offensive he had every opportunity to remove it before releasing it for publication. The weight of the evidence suggests that, rather than objecting to them, Edgar Chamorro was quite possibly the originator of some of the most objectionable passages in the manual.

There is also circumstantial evidence that Chamorro may have been the source of the copy of the manual that was given to the American press during the 1984 election campaign. As he notes in the above excerpt, the two thousand copies that were distributed to FDN troops had two pages replaced. Other knowledgable individuals told the author that only about half-a-dozen copies of the Chamorro edition were not changed—and Chamorro was known to have at least one of those copies. The copy that was given to the American press was a "Chamorro edition"—with the offending pages still intact.

These were some of the facts which led the author in late 1984 to surmise privately that Chamorro might have been either a Sandinista "mole" or at least a sympathizer determined to undermine the FDN, and that he may have altered the original manuscript by inserting sentences which could embarrass the Contras. By this theory, he would have been a likely candidate to leak the manual to the U.S. press during the 1984 presidential campaign. Nearly a year later, an event occurred in the Netherlands which greatly strengthened that suspicion.

A key portion of the Government of Nicaragua's case in its suit against the United States before the International Court of Justice turned out to be a sworn affidavit from Edgar Chamorro. His statement seemed carefully crafted to do the maximum damage to the United States and Contra positions, and he blatantly misrepresented the overall contents of the manual. He testified:

A major part of my job as communications officer was to work to improve the image of the FDN forces. This was challenging, because it was standard FDN practice to kill prisoners and suspected Sandinista collaborators. In talking with officers in the FDN camps along the Honduran border, I frequently heard offhand remarks like, "Oh, I cut his throat." The CIA did not discourage such tactics. To the contrary, the Agency severely criticized me when I admitted to the press that the FDN had regularly kidnapped and executed agrarian reform workers and civilians. We were told that the only way to defeat the Sandinistas was to use the tactics the Agency attributed to "Communist" insurgencies elsewhere: kill, kidnap, rob and torture.

These tactics were reflected in an operations manual prepared for our forces by a CIA agent who used the name "John Kirkpatrick." . . . The manual was entitled: "Psychological Operations in Guerrilla Warfare." It advocated "explicit and implicit terror" against the civilian population, including assassination of government employees and sympathizers. . . . In fact, the practices

[72] See p. 127, fn.69.

advocated in the manual were employed by FDN troops. Many civilians were killed in cold blood. Many others were tortured, mutilated, raped, robbed or otherwise abused. . . .[73]

The Nicaraguan Government provided the World Court with a copy of the manual—the Chamorro edition, of course. After studying the manual, the Court majority wrote:

That this . . . manual was prepared by the CIA appears to be clearly established: a report published in January 1985 by the Intelligence Committee contains a specific statement to that effect. It appears from this report that the manual was printed in several editions; only one has been produced and it is of that text that the Court will take account. The manual is devoted to techniques for winning the minds of the population, defined as including the guerrilla troops, the enemy troops and the civilian population. *In general, such parts of the manual as are devoted to military rather than political and ideological matters are not in conflict with general humanitarian law;* but there are marked exceptions. . . . In his affidavit, Mr. Chamorro reports that the attitude of some unit commanders, *in contrast to that recommended in the manual,* was that "the best way to win the loyalty of the civilian population was to intimidate it"—by murders, mutilations, etc.—"and make it fearful of us."[74]

As the World Court noted, there were "marked exceptions" to the general humanitarian theme of the manual. One of these, for example, suggested that demonstrations be used to provoke the government to shoot into the crowd— in the hopes of creating one or more "martyrs" for the revolution. The U.S. Army lesson plan from which the manual was prepared—and, by all accounts except Chamorro's, the original draft of the Nicaraguan manual—did not include this language. Instead, it stated that *if* during a demonstration the government forces were to shoot into the crowd and kill someone, that event should be widely publicized and the victim turned into a martyr. The suggestion in the Chamorro edition that the guerrillas would intentionally try to get one of their own supporters killed outraged the FDN leaders, and this was one of the pages that was removed from the copies actually distributed to FDN forces. The World Court, of course, did not know that.

Unfortunately, the Contra leaders did not catch all of the possibly objectionable sentences in the Chamorro edition of the manual. In particular, one passage that was not deleted referred to the possibility to "neutralize carefully selected and planned targets" such as "state security officials." This was widely interpreted as advocacy of "assassination,"[75] which might conflict with a legal

---

[73] Chamorro ICJ Affidavit, op. cit., p.270.

[74] International Court of Justice, Military and Paramilitary Activities in and Against Nicaragua, Merits, June 27, 1986, paras.118-119. (Emphasis added.)

[75] Part of the reasoning behind this interpretation was the belief that the word "neutralize" was a term of art for "assassinate." For example, the *Los Angeles Times* (October 23, 1984) reported that "the term *neutralize* is widely used within the intelligence community as a euphemism for political killings. . . ." This is not accurate. The term "neutralize" is widely used to encompass a broad range of measures which make an individual "neutral" or ineffective. While this can include execution, it also includes such alternatives as persuasion, defamation (e.g., spreading a rumor that the individual is paid by the CIA or KGB), bribery (not only with money or sexual favors, but by offering the individual a position of power in a new government), intimidation, and various degrees of actual violence (e.g., fire-bombing a target's office during the night).

prohibition embodied in a 1981 Executive Order,[76] although other interpretations were possible.[77] While this passage was at best unfortunate, and has received a great deal of publicity, it does not alter the fact that the overwhelming majority of the manual was directed at encouraging respect for human rights and discouraging abuses. Indeed, given the fact that in their fight against Somoza the Sandinistas used to brag about their success in assassinating some of these same categories of government officials,[78] and the fact that the Salvadoran guerrillas they finance and support continue even today to openly advocate a policy of assassination,[79] there is something disingenuous about Nicaragua's lawyers calling publication of this manual "the most shameful episode" in the whole affair. In reality, the manual in many respects is patterned after a number of Marxist guerrilla warfare manuals—minus most of the emphasis on violence traditionally found in such works.[80]

Consider, for example, how the term is used in General Vo Nguyen Giap's classic study on guerrilla warfare, *People's War: People's Army*. "The National United Front was to be a vast assembly of all the forces capable of being united, neutralising all those which could be neutralised, dividing all those it was possible to divide in order to direct the spearhead at the chief enemy of the revolution, invading imperialism." Giap is not here using "neutralize" to mean kill. When he wishes to indicate "assassination" or "killing," he says things like "eliminated traitors," "exterminate. . . the traitors," and "annihilate. . . the traitors." Even Edgar Chamorro admitted that the term can mean "anything from public embarrassment to physical elimination." *Baltimore Sun*, October 20, 1984.

[76] Executive Order 12333 (December 1981).

[77] At least one contextual argument goes against interpreting "neutralize" in this instance to mean "assassinate." In the section on "Implicit and Explicit Terror," the manual says "the guerrillas should be careful not to become an explicit terror, because this would result in a loss of popular support." It says that after a town is occupied, a "public tribunal" (i.e., people's court) should be held to "[s]hame, ridicule and humiliate the 'personal symbols' of the government of repression in the presence of the people. . . ." In so doing, the guerrillas are taught to "[r]educe the influence of individuals in tune with the regime, pointing out their weaknesses. . .without damaging them publicly." A public meeting is then held, concluded by a speech by the most dynamic guerrilla cadre "which includes explicit references to: The fact that the 'enemies of the people'—the officials or Sandinista agents—must not be mistreated in spite of their criminal acts, although the guerrilla force may have suffered casualties, and that this is done due to the generosity of the Christian guerrillas." (*Psychological Operations in Guerrilla Warfare*, op.cit., pp.52-55.) Two pages later the manual talks of "neutralizing" certain targets, but stresses that "it is absolutely necessary to gather together the population affected, so that they will be present, take part in the act, and formulate accusations against the oppressor." (Ibid., pp.57-58.) Given the explicit instructions *not* to harm regime supporters *publicly*, and to tell the population that "enemies of the people" should "not be mistreated," the insistence that the people be present and take part in the "neutralization" of certain targets suggests that something other than assassination is being contemplated. Nevertheless, even though it is widely used, "neutralization" is at best an ambiguous term, and, whatever the intention, it is unfortunate that it was included in what was otherwise generally an admirable enterprise.

[78] See, e.g., Nolan, op.cit., pp.46, 49, who quotes Comandante Henry Ruiz, who later became the Sandinista regime's Minister of Planning, as bragging that his guerrilla column alone "killed 50-60 *jueces* [judges] in 1975 while avoiding combat with the GN [National Guard]." Nolan adds: "The Sandinistas use the verb 'ajusticiar' (to bring to justice) to describe their assassinations." Ibid., p.49.

[79] The evidence is set forth on pp.93, 96–97.

[80] For example, there is nothing in the manual comparable to Truong Chinh's admonition in *The August Revolution* (Hanoi: Foreign Languages Publishing House, 1946): "[I]t is to be regretted that energetic, timely and necessary measures to counteract all possible dangers in the future were not taken immediately upon the seizing of power. . . . We regret only that the repression of the reactionaries during the August Revolution was not carried out fully within the framework of its possibilities. . . . For

The fact that on their own initiative Contra leaders insisted that certain pages containing objectionable material be torn from the manual and replaced with inoffensive language suggests that they may be quite sensitive to human rights concerns. Nevertheless, human rights abuses clearly have taken place—and probably are continuing. Fortunately, there is some evidence that progress is being made in this area. Contra leaders claim that nearly two dozen of their soldiers were court-martialed for human rights abuses in the latter half of 1985, with a 90 percent rate of conviction.[81] Continued U.S. support for the promotion of human rights by Contra soldiers was evidenced by the fact that, at the request of President Reagan, the 1986 Congressional appropriation of funds for the Contras included three million dollars to be used "exclusively for strengthening the observance and advancement of human rights."[82]

If the theory set forth above is accurate, and the objectionable language in the Chamorro edition of the manual was essentially a Sandinista "dirty trick" to discredit the Contras, it is a great tragedy. Respect for human rights is extremely important, and by virtually all accounts there were serious shortcomings among FDN forces in this area. The CIA made a major effort to train FDN guerrillas to be more respectful of the rights of prisoners and civilian noncombatants, and by most accounts on the scene the program was having very positive results. When Mr. Chamorro—or, perhaps, someone else—persuaded the American press that the CIA had instead prepared an "assassination manual," the training program was terminated and all copies of the manual were recalled. This was a serious setback for the cause of human rights.[83]

United States Aid to Contras is Proportional

In order to be legal, force used in self-defense must be both proportional and necessary. Professors McDougal and Feliciano, in their classic treatise, *Law and Minimum World Public Order*, explain that "Proportionality in

---

suicide." (p.41.) See also, John Gerassi, editor, *Venceremos! The Speeches and Writings of Che Guevara* (New York: Simon and Schuster, 1968); and "Report on an Investigation of the Peasant Movement in Hunan," in *Selected Works of Mao Tse-tung* (Peking: Foreign Languages Press, 1967), Vol. 1, p.29: "To put it bluntly, it is necessary to create terror for a while in every rural area, or otherwise it would be impossible to suppress the activities of the counter-revolutionaries. . . . Proper limits have to be exceeded in order to right a wrong, or else the wrong cannot be righted."

[81] *Washington Times*, December 6, 1985, pp.A-1, A-8.

[82] White House Press Release, February 25, 1986.

[83] After personally investigating U.S. training programs in South Vietnam and Central America, the author remains unable to explain how easy it seems to be for critics of the United States to persuade otherwise reasonable members of Congress and the press that a continuation of U.S. training programs will undermine the cause of human rights. As the El Salvador experience demonstrates, U.S. training can have a dramatic and positive impact upon human rights practices. See Editorial, "The Case for the Contras," *New Republic*, March 24, 1986, p.7.

coercion constitutes a requirement that responding coercion be limited in intensity and magnitude to what is reasonably necessary promptly to secure the permissible objectives of self-defense."[84]

United States support for Nicaraguan insurgents is not only proportional, but in many respects is a "mirror image"[85] of the support Nicaragua has been giving to Salvadoran guerrillas. The most obvious difference is that Nicaragua acted first with the intent of overthrowing neighboring governments, while the United States acted in defense of victims of aggression and for the purpose of bringing an end to Nicaragua's unlawful conduct. A few of the similarities between the two situations are apparent from a review of Nicaragua's testimony before the World Court:

- As already noted in Chapter 3, prior to the Sandinista victory in 1979 the five small Salvadoran insurgency groups were disorganized, feuding, and ineffective. Their primary activities were occasional bank robberies, bombings, and assassinations. Similarly, a Nicaraguan witness told the World Court that when the United States decided in late 1981 to give support to the Contras, "the ex-National Guardsmen were divided into several small bands operating along the Nicaragua-Honduras border. . . the bands were poorly armed and equipped, and thoroughly disorganized. They were not an effective military force and represented no more than a minor irritant to the Nicaraguan Government."[86]

- In December 1979, Nicaragua joined with Cuba in bringing together the leaders of the Salvadoran insurgent groups and promised them arms, equipment, and training, if they would set aside their differences and join in a united effort.[87] Assessing the success of the revolution, Fermán Cienfuegos, leader of the FARN guerrilla group and head of external relations for the FMLN, said in August 1985 that "Nothing would have been possible without that unification."[88] And yet Nicaragua's counsel complained to the World Court that "a senior United States Government official, General Vernon Walters, personally met with the leaders of these bands [of Nicaraguan Contras] and promised

[84] Myres S. McDougal and Florentino P. Feliciano, *Law and Minimum World Public Order* (New Haven, Conn.: Yale University Press, 1961), p.242.

[85] "In Central America, the governments of El Salvador and Nicaragua hold the upper hand in their mirror-image wars." Charles Hanley, "Number of wars is rising; cost is beyond counting," *Richmond Times-Dispatch*, October 25, 1986, p.2.

[86] Affidavit of Edgar Chamorro, quoted by Nicaraguan Counsel Paul S. Reichler in oral argument before the International Court of Justice, *Nicaragua v. United States*, Uncorrected Verbatim Record, September 18, 1985, CR 85/24, p.16. Quoted also in Leiken and Rubin, op.cit., p.265.

[87] See p. 49.

[88] Speech by Comandante Fermán Cienfuegos, member of the FMLN general command, at foreign debt conference in Havana; FBIS, Daily Report, Latin America, August 5, 1985, p.Q-11.

that they would receive United States assistance and support if they joined together in a single organization. . . ."[89]

- It has already been shown in Chapter 3 that Nicaragua has supported the Marxist guerrillas in El Salvador, *inter alia*, by providing arms, equipment, money, training, command-and-control assistance, and a headquarters and radio station on Nicaraguan soil. Nicaraguan Vice Minister of Interior Luis Carrión told the International Court of Justice that the United States was assisting the Contras "mainly by funds, intelligence, communications, weapons and logistics."[90]

The tactics of the Salvadoran and Nicaraguan insurgent groups also exhibit many similarities. Consider, for example, Nicaraguan complaints about the Contra attack on the Managua airport in 1983. The greatest difference between this attack and the January 1982 attack against the Ilopango airfield outside San Salvador—by a band of ERP guerrillas trained in Nicaragua and Cuba expressly for this attack[91]—was that the Managua attack was far less damaging. The Ilopango attack destroyed more than a dozen airplanes and helicopters—a substantial portion of the Salvadoran Air Force.

Furthermore, the damage caused by U.S.-supported insurgents inside Nicaragua has certainly not been disproportionate to that attributable to Nicaragua through its support of insurgents in El Salvador. In this regard it is worth noting that when Nicaragua filed its case against the United States before the International Court of Justice in April 1984, it alleged that the Contras had caused damage valued at $370,200,000.[92] By way of comparison, during the same period direct damage to the economy of El Salvador by Nicaraguan-supported insurgents totaled nearly $1 billion—more than two-and-a-half times the damage the Government of Nicaragua alleged could be attributed to the Contras.[93]

The fact is that Nicaraguan-supported guerrillas in El Salvador have been attacking the country's economic heartland, while U.S.-supported Contras

---

[89] Nicaraguan Counsel Paul S. Reichler in oral argument before the International Court of Justice, *Nicaragua v. United States*, Uncorrected Verbatim Record, September 18, 1985, CR 85/24, p.17.

[90] International Court of Justice, *Nicaragua v. United States*, Uncorrected Verbatim Record, September 12, 1985, CR 85/19, p.39.

[91] See p. 70.

[92] International Court of Justice, *Nicaragua v. United States*, Uncorrected Verbatim Record, September 20, 1985, CR 85/27, p.79. On September 17, 1985, Nicaraguan Minister of Finance, William Hupper, told the World Court that "the overall impact between 1981 and 1984 just of production losses, is a little higher than $300 million." Ibid., CR 85/23, p.10.

[93] For a discussion of damage by insurgents to the Salvadoran economy during the early years of the conflict, see Richard J. Meislin, "Economic Losses High in Salvador," *New York Times*, December 5, 1982, p.19; and Virginia Prewett, "Curious Truths About El Salvador's Economy," *Wall Street Journal*, September 7, 1984, p.27.

in Nicaragua have largely avoided the more important economic zones. Consider this mid-1983 report from the *Christian Science Monitor*:

[T]he vital economic heartland of Nicaragua, the swath of territory stretching along the west coast of the country from the city of Leon down to Granada, had hardly been touched by the *contras'* attacks. And that is the part of the country where many of the people live and much of the cotton, corn, and sugar is grown. . . .

[E]ach of the three regions affected by the fighting is relatively lightly populated and among the least important to the country in economic terms. . . . Last year's drought and floods have damaged the nation's economy much more than the *contras* have.[94]

According to the Nicaraguan electric company in Managua, "in all of 1986 only two electric power pilons were destroyed by contras."[95] By contrast, a central focus of the FMLN attack in El Salvador has from the start been against the country's economic infrastructure. Professor Robert S. Leiken, a Senior Associate at the Carnegie Endowment for International Peace and a former Sandinista supporter, notes that in El Salvador, "The guerrillas' onslaught on the economy has destroyed factories, stores, buses, private cars, and public utilities, causing widespread disruption, unemployment and misery."[96]

FMLN leaders are reasonably open about their strategy to destroy El Salvador's economy by attacking nonmilitary economic targets. Indeed, they have been quite creative in explaining the practice. FMLN spokesman Fermán Cienfuegos told Professor Leiken in a March 1982 interview that there was a "political explanation" to burning buses. He explained that certain bus routes "transport workers to factories," and reasoned: "Therefore, the workers do not get to work and can justify their absence by guerrillas' bus-burning. Therefore, the workers are not reprimanded. . . this is an indirect way of allowing the worker to go on strike. . . ."[97]

One year later the ERP issued a communique which explained its strategy of economic sabotage. It argued: "Sabotaging the economy within the framework of a war is not terrorism. It is a weapon used in any military confrontation."[98]

---

[94] Daniel Southerland, "CIA-backed rebels scarcely dent the Nicaraguan military machine," *Christian Science Monitor*, June 29, 1983, p.1. For a more recent account making the same point, see Forrest D. Colburn, "Nicaragua under Siege," *Current History*, March 1985, pp.108-132. He reported that "The areas of fighting are relatively marginal to the economy. The bulk of Nicaragua's gross national product (GNP) is generated in the Pacific region, which has been free from fighting. To date, the most consequential material cost to the new regime of the counterrevolution has been the cost of devoting attention and resources to defeating the counterrevolutionaries, and to preparing for a feared United States intervention."

[95] Julia Preston, "Nicaraguan Rebels Increase Pace of Sabotage Attacks," *Washington Post*, April 3, 1987, p.A-29.

[96] Robert S. Leiken, "The Salvadoran Left," in Robert S. Leiken, editor, *Central America: Anatomy of Conflict* (New York: Pergamon Press, 1984), p.119.

[97] Leiken and Rubin, op. cit., p.413.

[98] Quoted in Leiken, *Central America: Anatomy of Conflict*, op. cit., p.128, n. 21.

Casualty figures are difficult to estimate, but a spokesman for Nicaraguan-supported Salvadoran guerrillas stated in Havana in August 1985 that FMLN forces had inflicted over 18,000 casualties on the Salvadoran Army alone—presumably not including the thousands of civilian noncombatants assassinated by the guerrillas or killed in hostilities produced by guerrilla attacks. By this account, guerrilla-inflicted casualties in the first six months of 1985 were averaging 400 per month.[99] By contrast, Nicaraguan Defense Minister Humberto Ortega released figures at the end of 1985 indicating that total casualties caused by the Contras were slightly over 2,400, including 281 civilians killed.[100] Three months earlier Nicaraguan Vice Minister of Interior Luis Carrión told the ICJ: "Since the end of December 1981 to August 1985, there have been 3,886 people killed on the Nicaraguan side, on the government side. . . . And we had 4,731 wounded people. . . . I would add that more than 40,000 people have been forced to abandon their houses because of the *contras*."[101]

Although this study has not focused heavily upon human rights violations,[102] the casualty figures given by the Nicaraguan officials may provide useful insight into at least one human rights issue. Much effort is devoted to portraying the Contras as terrorists who devote most of their efforts to attacking the civilian population. But according to the figures provided by Defense Minister Ortega, during 1985 only 281 Nicaraguan civilians "died in the conflict."[103] Even if every one of these can be attributed to Contra actions and not one civilian was even accidentally caught in the cross-fire by a Sandinista bullet, by Ortega's own figures, for each civilian death the Contras killed more than four Sandinista soldiers.[104] That hardly supports a claim that the Contras are primarily attacking innocent civilians.

---

[99] Speech by Comandante Fermán Cienfuegos at foreign debt conference in Havana; FBIS, Daily Report, Latin America, August 5, 1985, p.Q-11. In its Declaration of Intervention in the case, the Government of El Salvador told the World Court that Nicaraguan-supported guerrillas had displaced "half-a-million persons" and that "over 30,000 persons have been killed in the conflict since it was unleashed in 1979." Reprinted in *International Legal Materials*, Vol. 24 (January 1985), pp.38,40.

[100] "Nicaraguan Says Contras Weakening," *Washington Post*, December 31, 1985, p.A-10. In 1985 Nicaraguan President Daniel Ortega stated that 7,968 casualties had resulted from four years of Contra activity. Vargas Llosa, op.cit., p.41.

[101] International Court of Justice, *Nicaragua v. United States*, Uncorrected Verbatim Record, September 12, 1985, CR 85/19, p.53.

[102] In the author's view there has been tragic disrespect for human rights on both sides in both Nicaragua and El Salvador. Some legal scholars argue that gross violations of fundamental international human rights may, under certain circumstances, justify a use of armed force under the doctrine of "humanitarian intervention." However, in the author's view U.S. policy in Nicaragua should be viewed as a defensive response to Nicaraguan armed aggression against its neighbors rather than as a response to human rights abuses or to the fact that the Sandinista leaders are Marxist-Leninists (which, under international law, would provide no legal grounds for armed intervention).

[103] "Nicaraguan Says Contras Weakening," *Washington Post*, December 31, 1985, p.A-10.

[104] Ortega claimed that about 1,140 Sandinista soldiers were killed. Ibid.

In contrast, the FMLN in El Salvador is clearly intentionally attacking civilians. In addition to a major campaign of assassination which has already been discussed,[105] Nicaraguan-supported guerrillas in El Salvador make extensive use of land mines which are incapable of distinguishing between military personnel and civilians. A United Press International story reported in early 1986 from San Salvador:

> The insurgents' clandestine Radio Venceremos . . . said half of the army's recent casualties were a result of the rebel-planted land mines. The guerrillas' campaign to use the mines has sparked fierce criticism from the Roman Catholic Church, which has said civilians are often maimed.
>
> Some 55,000 people, most of them non-combatants, have been killed in the country's 6-year-old civil war between Marxist-led guerrillas and the U.S.-backed government.[106]

Consider also this January 1987 *Washington Post* account, written by Frederick Downs, Jr., a health-care professional who had recently returned from El Salvador:

> The Government of El Salvador has been winning the war against its communist guerrillas. In desperation, the communists have indiscriminately used land mines against both the military and civilian populations.
>
> I recently returned from El Salvador, where I helped set up a program for amputees. Communist mines have blown one or more limbs off about 1,600 people, 950 military and 650 civilian. Of the civilians, it's estimated that a quarter to a third are children.
>
> This catastrophe results from a guerrilla program of deliberately mining farm areas and places frequented by civilians. Guerrilla radio broadcasts acknowledge responsibility for indiscriminate land-mine warfare, declaring it an integral part of their revolutionary strategy. . . . Guerrilla leader Shafik Handal said [in a *New York Times* interview]: "The use of land mines is a very important weapon for us." . . .
>
> Contrast this with the situation in Nicaragua, [where] . . . neither side has an avowed policy to kill and maim civilians with land mines. Tragically, this is not the case in El Salvador. . . .
>
> [T]he maiming and terrorizing of civilians is specifically aimed at demoralizing the government and eroding the people's faith in its ability to protect them and to provide care for them— a tactic used very effectively by the communists in Vietnam. . . .[107]

Mr. Downs notes further:

> The guerrillas have taken a toll other than combat injuries. Medical facilities have been closing, and health personnel fear for their lives. In 1983, the guerrillas assassinated the director and head nurse of Chalatenango Hospital. At Usulanton Hospital the guerrillas assassinated two residents, leaving the other four to wonder if they would be next.
>
> Assassination of government officials or anyone connected to the government is an accepted guerrilla tactic. Many wounded soldiers are afraid to return home for fear they will be killed.[108]

---

[105] See pp. 96-97.

[106] "U.S. military adviser lost leg in land mine blast, rebels say," *Washington Times*, February 17, 1986, p. A-6.

[107] Frederick Downs, Jr., "A Dirty War in Central America: The Salvadoran Communists Are Using Land Mines," *Washington Post*, January 18, 1987, p.C-5.

[108] Ibid.

Because the Sandinistas and their allies have a sophisticated propaganda network, and because many Americans are understandably more interested in learning about human rights abuses which are in some way attributable to their own government, the record of war crimes and other abuses by the Sandinistas and their Salvadoran proteges is not as well known as are allegations of Contra abuses. But the evidence is there, for anyone who wishes to take the time to look at it.

In summary, United States support for the Contras has been essentially a mirror image of the aid the Government of Nicaragua has been giving to Salvadoran insurgents. The U.S. program began as a defensive response to Sandinista aggression at the request of El Salvador, and its consequences have been far less damaging to Nicaragua than would be permissible under the doctrine of proportionality in international law. The Contras clearly have on occasion been disrespectful of human rights, but the United States has worked hard to promote better education and training to bring such conduct to an end. In contrast, the Sandinista-supported FMLN in El Salvador is increasing its reliance upon assassination and other forms of terrorism—in flagrant violation of fundamental principles of international law.

United States Aid to the Contras is Necessary

The initial U.S. efforts at constructive engagement with Nicaragua were dismally unsuccessful in deterring that country's aggression against its neighbors.[109] In view of the growing Nicaraguan military capability, and the apparently almost inexhaustible supply of weapons and ammunition available to Nicaragua, it quickly became apparent that if the United States did not become involved in trying to deter the ongoing Nicaraguan aggression, El Salvador and perhaps other countries as well were in danger of being conquered by armed force.

In addition to providing limited amounts of military assistance to permit El Salvador to defend itself, the United States also provided economic assistance to try to offset some of the damage done to El Salvador's economy by the Nicaraguan-supplied and -supported insurgents. It is worth noting, however, that U.S. economic assistance to El Salvador during the 1980-1984 time period was insufficient to offset fully the amount of damage

---

[109] Assistant Secretary of State Thomas O. Enders told the Senate Committee on Foreign Relations on April 12, 1983: "Nicaragua is a country of some 2.5 million people. Since 1979 it has received from the democracies and multilateral agencies $1.6 billion in economic assistance or $640 for every man, woman, and child. The United States supplied $125 million. . . . Yet this same period marks the big buildup of the EPS, direct support for violence in El Salvador, and the consolidation of internal repression. It is clear that constructive engagement has not worked in Nicaragua." State, *Nicaragua: Threat to Peace*, op.cit., p.2.

done to the economy of El Salvador by Nicaraguan-supported insurgents.[110] Indeed, the *Washington Post* reported in 1987:

According to a study by the U.S. Agency for International Development, the economic costs of the war between 1981 and 1985 exceeded $1.5 billion, about $100 million more than the value of U.S. *economic aid during that period.*[111]

While important as a means of buying time and keeping El Salvador stable in the face of the ongoing armed attack, it was clear that simply rebuilding the Salvadoran economy following insurgent attacks was an insufficient incentive to Nicaragua to produce an end to its armed aggression. It was apparent that Nicaragua would moderate its policies and observe its solemn international obligations not to contribute to the use of armed force against its neighbors only if the Sandinistas perceived it to be in their own self-interest to do so. Some sort of direct pressure was necessary.

United States Policy is Working

In retrospect, it is now clear that the Nicaraguan government is susceptible to credible external pressure. For example, as has already been noted, Nicaragua suspended arms shipments to El Salvador for a one-month period beginning in late September 1980 following a visit by Deputy Assistant Secretary of State James Cheek, during which the Nicaraguans were warned that if they did not cease their intervention in El Salvador the United States might be forced by law to terminate its aid program, and that U.S.-Nicaraguan relations could be seriously damaged. Shortly thereafter, according to a captured FMLN document, an individual identified as "Gustavo" informed the Salvadorans "of the [Sandinista] Front's decision to suspend shipments during a period of approximately one month."[112] While the document made it clear that the decision to suspend Nicaraguan arms shipments to Salvadoran insurgents was at least in part a direct response to the Cheek visit, it was equally clear that Nicaragua had no intention of permanently ceasing its intervention in the Salvadoran struggle. After noting the Nicaraguan decision to "suspend shipments" for a one-month period, the captured FMLN document notes:

They [the Sandinista Front] brought up a security problem beginning with a meeting which they said they had with one James Cheek, a representative of the North American Department of State. They said that he manifested knowledge about shipments via land through Nicaragua . . . in small vehicles and that we carried out attempts by sea. They raise the question of possible bad management of the information on the part of personnel working on this and that

---

[110] State/Defense, *Soviet-Cuban Connection*, op.cit., p.33. The chart on page 33 indicates that between 1980 and 1984 Salvadoran guerrillas did $1 billion in damage, while during the same period the United States gave $927 million in economic aid to El Salvador.

[111] William Branigin, "Rebels Impose Economic Toll in El Salvador," *Washington Post*, March 27, 1987, p.A-29.

[112] Captured letter from "Fernando" to "Federico," dated September 30, 1980, translated and reprinted in State, *Communist Interference in El Salvador*, op.cit., Document I, p.5.

they are going to carry out an investigation. . . . This is on one side and on the other is that it has to do with a political decision related to the U.S. elections, that is a possible understanding in order not to cause problems to Carter before November.[113]

Near the end of October 1980, with the investigation apparently concluded, Nicaragua began once again to ship large amounts of arms and military equipment to El Salvador. While this account suggests that U.S. diplomatic pressure and the threat to terminate aid were not sufficient to bring an end to Nicaraguan support for neighboring insurgency movements, it does demonstrate that even this type of pressure can have at least short-term consequences and that the Sandinistas are not immune to external pressure.

There are occasional examples of the successful use of internal pressure to moderate Nicaraguan behavior as well. Michael Kramer, writing in *New York* magazine, argued in 1983: "The critics are wrong: Pressure *can* moderate the Sandinistas' behavior, even internal pressure. Last year, for example, when the church protested the Sandinistas' curtailment of Holy Week observances, the regime backed down."[114]

Unfortunately, experience has also demonstrated that by far the most effective pressure on the Government of Nicaragua has been of a military nature. Consider, for example, the sequence of events in the second half of 1983, as the anti-government guerrillas in Nicaragua became more active and the United States increased its military presence in the region. In mid-July the United States deployed the aircraft carrier *Ranger* into international waters off the coast of Central America. Shortly thereafter, joint military exercises were conducted in Honduras, involving the presence of several thousand U.S. military personnel. On October 25 the United States participated in a joint military operation under the auspices of the Organization of Eastern Caribbean States (OECS) to rescue endangered American students and help restore order on the island of Grenada.[115] At about the same time, anti-government guerrillas inside Nicaragua intensified their attacks on airfields and other targets of importance to the Sandinista regime.

Clearly troubled by the increased pressure, Nicaragua took a number of steps. They announced an amnesty program for certain Miskito Indians who had taken up arms against the government in response to repressive policies implemented by the Managua regime, and a "safe-conduct" program for other members of the armed opposition. There were hints that

---

[113] Ibid.

[114] Kramer, op.cit., p.43. (Emphasis in original.)

[115] For a discussion of this operation, see John Norton Moore, *Law and the Grenada Mission* (Charlottesville, Va.: Center for Law and National Security, 1984); and Department of State and Department of Defense, *Grenada: A Preliminary Report*, December 16, 1983.

some Cuban civilian advisors would soon leave Nicaragua,[116] and it was asserted that some Salvadoran guerrilla leaders had been asked to leave Nicaragua.[117] As already discussed, the presence of U.S. armed forces on military exercises in Honduras was apparently a factor in Managua's decision not to provide promised air-dropped logistical support to the 96 Honduran guerrillas who had been trained in Cuba and Nicaragua and infiltrated from northern Nicaragua into the Olancho area of Honduras in mid-1983.[118]

There was also a temporary relaxation of press censorship inside Nicaragua, and it was announced that elections would be held in November 1984. Thanks to the publication of the very candid secret speech of May 1984 to the Nicaraguan Socialist Party[119] by Junta Political Coordinator Bayardo Arce—the authenticity of which was publicly confirmed by Junta Coordinator (and now President) Daniel Ortega himself[120]—it is clear that U.S. pressure was the primary reason for the scheduling of the 1984 Nicaraguan elections.[121] Comandante Arce said that in order to be assured of international support during the fight against Somoza the FSLN had "launched what we called the program of national reconstruction." He explained:

As part of that program we spoke of bringing about revolutionary change based on three principles which made us presentable in the international context and which, as far as we were concerned, were manageable from the revolutionary standpoint.

Those principles were non-alignment abroad, a mixed economy, and political pluralism. With those three elements . . . we got a number of governments of various tendencies to back the position of Nicaragua, the position of the Sandinista Front and of the revolutionary forces.

Of course, once defined in specific terms, this imposed certain commitments. One was that we said we were going to elect a constituent assembly, that we were going to have elections. While we might view those commitments as negative, if we analyze our revolution in black and white, we still consider them to be positive at this time. Of course, if we did not have the war situation imposed on us by the United States, the electoral problem would be totally out of

---

[116] Most if not all of the departing Cubans were thought to have been already scheduled for normal rotation back to Cuba at this time.

[117] Subsequently, although the command-and-control activities in support of the Salvadoran insurgency continued, the senior Salvadoran guerrillas who remained in the Managua area maintained a substantially lower profile than had earlier been the case.

[118] See pp. 100–101.

[119] The Nicaraguan Socialist Party (PSN) has been the official Moscow-line Marxist-Leninist party in Nicaragua since it was founded in 1937.

[120] See p. 89.

[121] Despite their pledge to the OAS to hold elections, the Sandinistas made little effort even in the early years to hide their general disdain for the electoral process. See, e.g., "Nicaragua: A Revolution Stumbles," *Economist*, May 10, 1980, p. 22 ("[T]he Sandinists proclaim that they too have been elected—in battle. 'The people have already had their election' says one: 'With their blood and with the guns in their hands, the people have cast their votes.' Mr Ramirez breezily told your correspondent that no date had been set for the election originally promised by the Sandinists because elections 'are not a priority for the government. . . .'"); and "Fidel's Pupils Do It Their Way," ibid., July 26, 1980, p. 31 ("[T]he Sandinists throw cold water on the virtues of 'bourgeois' democracy.").

place in terms of its usefulness. What a revolution really needs is the power to act. The power to act is precisely what constitutes the essence of the dictatorship of the proletariat—the ability of the [working] class to impose its will by using the means at hand [without] bourgeois formalities.

For us, then, the elections, viewed from that perspective, are a nuisance, just as a number of things that make up the reality of our revolution are a nuisance.

But from a realistic standpoint, being in a war with the United States, those things become weapons of the revolution to move forward the construction of socialism. . . .

We are using an instrument claimed by the bourgeoisie, which disarms the international bourgeoisie, in order to move ahead in matters that for us are strategic. . . .[122]

It is perhaps worth noting that Nicaraguan officials have admitted to American journalists that some of these steps have been taken "in response to American pressures."[123] Certainly Peruvian writer Maria Vargas Llosa was correct when he argued in the *New York Times* Magazine in April 1985 that "deprivations caused by rebel terrorism and sabotage" in Nicaragua had "served to moderate the Sandinistas' Communist stance."[124]

Senior Salvadoran guerrilla leaders who have been captured or have defected have also noted the impact of U.S. pressure on Nicaragua on the supply of arms to Salvadoran insurgents. For example, Napoleón Romero García, Secretary General of the Metropolitan [San Salvador] Front of the Popular Liberation Forces (FPL) in El Salvador at the time of his capture in early 1985, has said that Nicaragua is providing Salvadoran insurgents with only about 30 percent of the level of materiel that it was providing in previous years. In part this is because the number of guerrillas has significantly decreased, and the guerrillas already have enough small arms to meet their basic needs. But Romero claims that following the October 1983 U.S. and OECS operation in Grenada the Sandinistas temporarily suspended all arms shipments, and when they were resumed later that year they were at a significantly lower level. Another factor in the decrease in supplies for the insurgents, according to Romero, is the increased surveillance by the armed forces of El Salvador.

Romero stated that in 1983 the guerrillas received as much as 50 tons of supplies every three months from Nicaragua. Even in early 1984, the FPL

---

[122] State, *Bayardo Arce's Secret Speech*, op.cit., p.4.

[123] See, e.g., Gutman, op.cit., p.18. Cf. "Pros, Cons, and Contras," *Time*, June 6, 1983, p.16: "Ortega and Ramirez . . . offered perhaps the clearest official admission to date that the *contras* have become a major worry for Nicaragua. Said Ramirez: 'What we would like to talk about with the U.S. is a mutual commitment'—an end to U.S. backing of the *contras* in exchange for the Sandinistas' stopping any support that the U.S. can prove they are providing for Salvadoran guerrillas based in Nicaragua. It remains questionable just what the Sandinistas would accept as proof and how they could be kept to the terms of a possible deal."

[124] Vargas Llosa, op.cit., p.38. See also, "Uneasy over a Secret War," *Time*, May 16, 1983, p.12: "At the moment, the paramilitary pressure being brought to bear on Nicaragua seems to be working."

alone was receiving an average of 20,000 to 30,000 rounds of ammunition per month (primarily 5.56mm ammunition for M-16 rifles, and .50 caliber ammunition for machine guns used as anti-aircraft weapons)—although not much in the way of new weapons, since by the end of 1983 they had more weapons in storage than personnel to use them. While the guerrillas were seeking advanced weapons such as SAM-7 surface-to-air missiles, and these had been approved in principle for delivery by both the Cubans and Nicaraguans, Romero believed that the Nicaraguans were hesitant to provide such weapons out of fear that it would produce a strong reaction from the United States.

According to Romero, following the U.S.-OECS intervention in Grenada the Sandinista leadership was split on the issue of continuing assistance to the insurgents in El Salvador. He identified Nicaraguan Defense Minister Humberto Ortega, Interior Minister Tomás Borge, and Coordinator General for Foreign Affairs Bayardo Arce as the leaders of the faction most strongly favoring what Romero described as the "Cuban position"—that Nicaragua has an "international duty" to support wars of national liberation.

Romero noted that the decrease in Nicaraguan assistance since late 1983 has been noticed by rank-and-file Salvadoran insurgents, and has been a significant factor in morale problems and a growing desertion rate. During 1984 his FPL guerrilla faction suffered between 200 and 300 desertions. He stated that, at a meeting of the FPL high command in Chalatenango Department in February 1985, Comandante Leonel Gonzalez—the FPL Secretary General—presented a report of FMLN strength levels. According to Romero, over the years the FMLN had grown from about 6,000 full-time combatants and service personnel in 1981-1982[125] to a peak of about 9,000-10,000 in 1983. In large part because of desertions, by December 1984 the comparable figure for FMLN guerrilla strength was about 6,500[126]—a drop of nearly one-third. Romero indicated that this drop in troop strength was accompanied by a significant loss of popular support for the insurgents as well, making it more difficult for guerrillas to obtain food, shelter, and intelligence information from the population, and further contributing to a drop in guerrilla morale.[127]

---

[125] FMLN leaders at the time of the January 1981 "final offensive" stated that there were about 5,000 guerrillas. See, e.g., Raymond Bonner, "Salvadoran Rebels Still Predict an Offensive," New York Times, January 3, 1981, p.3; Le Monde (Paris), January 9, 1981, p.7.

[126] Romero gave a range of between 5,850 and 6,850. More recently, General Blandon of the Armed Forces of El Salvador stated that "there were anywhere between 11,000 and 12,000 armed terrorists in the national territory in 1983, while there are between 6,000 and 6,500 estimated here now." FBIS, Daily Report, Latin America, August 1, 1985, p.P-7.

[127] According to a recently declassified interrogation report: "Romero explained that many factors enter into a lessening of popular support for the FMLN. Among them is the indiscriminate sabotage of the electrical system; unwanted transportation strikes; the campaign to take away individual identity cards; and forced recruitments, by some FMLN factions. On top of this, many prospective members do not see a victory for the FMLN in the near term and are not interested in dedicating themselves to the rigors of an insurgent's

According to one recently declassified cable summarizing a debriefing interview with Romero:

> Romero considers the FMLN to have lost the strategic initiative militarily and to be in a declining state. He said if pressure on the Nicaraguan government continues, the Sandinistas will have to cut logistical support to the FMLN. This would, in his view, cause an additional increase in desertions and be an indication of the declining capability of the insurgent forces.[128]

Unfortunately, the effectiveness of the American pressure was somewhat diluted by the perception in Managua that the United States was divided on the question of pressuring Nicaragua to cease its aggression against its neighbors, and in particular by the consistent opposition of the House of Representatives and its intelligence committee to providing financial assistance to anti-government forces in Nicaragua—this despite the formal findings by both the committee and the full Congress that Nicaragua was providing substantial assistance to anti-government guerrillas in El Salvador.[129] Nicaraguan leaders are very much aware that an effective political warfare campaign during the Vietnam War ultimately led Congress to terminate aid to South Vietnam and helped to secure victory for communist North Vietnam.[130] They are unlikely to abandon totally their goal of destabilizing neighboring states if they believe there is a reasonable likelihood that a similar propaganda offensive can produce the same result

---

life. . . ." While many Salvadorans have had grievances against their various central governments over the years, there is little evidence the FMLN guerrillas have ever had widespread support from among the population. Alejandro Montenegro, former Commander-in-Chief of the National Central Guerrilla Front of the People's Revolutionary Army (ERP), was asked whether during the January 1981 "final offensive" the guerrillas under his command had received "popular support." He responded: "None whatsoever. That, too, was a disaster. I urged the chief of the Ligas Populares 28 Febrero to ask people to come help us. He went out in the middle of the street, shouting that what we were doing was for them and on their behalf. No one came out of the house, and I clearly saw that the popular support of which Villalobos and Managua had assured us was a pipe-dream." State, *Interview with Montenegro*, op.cit., p.13.

[128] Romero debriefing, op. cit.

[129] See pp. 83–86. The committee's opposition in 1983 appeared to be based largely on a perception that U.S. policy was not working. After acknowledging the massive Nicaraguan effort to destabilize its neighbors, the committee report concluded that the Contra program "has not interdicted arms. . . ." It continued: "In 18 months the Committee has not seen any diminishment of arms flow to the Salvadoran guerrillas. . . ." (House Report 98-122, op.cit., p.11.) On the basis of the testimony of Napoleón Romero and other prisoners and defectors, it now seems reasonably clear that in large part as a result of the Contra program there has been a very significant drop in the arms flow from Nicaragua to El Salvador since this House Report was written.

On July 28, 1983, the House of Representatives voted 228-195 to block covert assistance to the Contras. Three months later, on October 20, the House reaffirmed its opposition to the Contra program by a vote of 227-194. "House: No 'Covert' Aid to Nicaraguan Rebels," *Congressional Quarterly*, October 22, 1983, p.2163. See also, Don Oberdorfer, "House Acts to Bar CIA Rebel Aid," *Washington Post*, July 29, 1983, p.1.

[130] See p. 42, especially the statement by Tomás Borge that the American people "knew their great historical responsibility during the war in Vietnam." For a discussion of FMLN views on this subject, see p. 51.

vis-a-vis aid to El Salvador and especially assistance to the Contras. The key to the success of U.S. policy remains—as it did in Vietnam—on Capitol Hill. Thus far, Congress has fluctuated from year to year, shifting from authorizing aid for the Contras, to allowing no aid, then allowing only humanitarian aid, then military aid, and who knows what will come next. All in all, there have been something like six changes in Congressional policy toward the Contras.[131] This on-again, off-again, partisan approach not only produces an incredibly immoral and inconsistent national policy—encouraging the Contras to fight, cutting off their supplies, and then urging the survivors to fight again—but it also gives the Sandinistas just enough encouragement to dismiss U.S. policy as a deterrent to their unlawful international aggression.

Given the historic commitment of the Sandinistas and their allies to promoting "armed struggle" and "wars of national liberation" in Central America, it is unlikely that they are going to abandon this objective if they believe Congress will keep the American President in check. If the Contra program fails, the Sandinistas can be expected to increase their assistance to the Salvadoran guerrillas, and also to continue their efforts to bring about revolutionary changes in Honduras, Costa Rica, and elsewhere in the region. Each successful change can be expected to produce what might be characterized as a "psychological domino effect"—encouraging dissident elements in other nations to seek Sandinista, Cuban, and Soviet assistance to gain power, while at the same time persuading potential victims that the United States is not a reliable long-term friend.

This is not to say that if the Contra program fails all of Central America will inevitably fall to the Marxist-Leninists. That is, in the author's view, highly unlikely—at least in the short run. History suggests that at some point there will be a national awakening in the United States, and Congress can be expected to yield to clear public pressure for strong action.

---

[131] When the Administration's program was first reported to Congress in 1981 it was generally supported. Then on December 21, 1982, the first Boland Amendment was adopted, essentially permitting the program to continue but stipulating that none of its funds could be provided for the purpose of overthrowing the Nicaraguan government or promoting a confrontation between Nicaragua and Honduras. This language was continued in subsequent laws, expiring on December 8, 1983. On that date Congress authorized another $24 million for military aid to the Contras. Between October 1 and October 11, 1984, there was a full prohibition on aid to the Contras. This was continued in various other statutes. On October 12, 1984, Congress stipulated that the President would be able to provide $14 million to the Contras after February 28, 1985, if he provided specific reports to Congress and the aid was approved by joint resolution. For fiscal year 1986, $27 million in humanitarian aid to the Contras was provided, and for fiscal year 1987 $100 million was appropriated—the bulk of which was available for military aid to the Contras. However—as if to reassure the Sandinistas that they need only hold out and eventually the United States will "pull the plug" on the Contras—the House of Representatives went on record in 1987 as favoring a termination of that aid (knowing at the time that the vote would never become law).

The remaining question is whether that awakening will occur in time for the United States to deter further aggression by funding others who seek to defend themselves. If not, the United States may find itself even further isolated and discredited—forced in the end to choose between playing witness to further aggression or trying to reestablish its own national credibility with the lives of another generation of its own young men. That would be a great tragedy.

Glossary

AFP	Agence France Presse
ARDE	Democratic Revolutionary Alliance (Contras)
BPR	Popular Revolutionary Bloc (El Salvador)
CIA	Central Intelligence Agency
COFIN	FMLN Finance Commission (El Salvador)
CPSU	Communist Party of the Soviet Union
CRM	Revolutionary Coordinator of the Masses (El Salvador)
DGSE	General Directorate for State Security (Nicaragua)
DNC	Combined National Directorate (Nicaragua)
DNU-MRH	National Unity Directorate of the Revolutionary Movement of Honduras
DRU	Unified Revolutionary Directorate (El Salvador)
EMGC	Guerrilla Joint General Staff (El Salvador)
EPS	Sandinista People's Army
ERP	People's Revolutionary Army (El Salvador)
ETA	Basque Homeland and Liberty (BHL)
FARN	Armed Forces of National Resistance (El Salvador)
FBIS	Foreign Broadcast Information Service
FDN	Nicaraguan Democratic Force (Contras)
FDR	Revolutionary Democratic Front (El Salvador)
FMLN	Farabundo Marti National Liberation Front (El Salvador)
FPL	Farabundo Marti Popular Liberation Forces (El Salvador)
FPR-LZ	Revolutionary Popular Front Lorenzo Zelaya (Honduras)
FSLN	Sandinista National Liberation Front
GMT	Greenwich Mean Time
GN	National Guard (Somoza's)
GNP	Gross National Product
GPP	Prolonged Popular War (Nicaragua)
ICJ	International Court of Justice
IRA	Irish Republican Army
KGB	Committee for State Security (USSR)
LP-28	Popular Leagues of February 28 (El Salvador)
MLP	Movement of Popular Liberation (El Salvador)
MNR	National Revolutionary Movement (El Salvador)
MPSC	Popular Socialist Christian Movement (El Salvador)
NATO	North Atlantic Treaty Organization

NSC	National Security Council
OAS	Organization of American States
OECS	Organization of Eastern Caribbean States
PCES	Communist Party of El Salvador
PLN	National Liberation Party (Costa Rica)
PLO	Palestine Liberation Organization
PRTC	Revolutionary Party of Central American Workers
PSN	Socialist Party of Nicaragua
PVP	Popular Vanguard Party (Costa Rica)
SAHSA	Honduran National Airline
SOUTHCOM	U.S. Army Southern Command
TI	Insurrectional Tendency (Nicaragua)
TP	Proletarian Tendency (Nicaragua)
UDN	National Democratic Union (El Salvador)

Index

Cienfuegos, Fermán, 48, 48n.10, 49n.16, 93, 95-96, 133, 135

Coleman, Thomas, 85

Columbia: Cuban intervention in, 22-23n.3, 24n.13; M-19 terrorist group, 45, 105-106

"Comandante Cero." *See* Pastora Gómez, Edén.

"Comandante Marcial." *See* Carpio, Salvador Cayetano.

Communist International (Third), 26n.20, 47

Congress, United States. *See* United States: Congress.

Contadora Group, 90

Contras: damage caused by, 134-136; Democratic Revolutionary Alliance (ARDE), 36, 106, 121n.41; "Fifteenth of September" radio station, 123; first operations, 17, 121-122; inclusion of former National Guardsmen, 120-123; inclusion of former Sandinistas, 32-34, 122; La Concha attack, 65-66; "mercenaries," 120-121; "murder manual," 123-132; support for in neighboring states, 20-21, 81; U.S. support for, 17, 21, 119-123, 132-134, 138-139, 144-145; and *passim*

Costa Rica: 13, 33, 48n.10,; assistance to Sandinistas, 4, 12n.62, 36n.75, 37, 37n.83, 69, 69n.92; intervention by Sandinistas, 104-108; military forces of, 18, 18n.92; Popular Vanguard Party (PVP), 107; public opinion in, 20; SAHSA bombing, 105-107; Sandinista weapons transported through, 37-38; and *passim*

Craxi, Bettino, 45

Cruz Porras, Arturo José, 33, 34-35, 117

Cuarda, Joaquin, 71

Cuba: advisers in Nicaragua, 11-12, 11-12n.57, 141, 141n.116; arms shipments to El Salvador, 24-25n.13, 25; arms shipments to Guatemala, 25; arms shipments to Honduras, 25; constitution, 24; "Esmeralda," 56, 60, 75; forces in Africa, 2; intervention in Nicaragua, 23-24; military buildup, 2-3; role in establishment of FSLN, 24; role in overthrow of Somoza, 11, 37, 38; support for "wars of national liberation," 1, 22, 23-25, 115; training of FMLN guerrillas, 69-70, 95n.195; and *passim. See also* Castro, Fidel.

Czechoslovakia, 11-12n.57, 58n.49

Democratic Revolutionary Alliance. *See* Contras: Democratic Revolutionary Alliance—ARDE.

D'Escoto Brockman, Miguel, 33, 46-47n.3, 90, 90n.167, 110, 110n.3, 121n.40

"Diplomatic struggle": in El Salvador, 52, 52n.26; in Nicaragua, 118; in Vietnam, 40

Dominican Republic, Cuban intervention in, 22-23n.3

DRU. *See* El Salvador: Unified Revolutionary Directorate (DRU).

Duarte, José Napoleón, 51n.24, 79, 80-81

Echeverria, Johnny, 4n.18, 37n.83

Ecuador, 1

Elections: Contra view on, 123; in El Salvador, 48n.12; FMLN views on, 51n.25; in Nicaragua, 1n.3, 89, 89n.163, 141, 141n.121; Sandinista views on, 29, 29-30n.39; trends in Latin America, 1; in United States, 41, 139-140

El Salvador: Contras, 81, 102; cost of war 139-144, 139n.110; death squads, 95; democratic trends in, 1; denunciation of Nicaraguan aggression, 78-81; guerrilla damage to economy, 93-97, 95n.191/192/193/195, 134-137; guerrilla groups in, 46-47n.3, 48-49, 49n.19, 50, 51, 51n.24, 52, 92-97; guerrilla Joint General Staff (EMGC) meeting, 50n.21, 59, 65; guerrilla leaders and Fidel Castro, 36, 36n.75, 49; Handal, Jorge Roberto Shafik, 50, 50n.20, 55-56, 58-59, 58n.49; Ilopango airfield, 70, 95n.195, 134; International Court of Justice, 72, 115-116; La Concha attack, 65-66; M-16 rifles in, 53-57, 61, 67, 143; Nicaraguan C^3 assistance to Salvadoran guerrillas, 70-73; Nicaraguan and Cuban provision of arms to guerrilla insurgents, 9-10n.46, 41, 46-47n.3, 53, 59, 60-68, 68n.87, 74-78, 80, 81, 144, 144n.129; Nicaraguan financial support to insurgents, 68-69, 68n.90, 69n.91; Nicaraguan intervention in internal affairs of, 9, 20, 46-47, 90, 95; Nicaraguan leaders defend support for, 87-90, 90n.167; Nicaraguan training of Salvadoran guerrillas, 69-70; People's Revolutionary Army (Ejercito Revolucionario del Pueblo—ERP), 48, 48n.12, 52, 53, 70, 75, 135; PLO aid to insurgents, 14n.70; public opinion,

154

Bibliography

Books, Journal Articles, and Government Documents

Anderson, Thomas P. "The Roots of Revolution in Central America." In *Rift and Revolution: The Central America Imbroglio*, edited by Howard J. Wiarda. Washington, D.C.: American Enterprise Institute, 1984.

Arostegui, Martin. "Revolutionary Violence in Central America." *International Security Review* (Spring 1979).

Belli, Humberto. *Three Nicaraguans on the Betrayal of Their Revolution*. Heritage Lectures, No. 41. Washington, D.C.: The Heritage Foundation, October 11, 1984.

Bolaños, Miguel. "Inside Communist Nicaragua: The Miguel Bolanos Transcripts." *Backgrounder*, No. 294. Washington, D.C.: The Heritage Foundation, September 30, 1983.

"The Case for the Contras." Editorial, *New Republic* (March 24, 1986).

Christian, Shirley. *Nicaragua: Revolution in the Family*. New York: Random House, 1985.

Colburn, Forrest D. "Nicaragua Under Siege." *Current History* (March 1985).

Costa Rica, Ministry of Foreign Relations and Worship. *Las Relaciones Entre Costa Rica Y Nicaragua*, July 28, 1982. Translated in United States of America. Counter-Memorial submitted to the International Court of Justice in the case of Nicaragua v. United States of America (Jurisdiction), August 17, 1984, Annex 57.

Cruz, Arturo J. "Nicaragua's Imperiled Revolution." *Foreign Affairs*, Vol. 61, No. 5 (Summer 1983).

Dickey, Christopher. "I Obey But I Do Not Comply." In *The Central American Crisis Reader*, edited by Robert S. Leiken and Barry Rubin. New York: Summit Books, 1987.

_____ . *With the Contras: A Reporter in the Wilds of Nicaragua*. New York: Simon and Schuster, 1986.

Dreifus, Claudia. "Playboy Interview: The Sandinistas." *Playboy* (September 1983).

Evans, Ernest. "Revolutionary Movements in Central America: The Development of a New Strategy." In *Rift and Revolution: The Central American Imbroglio*, edited by Howard J. Wiarda. Washington, D.C.: American Enterprise Institute, 1984.

Ezell, Edward C. *Small Arms Today: Latest Reports on the World's Weapons and Ammunition*. Harrisburg, Pa.: Stackpole Books, 1984.

Fonseca Amador, Carlos. *A Nicaraguan in Moscow*. 1958. Republished in *Barricada* (Managua), November 8, 1980.

García-Amador, Francisco V. "The Rio de Janeiro Treaty." *University of Miami Inter-American Law Review*, Vol. 17 (1985).

Gerassi, John, editor. *Venceremos! The Speeches and Writings of Che Guevara*. New York: Simon and Schuster, 1968.

Gutman, Roy. "America's Diplomatic Charade." *Foreign Policy* (Fall 1984).

Harrison, Lawrence E. "We Tried to Accept the Sandinista Revolution." *Encounter* (December 1983).

Ho Chi Minh. *Selected Works*. Four Volumes. Hanoi: Foreign Languages Publishing House, 1962.

International Court of Justice. *Military and Paramilitary Activities in and against Nicaragua* (Nicaragua v. United States of America), Merits, 1986.

_____ . *Nicaragua v. United States*, Uncorrected Verbatim Record. September 12, 1985, CR 85/19—September 20, 1985, CR 85/27.

International Institute for Strategic Studies. *The Military Balance, 1981-1982*. Colchester, U.K.: Spottiswoode Ballantyne Ltd., 1981.

_____ . *The Military Balance 1986-1987*. London: Garden City Press, 1986.

Kramer, Michael. "The Not-Quite War." *New York* (September 12, 1983).

Leiken, Robert S., editor. *Central America: Anatomy of a Conflict*. New York: Pergamon Press, 1984.

_____ . "Eastern Winds in Latin America." *Foreign Policy* (Spring 1981).

_____ . "Nicaragua's Untold Stories." *New Republic* (October 5, 1984).

_____ . "The Salvadoran Left." In *Central America: Anatomy of a Conflict*, edited by Robert S. Leiken. New York: Pergamon Press, 1984.

_____ and Barry Rubin, editors. *The Central American Crisis Reader*. New York: Summit Books, 1987.

Lenin, V.I. *"Left-Wing" Communism: An Infantile Disorder*. Moscow: Books for Socialism, n.d.

McColm, R. Bruce. "The Nicaraguan Revolution: Slouching Toward Oblivion." *Freedom at Issue* (September-October 1981).

McDougal, Myres S., and Florentino P. Feliciano. *Law and Minimum World Public Order*. New Haven, Conn.: Yale University Press, 1961.

"Miguel Bolaños Transcripts." Interview with Miguel Bolaños by two *Washington Post* journalists. Washington, D.C.: The Heritage Foundation, June 16-17, 1983 (typescript).

Moore, John Norton. *Law and the Grenada Mission*. Charlottesville, Va.: Center for Law and National Security, 1984.

_____ . *The Secret War in Central America*. Frederick, Md.: University Publications of America, 1987.

_____ . "The Secret War in Central America and the Future of World Order." *American Journal of International Law*, Vol. 80 (January 1986).

_____ , and Robert F. Turner. *International Law and the Brezhnev Doctrine*. Lanham, Md.: University Press of America, 1987.

Nolan, David. *The Ideology of the Sandinistas and the Nicaraguan Revolution*. Coral Gables, Fl.: University of Miami, North/South Center, 1984.

Pastora Gómez, Edén. "Nicaragua 1983-1985: Two Years' Struggle Against Soviet Intervention." *Journal of Contemporary Studies* (Spring/Summer 1985).

Payne, Douglas. "Sandinistas Bid 'Farewell to the West.'" *Freedom at Issue* (November-December 1985).

Poelchau, Warner, editor. *White Paper Whitewash: Interviews with Philip Agee on the CIA and El Salvador*. New York: Deep Cover Books, 1981.

Psychological Operations in Guerrilla Warfare. With essays by Joanne Omang and Aryeh Neier. New York: Vintage Books, 1985.

Radu, Michael S. *The Origins and Evolution of the Nicaraguan Insurgencies, 1979-1985*. Philadelphia, Pa.: Foreign Policy Research Institute, 1986.

Richardson, James D., editor. *Messages and Papers of the Presidents*. Washington, D.C.: U.S. Government Printing Office, 1986.

Report of the President's National Bipartisan Commission on Central America. January 10, 1984. Washington, D.C.: U.S. Government Printing Office, 1984.

Republican Study Committee, U.S. House of Representatives. *Republican Study Committee Task Force on Central America Briefing with Alejandro Montenegro*, Thursday, July 12, 1984.

Rudolph, James D., editor. *Nicaragua : A Country Study*. Washington, D.C.: U.S. Government Printing Office, 1982.

Sandinist National Liberation Front (FSLN). *Analysis of the Situation and Tasks of the Sandinist People's Revolution* (Seventy-Two-Hour Document). October 5, 1979.

Schlesinger, Arthur M., Jr. *The Dynamics of World Power: A Documentary History of U.S. Foreign Policy, 1945-1973*. Ten volumes. Edgemont, Pa.: Chelsea Hse. Pubs., 1983.

Selected Works of Mao Tse-tung. Four Volumes. Peking: Foreign Languages Press, 1967.

Starr, Richard F., editor. *1969 Yearbook on International Communist Affairs*. Stanford, Calif.: Hoover Institution Press, 1969. (Also, subsequent yearbooks for 1970, 1971, 1972, and 1976.)

Truong Chinh. *The August Revolution*. Hanoi: Foreign Languages Publishing House, 1946.

_____ . *The Resistance Will Win*. Hanoi: Foreign Languages Publishing House, 1947.

Turner, Robert F. "Peace and the World Court: A Comment on the Paramilitary Activities Case." *Vanderbilt Journal of Transnational Law*, Vol. 20, No. 1 (1987).

_____ . *Vietnamese Communism: Its Origins and Development*. Stanford, Calif.: Hoover Institution Press, 1975.

United States of America. Counter-Memorial submitted to the International Court of Justice in the case of Nicaragua v. United States of America (Jurisdiction), August 17, 1984.

United States Information Agency. *Public Opinion in Four Countries of Central America, 1983*. Research Report R-1-84.

United States Army Southern Command (SOUTHCOM). *Cuban-Nicaraguan Support for Subversion in Honduras: El Paraiso, July 1984*.

U.S. Central Intelligence Agency. *The World Factbook 1981*. Washington, D.C.: U.S. Government Printing Office, 1981.

_____ . *The World Factbook 1984*. Washington, D.C.: U.S. Government Printing Office, 1984.

U.S. Congress, *Congressional Record*. Washington, D.C. (1979-1987)

U.S. Congress, House, Permanent Select Committee on Intelligence. *Amendment to the Intelligence Authorization Act for Fiscal Year 1983*. House Report 98-122, pt.1, 98th Congress, 1st Session, May 13, 1983.

U.S. Congress, Senate, Committee on Foreign Relations. *North Atlantic Treaty*. Report of the Committee on Foreign Relations, on Ex.L., 81st Congress, 1st Session, Senate Executive Report No. 8.

U.S. Department of Commerce, National Technical Information Service. Foreign Broadcast Information Service, Latin America. 1979-1987.

U.S. Department of Defense. *Soviet Military Power 1987*. Washington, D.C.: U.S. Government Printing Office, 1987.

U.S. Department of State and Department of Defense. *Background Paper: Nicaragua's Military Buildup and Support for Central American Subversion*. Washington, D.C.: U.S. Government Printing Office, July 18, 1984.

_____ . *The Challenge to Democracy in Central America*. Washington, D.C.: U.S. Government Printing Office, June 1986.

_____ . *Grenada: A Preliminary Report*. Released by U.S. Department of State and Department of Defense, December 16, 1983.

_____ . *News Briefing: Intelligence Information on External Support of the Guerrillas in El Salvador*. August 8, 1984.

_____ . *The Sandinista Military Buildup*. Washington, D.C.: U.S. Government Printing Office, Department of State Publication No. 9432, revised edition, May 1985.

_____ . *The Soviet-Cuban Connection in Central America and the Caribbean*. Washington, D.C.: U.S. Government Printing Office, March 1985.

U.S. Department of State. *Background Paper: Central America*. May 27, 1983.

_____ . *Comandante Bayardo Arce's Secret Speech Before the Nicaraguan Socialist Party (PSN)*. Department of State Publication No. 9422, Inter-American Series 118.

_____ . *Communist Interference in El Salvador: Documents Demonstrating Communist Support for the Salvadoran Insurgency*. February 23, 1981.

_____ . *Cuban Support for Terrorism and Insurgency in the Western Hemisphere*. Statement by Assistant Secretary of State Thomas O. Enders before the Subcommittee on Security and Terrorism of the Senate Committee on the Judiciary, March 12, 1982. Current Policy Series No. 376.

_____ . *Cuba's Renewed Support for Violence in Latin America*. Washington, D.C.: U.S. Government Printing Office, Special Report No. 90, December 14, 1981.

_____ . "Declassified Transcript of Debriefing with Napoleon Romero Garcia" (unpublished).

_____ . *Documents on the Nicaraguan Resistance*. Special Report No. 142, 1986.

_____ . Office of Public Diplomacy for Latin America and the Caribbean. *Inside the Sandinista Regime: A Special Investigator's Perspective*. 1985.

_____ . "Interview with Montenegro at Department of State" (unpublished). Division of Language Services, Transcript No. 112533.

_____ . *Nicaragua: Threat to Peace in Central America*. Current Policy Series No. 476.

_____ . *The Sandinistas and Middle East Radicals*. Washington, D.C.: U.S. Government Printing Office, August 1985.

_____ . *Statement and Background Papers Released by Department of State to Press*. Saturday, March 20, 1982.

_____ . *The United States and Cuba*. Address by Kenneth N. Skoug, Jr., Director of the Office of Cuban Affairs. Current Policy Series No. 646, December 17, 1984.

_____ . *U.S. Efforts to Achieve Peace in Central America*. Report Submitted Pursuant to Section 109(f) of the Intelligence Authorization Act for Fiscal Year 1984.

United States, *President's Report to the Congress* Pursuant to Section 8066 of the Continuing Resolution for FY 1985, PL 98-473, April 10, 1985: unclassified excerpts, "U.S. Support for the Democratic Resistance Movement in Nicaragua."

Valenta, Jiri, and Virginia Valenta. "Sandinistas in Power." *Problems of Communism* (September-October 1985).

Vargas Llosa, Mario. "In Nicaragua." *New York Times* Magazine (April 28, 1985).

Vo Nguyen Giap. *People's War, People's Army*. Hanoi: Foreign Languages Publishing House, 1961.

Whiteman, Marjorie M. *Digest of International Law*. Washington, D.C.: U.S. Government Printing Office, 1971.

Wiarda, Howard J., editor. *Rift and Revolution: The Central American Imbroglio*. Washington, D.C.: American Enterprise Institute, 1984.

Newspapers and Periodicals

Baltimore Evening Sun
Baltimore Sun
Barricada (Managua)
Bohemia (Caracas)
Business Week
Chicago Sun-Times
Chicago Tribune
Christian Science Monitor
Columbia Missourian
Congressional Quarterly
Congressional Record
Department of State Bulletin
El Nuevo Diario (Managua)
Economist
Encounter
Excelsior (Mexico City)
Freedom at Issue
Granma (Havana)
Houston Chronicle
International Legal Materials
La Nación (San José)
La Prensa (Managua)
La República (San José)
Le Monde (Paris)
London Times
Los Angeles Times
New Times (Moscow)
New York Times
Philadelphia Inquirer
Richmond Times-Dispatch
San Diego Union
St. Louis Post-Dispatch
Time
Tricontinental (Havana)
Wall Street Journal
Washington Post
Washington Star
Washington Times

PERGAMON-BRASSEY'S
International Defense Publishers

List of Publications
published for the
Institute for Foreign Policy Analysis, Inc.

Orders for the following titles should be addressed to: Pergamon-Brassey's, Maxwell House, Fairview Park, Elmsford, New York, 10523; or to Pergamon-Brassey's, Headington Hill Hall, Oxford, OX3 0BW, England.

Foreign Policy Reports

ETHICS, DETERRENCE, AND NATIONAL SECURITY. By James E. Dougherty, Midge Decter, Pierre Hassner, Laurence Martin, Michael Novak, and Vladimir Bukovsky. 1985. xvi, 91pp. $9.95.

AMERICAN SEA POWER AND GLOBAL STRATEGY. By Robert J. Hanks. 1985. viii, 92pp. $9.95.

DECISION-MAKING IN COMMUNIST COUNTRIES: AN INSIDE VIEW. By Jan Sejna and Joseph D. Douglass, Jr. 1986. xii, 75pp. $9.95.

NATIONAL SECURITY: ETHICS, STRATEGY, AND POLITICS. A LAYMAN'S PRIMER. By Robert L. Pfaltzgraff, Jr. 1986. v, 37pp. $9.95.

DETERRING CHEMICAL WARFARE: U.S. POLICY OPTIONS FOR THE 1990S. By Hugh Stringer. 1986. xii, 71pp. $9.95.

THE CRISIS OF COMMUNISM: ITS MEANING, ORIGINS, AND PHASES. By Rett R. Ludwikowski. 1986. xii, 79pp. $9.95.

TRANSATLANTIC DISCORD AND NATO'S CRISIS OF COHESION. By Peter H. Langer. 1986. viii, 89pp. $9.95.

THE REORGANIZATION OF THE JOINT CHIEFS OF STAFF: A CRITICAL ANALYSIS. Contributions by Allan R. Millett, Mackubin Thomas Owens, Bernard E. Trainor, Edward C. Meyer, and Robert Murray. 1986. xi, 67pp. $9.95.

THE SOVIET PERSPECTIVE ON THE STRATEGIC DEFENSE INITIATIVE. By Dmitry Mikheyev. 1987. xii, 88pp. $9.95.

ON GUARD FOR VICTORY: MILITARY DOCTRINE AND BALLISTIC MISSILE DEFENSE IN THE USSR. By Steven P. Adragna. 1987. xiv, 87pp. $9.95.

Special Reports

STRATEGIC MINERALS AND INTERNATIONAL SECURITY. Edited by Uri Ra'anan and Charles M. Perry. 1985. viii, 85pp. $9.95.

THIRD WORLD MARXIST-LENINIST REGIMES: STRENGTHS, VULNERABILITIES, AND U.S. POLICY. By Uri Ra'anan, Francis Fukuyama, Mark Falcoff, Sam C. Sarkesian, and Richard H. Shultz, Jr. 1985. xv, 125pp. $9.95.

THE RED ARMY ON PAKISTAN'S BORDER: POLICY IMPLICATIONS FOR THE UNITED STATES. By Anthony Arnold, Richard P. Cronin, Thomas Perry Thornton, Theodore L. Eliot, Jr., and Robert L. Pfaltzgraff, Jr. 1986. vi, 83pp. $9.95.

ASYMMETRIES IN U.S. AND SOVIET STRATEGIC DEFENSE PROGRAMS: IMPLICATIONS FOR NEAR-TERM AMERICAN DEPLOYMENT OPTIONS. By William A. Davis, Jr. 1986. xi, 71pp. $9.95.

REGIONAL SECURITY AND ANTI-TACTICAL BALLISTIC MISSILES: POLITICAL AND TECHNICAL ISSUES. By William A. Davis, Jr. 1986. xii, 54pp. $9.95.

DETERMINING FUTURE U.S. TACTICAL AIRLIFT REQUIREMENTS. By Jeffrey Record. 1987. vii, 40pp. $9.95.

NAVAL FORCES AND WESTERN SECURITY. By Francis J. West, Jr., Jacquelyn K. Davis, James E. Dougherty, Robert J. Hanks, and Charles M. Perry. 1987. xi, 56pp. $9.95.

NATO'S MARITIME STRATEGY: ISSUES AND DEVELOPMENTS. By E.F. Gueritz, Norman Friedman, Clarence A. Robinson, and William R. Van Cleave. 1987. xii, 79pp. $9.95.

NATO'S MARITIME FLANKS: PROBLEMS AND PROSPECTS. By H.F. Zeiner-Gundersen, Sergio A. Rossi, Marcel Duval, Donald C. Daniel, Gael D. Tarleton, and Milan Vego. 1987. xii, 119pp. $9.95.

SDI: HAS AMERICA TOLD HER STORY TO THE WORLD? By Dean Godson. Report of the IFPA Panel on Public Diplomacy. 1987. xviii, 67pp. $9.95.

Books

ATLANTIC COMMUNITY IN CRISIS: A REDEFINITION OF THE ATLANTIC RELATIONSHIP. Edited by Walter F. Hahn and Robert L. Pfaltzgraff, Jr. 1979. 386pp. $43.00.

REVISING U.S. MILITARY STRATEGY: TAILORING MEANS TO ENDS. By Jeffrey Record. 1984. 113pp. $16.95 ($9.95, paper).

SHATTERING EUROPE'S DEFENSE CONSENSUS: THE ANTINUCLEAR PROTEST MOVEMENT AND THE FUTURE OF NATO. Edited by James E. Dougherty and Robert L. Pfaltzgraff, Jr. 1985. 226pp. $18.95.

INSTITUTE FOR FOREIGN POLICY ANALYSIS, INC.
List of Publications

Orders for the following titles in IFPA's series of Special Reports, Foreign Policy Reports, National Security Papers, Conference Reports, and Books should be addressed to the Circulation Manager, Institute for Foreign Policy Analysis, Central Plaza Building, Tenth Floor, 675 Massachusetts Avenue, Cambridge, Massachusetts 02139-3396. (Telephone: 617-492-2116.) Please send a check or money order for the correct amount together with your order.

Foreign Policy Reports

DEFENSE TECHNOLOGY AND THE ATLANTIC ALLIANCE: COMPETITION OR COLLABORATION? By Frank T.J. Bray and Michael Moodie. April 1977. vi, 42pp. $5.00.

IRAN'S QUEST FOR SECURITY: U.S. ARMS TRANSFERS AND THE NUCLEAR OPTION. By Alvin J. Cottrell and James E. Dougherty. May 1977. 59pp. $5.00.

ETHIOPIA, THE HORN OF AFRICA, AND U.S. POLICY. By John H. Spencer. September 1977. 69pp. $5.00.

BEYOND THE ARAB-ISRAELI SETTLEMENT: NEW DIRECTIONS FOR U.S. POLICY IN THE MIDDLE EAST. By R.K. Ramazani. September 1977. viii, 69pp. $5.00.

SPAIN, THE MONARCHY AND THE ATLANTIC COMMUNITY. By David C. Jordan. June 1979. v, 55pp. $5.00.

U.S. STRATEGY AT THE CROSSROADS: TWO VIEWS. By Robert J. Hanks and Jeffrey Record. July 1982. viii, 69pp. $7.50.

THE U.S. MILITARY PRESENCE IN THE MIDDLE EAST: PROBLEMS AND PROSPECTS. By Robert J. Hanks. December 1982. vii, 77pp. $7.50.

SOUTHERN AFRICA AND WESTERN SECURITY. By Robert J. Hanks. August 1983. vii, 71pp. $7.50.

THE WEST GERMAN PEACE MOVEMENT AND THE NATIONAL QUESTION. By Kim R. Holmes. March 1984. x, 73pp. $7.50.

THE HISTORY AND IMPACT OF MARXIST-LENINIST ORGANIZATIONAL THEORY. By John P. Roche. April 1984. x, 70pp. $7.50.

Special Reports

THE CRUISE MISSILE: BARGAINING CHIP OR DEFENSE BARGAIN? By Robert L. Pfaltzgraff, Jr., and Jacquelyn K. Davis. January 1977. x, 53pp. $3.00.

EUROCOMMUNISM AND THE ATLANTIC ALLIANCE. By James E. Dougherty and Diane K. Pfaltzgraff. January 1977. xiv, 66pp. $3.00.

THE NEUTRON BOMB: POLITICAL, TECHNICAL, AND MILITARY ISSUES. By S.T. Cohen. November 1978. xii, 95pp. $6.50.

SALT II AND U.S.-SOVIET STRATEGIC FORCES. By Jacquelyn K. Davis, Patrick J. Friel, and Robert L. Pfaltzgraff, Jr. June 1979. xii, 51pp. $5.00.

THE EMERGING STRATEGIC ENVIRONMENT: IMPLICATIONS FOR BALLISTIC MISSILE DEFENSE. By Leon Gouré, William G. Hyland, and Colin S. Gray. December 1979. xi, 75pp. $6.50.

THE SOVIET UNION AND BALLISTIC MISSILE DEFENSE. By Jacquelyn K. Davis, Uri Ra'anan, Robert L. Pfaltzgraff, Jr., Michael J. Deane, and John M. Collins. March 1980. xi, 71pp. $6.50. (Out of print).

162

ENERGY ISSUES AND ALLIANCE RELATIONSHIPS: THE UNITED STATES, WESTERN EUROPE AND JAPAN. By Robert L. Pfaltzgraff, Jr. April 1980. xii, 71pp. $6.50.

U.S. STRATEGIC-NUCLEAR POLICY AND BALLISTIC MISSILE DEFENSE: THE 1980S AND BEYOND. By William Schneider, Jr., Donald G. Brennan, William A. Davis, Jr., and Hans Rühle. April 1980. xii, 61pp. $6.50.

THE UNNOTICED CHALLENGE: SOVIET MARITIME STRATEGY AND THE GLOBAL CHOKE POINTS. By Robert J. Hanks. August 1980. xi, 66pp. $6.50.

FORCE REDUCTIONS IN EUROPE: STARTING OVER. By Jeffrey Record. October 1980. xi, 91pp. $6.50.

SALT II AND AMERICAN SECURITY. By Gordon J. Humphrey, William R. Van Cleave, Jeffrey Record, William H. Kincade, and Richard Perle. October 1980. xvi, 65pp.

THE FUTURE OF U.S. LAND-BASED STRATEGIC FORCES. By Jake Garn, J.I. Coffey, Lord Chalfont, and Ellery B. Block. December 1980. xvi, 80pp.

THE CAPE ROUTE: IMPERILED WESTERN LIFELINE. By Robert J. Hanks. February 1981. xi, 80pp. $6.50. (Hardcover, $10.00).

POWER PROJECTION AND THE LONG-RANGE COMBAT AIRCRAFT: MISSIONS, CAPABILITIES AND ALTERNATIVE DESIGNS. By Jacquelyn K. Davis and Robert L. Pfaltzgraff, Jr. June 1981. ix, 37pp. $6.50.

THE PACIFIC FAR EAST: ENDANGERED AMERICAN STRATEGIC POSITION. By Robert J. Hanks. October 1981. vii, 75pp. $7.50.

NATO'S THEATER NUCLEAR FORCE MODERNIZATION PROGRAM: THE REAL ISSUES. By Jeffrey Record. November 1981. viii, 102pp. $7.50.

THE CHEMISTRY OF DEFEAT: ASYMMETRIES IN U.S. AND SOVIET CHEMICAL WARFARE POSTURES. By Amoretta M. Hoeber. December 1981. xiii, 91pp. $6.50.

THE HORN OF AFRICA: A MAP OF POLITICAL-STRATEGIC CONFLICT. By James E. Dougherty. April 1982. xv, 74pp. $7.50.

THE WEST, JAPAN AND CAPE ROUTE IMPORTS: THE OIL AND NON-FUEL MINERAL TRADES. By Charles Perry. June 1982. xiv, 88pp. $7.50.

THE RAPID DEPLOYMENT FORCE AND U.S. MILITARY INTERVENTION IN THE PERSIAN GULF. By Jeffrey Record. May 1983, Second Edition. viii, 83pp. $7.50.

THE GREENS OF WEST GERMANY: ORIGINS, STRATEGIES, AND TRANSATLANTIC IMPLICATIONS. By Robert L. Pfaltzgraff, Jr., Kim R. Holmes, Clay Clemens, and Werner Kaltefleiter. August 1983. xi, 105pp. $7.50.

THE ATLANTIC ALLIANCE AND U.S. GLOBAL STRATEGY. By Jacquelyn K. Davis and Robert L. Pfaltzgraff, Jr. September 1983. x, 44pp. $7.50.

WORLD ENERGY SUPPLY AND INTERNATIONAL SECURITY. By Herman Franssen, John P. Hardt, Jacquelyn K. Davis, Robert J. Hanks, Charles Perry, Robert L. Pfaltzgraff, Jr., and Jeffrey Record. October 1983. xiv, 93pp. $7.50.

POISONING ARMS CONTROL: THE SOVIET UNION AND CHEMICAL/BIOLOGICAL WEAPONS. By Mark C. Storella. June 1984. xi, 99pp. $7.50.

National Security Papers

CBW: THE POOR MAN'S ATOMIC BOMB. By Neil C. Livingstone and Joseph D. Douglass, Jr., with a Foreword by Senator John Tower. February 1984. x, 33pp. $5.00.

U.S. STRATEGIC AIRLIFT: REQUIREMENTS AND CAPABILITIES. By Jeffrey Record. January 1986. vi, 38pp. $6.00.

STRATEGIC BOMBERS: HOW MANY ARE ENOUGH? By Jeffrey Record. January 1986. vi, 22pp. $6.00.

STRATEGIC DEFENSE AND EXTENDED DETERRENCE: A NEW TRANSATLANTIC DEBATE. By Jacquelyn K. Davis and Robert L. Pfaltzgraff, Jr. February 1986. viii, 51pp. $8.00.

JCS Reorganization and U.S. Arms Control Policy. By James E. Dougherty. March 1986. xiv, 27pp. $6.00.

Strategic Force Modernization and Arms Control. Contributions by Edward L. Rowny, R. James Woolsey, Harold Brown, Alexander M. Haig, Jr., Albert Gore, Jr., Brent Scowcroft, Russell E. Dougherty, A. Casey, Gordon Fornell, and Sam Nunn. 1986. xiii, 43pp. $6.00.

U.S. Bomber Force Modernization. Contributions by Mike Synar, Richard K. Betts, William Kaufmann, Russell E. Dougherty, Richard DeLauer, and Dan Quayle. 1986. vii, 9pp. $5.00.

U.S. Strategic Airlift Choices. Contributions by William S. Cohen, Russell Murray, Frederick G. Kroesen, William Kaufmann, Harold Brown, James A. Courter, and Robert W. Komer. 1986. ix, 13pp. $5.00.

Books

Soviet Military Strategy in Europe. By Joseph D. Douglass, Jr. Pergamon Press, 1980. 252pp. (Out of print).

The Warsaw Pact: Arms, Doctrine, and Strategy. By William J. Lewis. New York: McGraw-Hill Publishing Co., 1982. 471pp. $15.00.

The Bishops and Nuclear Weapons: The Catholic Pastoral Letter on War and Peace. By James E. Dougherty. Archon Books, 1984. 255pp. $22.50.

Conference Reports

NATO and Its Future: A German-American Roundtable. Summary of a Dialogue. 1978. 22pp. $1.00.

Second German-American Roundtable on NATO: The Theater-Nuclear Balance. 1978. 32pp. $1.00.

The Soviet Union and Ballistic Missile Defense. 1978. 26pp. $1.00.

U.S. Strategic-Nuclear Policy and Ballistic Missile Defense: The 1980s and Beyond. 1979. 30pp. $1.00.

SALT II and American Security. 1979. 39pp.

The Future of U.S. Land-Based Strategic Forces. 1979. 32pp. $1.00.

The Future of Nuclear Power. 1980. 48pp. $1.00.

Third German-American Roundtable on NATO: Mutual and Balanced Force Reductions in Europe. 1980. 27pp. $1.00.

Fourth German-American Roundtable on NATO: NATO Modernization and European Security. 1981. 15pp. $1.00.

Second Anglo-American Symposium on Deterrence and European Security. 1981. 25pp. $1.00.

The U.S. Defense Mobilization Infrastructure: Problems and Priorities. The Tenth Annual Conference, sponsored by the International Security Studies Program, The Fletcher School of Law and Diplomacy, Tufts University. 1981. 25pp. $1.00.

U.S. Strategic Doctrine for the 1980s. 1982. 14pp.

French-American Symposium on Strategy, Deterrence and European Security. 1982. 14pp. $1.00.

Fifth German-American Roundtable on NATO: The Changing Context of the European Security Debate. Summary of a Transatlantic Dialogue. 1982. 22pp. $1.00.

Energy Security and the Future of Nuclear Power. 1982. 39pp. $2.50.

International Security Dimensions of Space. The Eleventh Annual Conference, sponsored by the International Security Studies Program, The Fletcher School of Law and Diplomacy, Tufts University. 1982. 24pp. $2.50.

PORTUGAL, SPAIN AND TRANSATLANTIC RELATIONS. Summary of a Transatlantic Dialogue. 1983. 18pp. $2.50.

JAPANESE-AMERICAN SYMPOSIUM ON REDUCING STRATEGIC MINERALS VULNERABILITIES: CURRENT PLANS, PRIORITIES, AND POSSIBILITIES FOR COOPERATION. 1983. 31pp. $2.50.

NATIONAL SECURITY POLICY: THE DECISION-MAKING PROCESS. The Twelfth Annual Conference, sponsored by the International Security Studies Program, The Fletcher School of Law and Diplomacy, Tufts University. 1983. 28pp. $2.50.

THE SECURITY OF THE ATLANTIC, IBERIAN AND NORTH AFRICAN REGIONS. Summary of a Transatlantic Dialogue. 1983. 25pp. $2.50.

THE WEST EUROPEAN ANTINUCLEAR PROTEST MOVEMENT: IMPLICATIONS FOR WESTERN SECURITY. Summary of a Transatlantic Dialogue. 1984. 21pp. $2.50.

THE U.S.-JAPANESE SECURITY RELATIONSHIP IN TRANSITION. Summary of a Transpacific Dialogue. 1984. 23pp. $2.50.

SIXTH GERMAN-AMERICAN ROUNDTABLE ON NATO: NATO AND EUROPEAN SECURITY—BEYOND INF. Summary of a Transatlantic Dialogue. 1984. 31pp. $2.50.

SECURITY COMMITMENTS AND CAPABILITIES: ELEMENTS OF AN AMERICAN GLOBAL STRATEGY. The Thirteenth Annual Conference, sponsored by the International Security Studies Program, The Fletcher School of Law and Diplomacy, Tufts University. 1984. 21pp. $2.50.

THIRD JAPANESE-AMERICAN-GERMAN CONFERENCE ON THE FUTURE OF NUCLEAR ENERGY. 1984. 40pp. $2.50.

SEVENTH GERMAN-AMERICAN ROUNDTABLE ON NATO: POLITICAL CONSTRAINTS, EMERGING TECHNOLOGIES, AND ALLIANCE STRATEGY. Summary of a Transatlantic Dialogue. 1985. 36pp. $2.50.

TERRORISM AND OTHER "LOW-INTENSITY" OPERATIONS: INTERNATIONAL LINKAGES. The Fourteenth Annual Conference, sponsored by the International Security Studies Program, The Fletcher School of Law and Diplomacy, Tufts University. 1985. 21pp. $2.50.

EAST-WEST TRADE AND TECHNOLOGY TRANSFER: NEW CHALLENGES FOR THE UNITED STATES. Second Annual Forum, co-sponsored by the Institute for Foreign Policy Analysis and the International Security Studies Program, The Fletcher School of Law and Diplomacy, Tufts University. 1986. 40pp. $3.50.

ORGANIZING FOR NATIONAL SECURITY: THE ROLE OF THE JOINT CHIEFS OF STAFF. 1986. 32pp. $2.50.

EIGHTH GERMAN-AMERICAN ROUNDTABLE ON NATO: STRATEGIC DEFENSE, NATO MODERNIZATION, AND EAST-WEST RELATIONS. Summary of a Transatlantic Dialogue. 1986. 47pp. $2.50.

EMERGING DOCTRINES AND TECHNOLOGIES: IMPLICATIONS FOR GLOBAL AND REGIONAL POLITICAL-MILITARY BALANCES. The Fifteenth Annual Conference, sponsored by the International Security Studies Program, The Fletcher School of Law and Diplomacy, Tufts University. 1986. 49pp. $2.50.

STRATEGIC WAR TERMINATION: POLITICAL-MILITARY-DIPLOMATIC DIMENSIONS. 1986. 22pp. $2.50.

SDI AND EUROPEAN SECURITY: ENHANCING CONVENTIONAL DEFENSE. 1987. 21pp. $2.50.

STRATEGIC DEFENSE: INDUSTRIAL APPLICATIONS AND POLITICAL IMPLICATIONS. 1987. ix, 29pp. $2.50.

FUTURE OF NATO FORCES. 1987. ix, 30pp. $2.50.